ENGAGING IN SOCIAL PARTNERSHIPS

Engaging in Social Partnerships helps practitioners advance democratic engagement by creating spaces where institutions of higher education, community groups, and other organizations can come together. This important book prepares higher education professionals to become reflective practitioners while working in collaborations that span not only the boundaries of organizations, but also borders created by the social divides of class, race, ethnicity, culture, professional expertise, and power. Through illustrative cases, Keith explores effective models of democratic engagement for border-crossing campus-community partnerships, as well as approaches to overcoming obstacles and assessing process and outcome. Current and future professionals in higher education will find this a valuable resource as they explore the power of engaging in collaborations that cross social divides, while enacting practices that are more equitable and democratic.

Novella Zett Keith is Professor Emerita of Urban Education at Temple University.

For my family and the family of border crossers, who help us see a *human* family and a less divided world as possibilities and not as illusions.

CONTENTS

List of Figure x
List of Tables xi
Preface xii
   Some Definitions xiii
   What This Book Is About xiv
   How the Book Is Organized and How It Can Be Read xv
   Chapter Summaries xv
   Who I Am and Why I Wrote This Book xvii
Acknowledgments xix

PART 1
Contexts   1

1 Social Partnerships Across Social Divides   3
   Higher Education and Social Partnerships in a Transitional Era   4
   Needed: A New Kind of Professional   13

2 Different Lenses for Understanding Partnerships: Learning
   from the Addams-Lincoln Family Center Case   17
   Case Narrative   18
   Understanding What Happened: Three *Moments*   23
   The Literature on Partnerships: Initial Case Analysis   28
   The Literature on Collaboration Across Borders   36
   Using Thinking Tools to Understand the Addams-Lincoln Case   37

3 Democratic Engagement in Higher Education: Between
   Modernity and Neoliberalism   44
   The Engaged University: Movement and Institutionalization   46
   Modernity and Neoliberalism as Meta-context   54
   Liberalism, Neoliberalism, and the Marketization of Higher
      Education   61
   Conclusion   67

PART 2
Thinking About Professional Practice   71

4 Crossing Borders: From Experts to Democratic Civic
   Professionals   73
   The Professional and the Profession   75
   The Democratic Civic Professional   83
   Communities of Practice and *Third Spaces*   91
   Summary and Conclusion: Weaving a Habit for
      the New Professional   96

5 Toward Wise Practice for University-Community
   Collaborations   99
   What Is Practice?   100
   Phronesis as an Alternative Guide for Professional Practice   104
   Becoming Wiser Practitioners   111
   The Practitioner and the Situation: The *Change from Within*
      Programme   116
   Conclusion   129

PART 3
Learning About Professional Practice
Through Cases   131

6 From Normal to Wiser Practice in a High-School,
   Community, and University Service-Learning Partnership   133
   Novella Zett Keith, with Fatima Hafiz and Jim Peterson
   Embodying the Virtues: The Leadership Team   135
   Sensemaking and Constructing the Good: Working with Students   140
   Enacting the Good   150
   Summary and Conclusion   156

Contents **ix**

7	Building Trust, Sharing Power, Crossing Borders: The Art Sanctuary–Temple/Tyler Partnership	161
	Billy Yalowitz, Karen Malandra, and Novella Zett Keith	
	The Setting, *Reflections in Brown*, Church of the Advocate, May 2004	162
	Building Trust, Sharing Power: *The North Cycle*	167
	Interlude: Becoming . . . *Allies*?	173
	Border Pedagogy as a Transformative Process	174
	Summary and Conclusion	185
8	Cultivating Civic Capacity for Democratic Collaboration: The Maville–TST Project for School Success	190
	The Setting	192
	TST and Collaboration: From Toxic Emotions to Democratic Dialogue	193
	The Maville–TST Project	198
	The Maville–TST Process	199
	Summary and Conclusion	210

PART 4
Going Forward 215

9	Looking Backward to Go Forward	217
	Looking Backward	217
	Three Processes for Collaborations across Borders	221
	Going Forward: Some Things to Remember and Questions to Keep Asking	228
	Conclusion	229

References	*231*
Index	*247*

FIGURE

4.1 From Professional as Expert/Social Trustee to Professional as
Democratic Civic Border Crosser   97

TABLES

2.1	Collaborative Dynamics	33
3.1	Timeline and Road Markers in University Engagement	47
3.2	Meta-contexts and their Supports for Modalities of Engagement and Professional Orientation	69
4.1	Comparison of Expert, Social Trustee, and Democratic Civic Professional	82
4.2	Civic-Minded Professional and Civic-Minded Graduate	85
4.3	Civic Learning Spiral: Expected Outcomes	89
5.1	Border-Crossing Partnership Framework: Practice Theory, Phronesis and Habitus-Field-Capital	115
6.1	The Good, the Normal to Be Interrupted, and Supports for Wise Practice	141
6.2	The Service-learning Process, Guiding Questions, and Course Requirements	143
8.1	Heuristic for TST Facilitator's Practice	195
8.2	Adult Action Proposals, First and Last Day	211
9.1	Main Focuses of Professional's Practice in Border-crossing Partnership Framework	222

PREFACE

If you are a current or future higher education practitioner—whether your practice involves teaching, leadership, administration, research—and your work brings you in contact with groups and communities beyond campus walls, this book is meant for you. The work I'm referring to takes place through social partnerships, collaborations that bring together organizations, neighborhood groups, or other entities in order to address issues that are public in nature. The focus of the book is on collaborations that span not only the boundaries of organizations but also *borders* created by the social divides of class, race, ethnicity, culture, professional expertise, power, and other markers of difference. Boundaries simply define the contours of a particular group or organization and what or who is included in it. Borders point to power asymmetries that allow easy passage for some—members of dominant groups, upper and middle classes, professionals, insiders—while others are held back and at times have to give up something—their language, culture, or identity—before being allowed through. Borders are especially but not uniquely present in urban neighborhoods, which is where most of the practice situations in the book are located.

Engaging in social partnerships, as used in this book, means working together in ways that open up these borders, creating *border-crossing* spaces for power sharing, communication, respectful relationships, and mutually beneficial action. The questions that guide the book, then, are about current and future professionals in higher education (administrators, staff, faculty, and students) as prospective partners in collaborations that cross social divides and how they might be helped in becoming the kind of professional who can engage successfully in these partnerships. The section immediately below briefly introduces two of the terms in the title: social partnerships and engagement. The next section explains what the book is about and in that context introduces the third term, democratic practices; it also suggests different ways the book can be read. A more detailed account of the book's themes and organization and the major ideas in each chapter come next. Finally, there's a bit about myself and how I came to write this book.

Some Definitions

Social partnerships are arrangements whereby formal and informal organizations, groups, and individuals voluntarily join and work together to address issues of mutual concern. They are different from typical partnerships in business and the professions (for example, a law or medical partnership) in that their work crosses organizational boundaries and is specifically identified with socially relevant and public purposes. In a foundational article on the topic, Sandra Waddock (1991) explains that social partnerships usually address complex and 'messy' problems that individual organizations can't tackle alone, involve a degree of power sharing, and are closer in organizational form to a network than a bureaucracy or hierarchy.

Identifiable benefits are important to all kinds of partnerships, but for social partnerships these may be intangible and at times they won't accrue directly to the people or organizations involved, but will further instead a broadly defined public good. Waddock provides some examples of social partnerships that yield concrete benefits: labor unions establishing a training institute, a corporation and a community college joining to provide needed technical skills for workers, and a broad coalition including researchers, advertisers, media outlets, and unions, the Partnership for a Drug-Free America. The cases in this book feature social partnerships that involve higher education and K–12 institutions and community-based groups but contain information that is useful for other collaborations across social divides. The main focus is not on the institutions but on the professional partners, because we need to understand better this important process-oriented aspect of collaboration across divides.

Engagement, in the context of higher education, pertains to both the institution and the professionals in it. Institutionally, it stands for a commitment to directing resources toward socially and civically responsible ends, with real and practical benefits accruing both within and beyond campus walls. This means, for instance, that the institution values the creation of knowledge and the education of students beyond their contribution to the individual, the profession, 'pure' research, or the institution itself: on an engaged campus, the learning of students and the work of faculty and staff also make contributions that are publicly valued and serve practical purposes, thus advancing human, social, political, and economic development. Engagement calls on higher education to make a civic contribution especially by working to alleviate social problems.

There are different ways for organizations and the researchers and professionals in them to enact engagement and one of the central differences involves how they see and use their core asset: knowledge. Certain forms of engagement draw from the practice of outreach and extension services, which is essentially a one-way street: expert professionals in higher education conduct research and gather information and provide it to clients who can benefit from it. Drawing from democratic practices, others see engagement as a two-way street where there is mutual sharing and an exchange of information and knowledge. Here knowledge from research meets local knowledge from experience and practice and mutual learning occurs. Community partners are seen as having resources and not only needs. →What I want to cultivate

What This Book Is About

Engagement has been described as civic, public, community, and democratic. In this book, I consider the possibilities of social partnerships furthering democratic engagement by creating spaces where institutions of higher education, community groups, and organizations come together around what Harry Boyte (2004) calls *public work*: citizens working together deliberately and democratically to accomplish some public purpose. As I treat partnerships in this book, they are not only about addressing pressing social problems but also about doing so in ways that are equitable and democratic and uphold an ethic of social justice that takes seriously the implied promise inherent in the notion of partnership. That is, I explore partnerships as spaces where we might learn how to work together in the spirit of mutual respect, power sharing, open communication, and democratic decision making. Democratic engagement thus becomes a stepping stone to building a more equitable democracy for all.

Making such partnerships work requires paying special attention to borders and to dynamics of power, culture, and difference. It means understanding who we and our partners are and what is real and possible in the particular situations we encounter in our partnership work. There are two kinds of challenges here. ① The first is present in any type of networked organizational arrangement; it involves stepping out of established roles, power structures, and organizational and professional cultures and entering a world that is about the enabling power of mutual relationships and shared motivations, interests, and purposes. The second is specific to partnerships that take higher education practitioners across social borders. This is uncommon work for which we tend not to be prepared, either in professional education or in our personal, social, and organizational lives; ② it thus requires interrupting ways of being, acting, and interacting that have acquired the status of normalcy. Doing so calls for becoming especially aware of how our organizational structures and our normal ways of communicating, using power (including the power of the expert and the professional) and engaging diverse others unwittingly create and sustain borders and hinder social justice agendas.

How the Book Is Organized and How It Can Be Read

The book is divided into four parts. Part 1 (Chapters 1 through 3), sets the context: it addresses the purpose and main themes of the book, the relevant literature, some theoretical tools, and offers a broad historical overview. Part 2 provides the conceptual framework: its two chapters (4 and 5) explore various meanings of being a professional and the meaning and cultivation of professional practice. Cases are an important way to learn in and through practice, and each of the three chapters in Part 3 (6, 7, and 8) describes and analyzes a border-crossing social partnership and how new professionals were cultivated in it. Part 4 is the last chapter. It pulls together the various threads, takes us back to the purposes of the book, and, in the spirit of what has been learned and ongoing inquiry, raises some new questions.

The book can be read in different ways. It is about theory and practice and, although references and explanations pertaining to both run through it, there are more materials that start with abstract ideas in Part 2 and more that start from experiences (practice) in Part 3. If experience or, here, cases, is your preferred starting point, instead of reading the book as I have laid it out, you might want to begin by reading the cases in Chapters 2, 5, 6, 7, and 8—although you will need to toggle back and forth through the other materials. The case in Chapter 2 is a negative example that explores some of the obstacles to partnerships. Chapter 5 includes a mini-case that grounds the book's theoretical framework. The cases in Part 3 provide generally positive examples: participants don't do everything right, but are able to learn from the experience and reach a measure of success. The endnotes and references include resources you can put to use immediately in your own partnership work. If you are like me and want a sneak preview, you could also begin at the end. The concluding chapter provides a summary that might serve as a backwards guide to the others. I strongly encourage you, however *practical* you might think you are, to make the more conceptual chapters your own.

Chapter Summaries

Chapter 1 elaborates the overall purpose and importance of the book. The purpose is to support the formation of a new kind of civic professional, a wise practitioner who can support campus-community border-crossing partnerships by engaging in practices that are democratic and oriented to social justice. Among the trends that support the importance of social partnerships are networked forms of organization, increasing social diversity and social injustice, and pressures on higher education to use its resources to address these and other challenges. The chapter also defines relevant terms and outlines important tasks for the new professional: interrupting oppressive normalcies, Self-Other transformation, and developing collective intelligence for pressing community and social problems.

Cases offer a storehouse of knowledge for practice. Chapter 2 introduces a negative case that illustrates how one may work with cases to learn for professional practice. The barriers that caused the partnership to fail are examined through three analytical lenses: the general literature on collaborations and partnerships, the more specialized literature on partnerships across social borders, and the use of thinking tools (or theoretical concepts)—here, social justice and power, especially the *power of the normal*. This teaching case highlights the problematic assumptions that come with normalcies built into the orientation to knowledge and practice of the expert professional and of the academy and other organizations that support this orientation.

The focus of Chapter 3 is on democratic engagement in higher education. After reviewing the path, issues, and accomplishments of the engagement movement, the chapter turns to two deep structures that are part of the meta-context the democratic project needs to consider: modernity (as a long historical period) and neoliberalism. The case in Chapter 2 showed that it is *normal* in the academy for expert professionals to enact engagement as outreach. This chapter looks at modernity's assumptions about knowledge, professional identity, and organizations and the continuities and divergences found in neoliberal policies and practices that are currently dominant in education and other social institutions. Would-be democratic civic professionals must learn to recognize these different orientations in social partnerships and engagement efforts.

Chapter 4 interrogates notions of the professional and profession. It details the constructs of the expert, social trustee, and democratic civic professional in the context of three components of professionalism: identity, knowledge, and associational life. The chapter reviews a number of constructs that are relevant for democratic civic professionalism. The purpose of the exercise is to clearly grasp what is involved in becoming the kind of professional who can engage in border-crossing partnerships and how to support this change.

Chapter 5 reviews the literature on practice and learning for practice and continues to develop the conceptual framework for the book. Traditional academic orientations to knowledge for practice are reviewed and contrasted to this emerging framework, which is developed from a number of sources: the most important are practice theory, the neo-Aristotelian concept of phronesis, and Bourdieu's interconnected thinking tools of habitus, field, and capital. All of these emphasize the nature of practice and practitioner knowledge as embodied, socially constructed, and situated in the particular. These contributions help us explore the path from the traditional to the 'new' professional who can engage in partnerships through border-crossing democratic practice. A mini-case illustrates this path, also showing how practitioner-driven action research can support the process.

Chapter 6 is the first of three chapters that are grounded in cases. It presents a campus-school-community collaboration that involved joint teams of high school and college students planning and carrying out service-learning projects in the high school and its inner-city neighborhood. The border-crossing partnership framework developed in Chapter 5 is used to identify some *normal* practices in the leadership team, the student teams, and between students and neighborhood members. Case analysis explores how these normalcies constituted barriers for partnerships and the ways they were interrupted, making room for wiser practitioners and wiser practice. The analysis reveals different understandings of leadership, the community, community needs and shows ways to support and enact *wiser* understandings of democratic engagement.

The arts have a special role to play in democratic engagement. Chapter 7 details a community-arts project that draws from community-based oral history research, culminating in a multimedia performance. The project brings the voices of an African American community out of the private world of memory and forgetting, reinserting its narratives into a public performance that builds on the struggles and strengths of the community. The chapter explores how to be in a partnership that de-centers the university partners and how to prepare students for this experience through what is termed border pedagogy. It uses the thinking tools and practice of sharing power, building trust, and transforming habitus for ongoing social justice work.

Chapter 8 takes us from the level of relationships between people and within teams to the level of institutions and the creation of community civic capacity. It details an intervention in one of France's most difficult and "volatile" neighborhoods, where there are severe barriers to collaboration, through a process called Transformational Social Therapy (TST). The case shows how facilitation informed by TST theory and practice helped create trust and genuine communication by healing relationships in the school and community. The information gathered through this unusual form of community-based research was used to plan and inform wiser practice. The case illustrates thinking tools associated with the TST process, especially creating healthy relationships, democratic dialogue, and collective intelligence.

Where have we been and what can we build together? Chapter 9 distills some of the main ideas presented in the book and reviews three processes and tasks for the democratic civic professional who engages in border crossing partnerships: disturbing and interrupting the normal, Self-Other transformation, and collective intelligence. The chapter ends with 10 points and questions to keep in mind as you go forward in this work.

Who I Am and Why I Wrote This Book

In 30-odd years in the academy, much of my time has been spent learning about theory and practice, gradually getting into the practice of experiential and community-based education, and learning and helping others learn from those experiences. I don't consider myself an expert: I have constantly struggled with broadening my own understanding of how we learn, lately getting in touch with what is now called wise practice, or phronesis. The 'wisdom' toward which my practice has been directed strives to bridge borders, reconnecting severed relationships across social groups and supporting understandings of how social institutions promote injustice, often unwittingly, but can also be places for healing and change.

My motivation to pursue wise(r) practice comes from my personal and professional life. Experiences during my childhood left me with attitudes and dispositions to want to fight perceived injustices and take the side of the underdog. I am giving myself away here: I often felt like both an underdog and a fighter as a child and young adult. My family migrated to the US from Italy when I was a teenager. Growing up in the in-between world of the immigrant adolescent, in a working-class family that 'did well'* (meaning that immigration helped us achieve social mobility), I often felt that my parents belonged to another era and at times, a culture that was foreign to me. When my father did not understand me, he tried to impose his will on me. When I did not understand or agree with his wishes and commands, I resisted. Some years later, through marriage, I joined another culture and experienced the in-between worlds of a mixed-race family as a wife (my husband is Jamaican) and as the white mother of a biracial child. This is to say that my experiences seem to have led me quite naturally down a path of wanting to break down barriers between people and change the institutions that support those barriers.

Although I did not always understand these patterns clearly, they informed my professional and personal decisions. From an educational start in the liberal arts and radical sociology, I eventually found my home teaching in an urban education program. When I became involved professionally with experiential learning, in several forms but especially as service learning, it seemed also quite natural for me to embrace a social justice and border-crossing orientation rather than ones that followed tenets of charity, volunteering, or community service. Trying to enact the principles I hold dear was and continues to be a struggle, as I discover in and around me orientations that unthinkingly and unknowingly hold on to what is *normal* in our world: my status as a white professional woman affords me privileges that I have come to take for granted and I don't recognize as such until a situation, at times a painful one, brings them to my awareness. My academic life has led me to learn much in selected areas, those that are in the province of the mind; I was well supported there. But I have had to struggle to learn, with much less institutional support though with caring and wonderful colleagues and friends, about the realm of the emotions, about empathy, about respectful, caring, and honest relationships across borders, and about the meaning of democratic practice in these contexts. I am still learning and still teaching, and the book in your hands is part of this quest.

* Being Afro-Caribbean & immigrating to US offers us a social mobility (access) that being African-American doesn't *

ACKNOWLEDGMENTS

It is quite *normal*—and also quite true—to say that this book could not have been written without the help and support of many people. I started thinking about it almost a decade ago and so there are lots of people who knowingly or unknowingly have contributed to its creation.

Among my Temple colleagues, my first thanks go to Erin Horvat, who believed in me and made space and time for me to write; James Davis and Trevor Sewell deserve similar thanks. Colleagues and students in the Urban Education Program, among whom I can only mention Will Jordan, Maia Cucchiara, Mike Dorn (and of course, Erin Horvat): thanks from the depths of my heart for what we created together. Avi Kaplan, you are there in spirit and I thank you for your immense energy, vitality, ideas, and excitement.

Other colleagues and friends read the work, gave me feedback, and kept me going. Special thanks go to Eric Hartman and my colleagues and co-conspirators, Fatima, Jim, Billy, Pauletta, Cindy, Jan, and the constant inspiration of Karen. My *diversity* buddies, you have taught me more than you will ever know: Charles, Nicole, Igor, Tchet, Marjory, Pamela, Tiff, Rhonda, and everyone in my own Diversity Certificate cohort: you are here in these pages as you will always be in my heart. Friends and colleagues in the Community Learning Network have been a constant source of inspiration. Thank you, especially, Eli Goldblatt: you are a master in this work! My students: I can't acknowledge you all, but your ideas, reactions, truths, made me think, feel, and see more. At times we upset and disturbed one another, in ways that I now see as good. My Sufi friends, Telema, Gayle, Birgit, Adrian, Kava, Nissa, LatifaNoor: thanks for listening and for all the different and supportive ways you found of asking, "is it finished?"

Nelson and Vanessa, my team, cheering gallery, and constant inspiration, how can I thank you? Perhaps a poet could find the right words. All I can say is that truly, honestly, I could not have done it without you.

PART 1
Contexts

1

SOCIAL PARTNERSHIPS ACROSS SOCIAL DIVIDES

> In a period of relentless change, all students need the kind of education that leads them to ask not just "how do we get this done?" but also "what is most worth doing?"
>
> (National Leadership Council for Liberal Education & America's Promise [NLC-LEAP], 2007, p. 13)

The starting point of this book is that one thing "most worth doing" in our times is learning to collaborate with others to reach toward goals and purposes that really matter to all of us. These goals and purposes are thus in the *public* realm. Doing so is especially important now for two reasons: first, the fast-paced and complex nature of the world in which we live makes traditional experts and their technical solutions unsuited to handle the task on their own; second, increasing social diversity in the context of increasing intolerance makes it imperative to create democratic spaces and practices that bridge these social divisions. The book puts forth social partnerships as grounds that hold great potential for this kind of learning, particularly when they create spaces where people who live, figuratively, in different worlds can come together and practice democratic work.

Writers across different fields strongly agree that a new partnership paradigm has emerged over the last 25 years and that this organizational change is with us for the foreseeable future. Whether in private, public, or civil society settings, leaders are confronted with the need to replace steep *command and control* hierarchies with *flat and nimble* networks that are characteristic of the ways partnerships are organized (see Austin, 2000; Salamon, Sokolowski, & List, 2003). Advocates across the political spectrum have been calling on higher education to engage with the 'real world' and social partnerships and collaborations provide paths to such engagement. The purposes of these partnerships run the gamut

4 Contexts

from contributing to knowledge markets through academic research, applying academic knowledge to public and community problems, and using the knowledge and resources of the academy to support democratic public work. The last is most closely aligned to the purpose of this book.

Knowing that something should be done does not mean knowing how to do it well, and this is the problem the book addresses:[1] how to cultivate a new kind of professional who can facilitate, lead, and learn through these partnerships, not as an expert but as a citizen—a civic professional who can work democratically across social divisions, creating and using both local and expert knowledge. An extensive literature on civic and democratic professionalism, reviewed in Chapter 4, has produced a good sense of the knowledge, skills, dispositions, values, and capabilities of this new professional; we also know that practices such as democratic classrooms, intergroup dialogues, and service- and community-based learning often result in changes in students that are in tune with these desired outcomes. But we know much less about what this professional practice entails and how to engage in it.

The preface has reviewed how the different chapters contribute to this objective. This chapter provides some background information. The first section presents major trends that contribute to the relevance of partnerships for higher education and the specific focus on partnerships across social divides. The second section introduces democratic civic professionalism and trains the spotlight on some of its tasks.

Higher Education and Social Partnerships in a Transitional Era

The authors of *College Learning for a New Global Century*, the report cited in the epigraph, remind us that we are in the midst of a ground shift. Widely known by now, the message is that we live in a world of "daunting complexity," "relentless change," ongoing economic innovation, and global engagement—all in the context of exponential technological change. Knowledge is central to this shift and thus educational institutions are deeply implicated in it; but what should these institutions hold as most worth learning?

The report calls for recasting and enhancing the relevance of the foundational values of liberal learning. Its data show that these themes are echoed in corporate and other settings that did not traditionally espouse such values but marched to the tune of command-and-control efficiency. According to the authors of the report, the knowledge we need is not only specialized and technical: it should enable us to "understand and navigate the dramatic forces—physical, cultural, economic, technological—that directly affect the quality, character, and perils of the world in which . . . [we] live" (NLC-LEAP, 2007, p. 13). These are the forces of turbulence that portend a world that is becoming ever more interconnected through communications and other technologies and ever more divided socially, economically, and ideologically. To navigate in these waters we must be prepared to ask what matters and not only what can be done. The challenge—a huge one—is to create responsible and informed citizens and civic professionals who can keep at the forefront a concern for the common good (multivocally and dialogically defined!) and a vision of diverse and globally engaged democracies.

Four important trends intersect with social partnerships and help explain their relevance for higher education: the ①emerging global network society, the ②increasing presence of social diversity in the context of social injustice, ③pressing social problems, and ④pressures on higher education to use its resources to make 'real world' contributions. I will address each in turn and later return to them selectively in the discussion of the new professional.

Network Society

Some 50 years ago, in an almost prescient way, Marshall McLuhan (1960, 1962) wrote and talked about the upcoming electronic age that was giving rise to a global village. More recently, we refer to our era as the Internet Age, the network society, or the global information economy. McLuhan used the global village metaphor to refer to changes emerging in the 1960s that would allow people to communicate, learn about, and become connected to one another through the postmodern equivalent of the beating of the drum—the electronic media. Just like the print age before it, the media of the electronic and Internet age favor certain tendencies that find their way into social arrangements. The speed of information flows, for instance, erases time and space and favors organizational forms that can respond quickly to rapid change.

In the network society, our world is interconnected through social systems that are based on the logic of networks. Manuel Castells's monumental three-volume work, *The Rise of the Network Society* (2010) has added information nodes (and much more) to McLuhan's now almost quaint idea of the electronic age. Instead of the vertical charts of bureaucratic organizational forms that characterize the print age, visualize crisscrossing lines and smaller or larger nodes indicating where few or many lines in the network intersect. In networks, power is distributed differently from the way it operates in bureaucratic organizations, where command and control flow downward to divisions and offices with specialized functions: network nodes can rise and fall based on their connectivity, on the information that passes through them, and on the degree of their interconnectedness or flow.

Thus, network society and the network economy seem to favor organizational forms that are horizontal and decentralized (which should not be equated with democratic forms), can link complementary resources, and shift at a moment's notice, according to rapidly emerging trends. Keeping up with these ever-changing and speeding flows of information is accomplished through flatness rather than hierarchical control and new forms of management or managerialism. Terms such as *smart and nimble* have gained currency, applying to organizational entities that are best able to collect and use information (and are thus information rich or smart) and can adapt quickly to changing environments (nimble), which best positions them to seize new opportunities. This is also the likely organizational form of social partnerships.

New organizational forms, in turn, require new forms of management and leadership.[2] A special issue of *Business Week* dedicated to *smart management* describes companies that are "testing fresh methods to develop global leaders while tapping innovative collaboration tools and social networks to speed up productivity and decision-making" (McGregor, 2009). In the same article, the CEO of Cisco Systems, one of the featured companies, explains the advantages of what he describes as democratizing management, which allows teams at various levels to make decisions: "When you have command and control by the top 10 people, you can only do one or two things at a time. The future is about collaboration and teamwork and making decisions with a replicable process that offers scale, speed, and flexibility." The role of the manager thus shifts from exercising command and control to being the enabler who coordinates through dynamic linking and communicates through conversation (Denning, 2011).

In this new global economy, people need to 'learn to learn,' as they are expected to take on changing rather than stable occupations: working in organizations that are not only smart and nimble, but also *lean* (that is, they adjust their workforce, inventories, and resource use according to changing needs), people are expected to be smart and nimble in turn. A survey of employers and college graduates conducted by Peter D. Hart Research Associates (2006) for the Association of American Colleges & Universities (AAC&U) found that employers looking for new hires highly valued skills in teamwork and the ability to collaborate with others in diverse group settings. More than two-thirds of employers think higher education should place more emphasis on these skills as well as on communication, applying knowledge to real-world settings, critical thinking and analysis, global issues, and solving complex problems. Generally, the preference is for well-rounded people with a balance of skills rather than a narrow, overly specialist focus. Some three-fourths of employers also think that the ability of firms to innovate is central to success in the global economy and that higher education must play an important role in this regard. Innovation requires the collection and smart management of information.

The logic of networks is also influencing the reform of public entities such as government agencies, educational institutions, and school systems. Writing about new approaches to public administration, Goldsmith and Eggers (2004) remark that *connectors* are needed, leaders who listen well, cultivate relationships, and appreciate others' assets and thus can bring together people from different backgrounds. Rather than running an entire operation, the role of the new type of leader is to activate and coordinate a network of resources involving any number of public and private partners or contractors. Public-private partnerships grew significantly as the government shed and outsourced functions that were previously the exclusive domain of public employees. This has been happening not only in the provision of public services but also in the prison system and the military: for instance, the wars in Iraq and Afghanistan have been described as network centric, as private contractors played an increasingly larger role in all aspects of military operations. The ratio of military personnel to private contractors grew from 55:1 in the Vietnam War to 1:1 in the Iraq Wars and 1:1.49 in Afghanistan (Hammes, 2010). Of course, there are issues and criticisms in these and other privatization ventures, but the main point for us is that Goldsmith and Eggers and others were on target with their claim that new organizational forms are evolving and replacing the bureaucratic model.

Social change and global justice movements are adding new twists to this network logic (Fung, 2006). Political movements—including the 1990s indigenous people's movement in Chiapas, Mexico, the 1999 'Battle of Seattle,' the World Social Forum, and the Occupy movements in Europe, the US, and elsewhere—have developed new participatory democratic practices that involve horizontal ways of coordinating the social actions of various autonomous groups, as well as information exchange and consensus decision making. Jeffrey Juris (2007) explains the new approach:

> While the command-oriented logic of traditional parties and unions involves recruiting new members, developing unified strategies, pursuing political hegemony, and organizing through representative structures, network politics revolve around the creation of "convergence spaces"...., where diverse collectives, organizations, and networks converge around a few common hallmarks, while preserving their autonomy and specificity. The objective becomes enhanced "connectivity" and horizontal expansion by articulating diverse movements within flexible, decentralized structures which facilitate transnational coordination and communication. Key "activist-hackers"... operate as relayers and exchangers, receiving, interpreting, and routing information out to diverse network nodes. Like computer hackers, activist-hackers combine and recombine cultural codes (in this case political signifiers), sharing information about projects, mobilizations, strategies, and tactics within global networks.
>
> (para. 18)

The logic of networks seems to be applying to all kinds of settings and activities. The importance of the role of the connector or, in the language of this book, the democratic civic professional, is thus assured for the foreseeable future. One of the questions will be how to engage in this role given the complexities of this historical moment. One factor that adds to complexity pertains to what is generally known as diversity.

Social Diversity

Globalization involves increasing world population movements, through migration, flows of refugees, student and professional exchanges, tourism, volunteer-service vacations, international nongovernmental organizations (INGOs), and the like. The result is that globalization is happening 'right here' as well as 'out there.' Along with other 'advanced' countries of the global North, the United States is becoming an increasingly diverse nation. Haub (2009) reports that in the US "immigrants arriving after 2005, and their children and grandchildren, will account for 82% of the population growth between 2005 and 2050" (p. 10). As Robert Putnam (2007) remarks, this trend is "one of the most important challenges facing modern societies, and at the same time one of our most significant opportunities" (p. 137). What does it portend?

On the challenge side, social heterogeneity often erodes social trust, a sense of community, and participation in civic life (see Pettigrew, 2008). This is particularly true where there are growing economic divides, which in turn spawn not only social insecurity but also public incivility, hate groups, and intergroup violence. The problem, thus, lies not in heterogeneity or diversity itself but in essentially ideological and political processes (where *political* refers to the use of power, not necessarily to government and related institutions) that transform diversity into binary categories involving dominance (Self) and subordination (Other), with attendant inequalities in the distribution of resources, including psychic ones: Self is an active subject and agent, a doer, while Other is a passive recipient, an object and nonagent. The issue, then, is not diversity but *difference*.

Diversity or Difference?

This question highlights the fact that power and privilege are implicated in creating social categories or identities. If mere diversity were at play, we could imagine a spectrum from which members of different groups would create their identity by selecting the qualities by which they want to define themselves. Instead, we find a play of opposites, where dominant groups construct their social identities by appropriating qualities they value while assigning their absence or their opposite to members of subordinate groups, through a collective projection of the shadow side, or those parts of the self that are rejected and feared. For instance, according to a binary classification, the traditional dominant group composed of upper-class heterosexual white males will ascribe to itself socially valued qualities such rationality, intelligence, willpower, and drive, while Others (e.g., women, nonwhites, lower classes, gays, despised ethnicities) may be described as irrational or overly emotional, violent, unintelligent, weak, immoral, unmotivated, and untrustworthy. Thus in the eyes of the dominant group and through dominant discourses the Other is what the Self is not, a being constructed in terms of deficits, as less valuable and ultimately less human or even as a demonized alien, with whom one cannot reason or even communicate. What is needed, then, is the transformation of the Self-Other relation into a relation of difference, that is, disrupting binary opposites in favor of multiplicity. Social action is clearly involved, as are democratic orientations, for instance, recognizing that there are multiple sources of knowledge and talents and that the expert's or dominant member's values are not the only ones that matter. As used in this book, Self-Other transformation invokes social justice, especially its recognitive aspect, which is explained below. I take up the practice of Self-Other transformation in the last section.

Social Justice

Social justice is generally conceptualized as having three aspects. The most familiar entails the fair distribution of goods and resources, also termed *distributive* social justice. Included under this umbrella are resources that level the playing field and provide all people the opportunity and capabilities for attaining a life they consider worth living. The United Nations Universal Declaration of Human Rights, for instance, contains a basic right to resources adequate for maintaining health and well-being, including literacy, education, and work, as well as other aspects of social justice such as dignity, freedom, and recognition as a person. The Human Development Index (HDI) reflects this orientation (Robeyns, 2005).

A second aspect of social justice pertains to what Iris Marion Young (2000) terms *self-determination*, or the ability "to participate in determining one's action and the condition of one's action" (p. 32). The essence of democracy, on this view, is that it provides the means for promoting justice through meaningful participation, which is especially important for marginalized groups and identities. For Young, social justice as self-determination involves communication, valuing, validation, and appreciation for cultural differences.

Self-determination shades into a third aspect, *recognition*. Its best known proponent, Axel Honneth, begins with the proposition that achieving mature autonomy as an adult requires the capacity to sustain one's own self-trust, self-respect, and self-esteem (Thompson, 2006). These self-conceptions are not just internal but are dependent on confirmation by others. If these conditions are absent, we are vulnerable to autonomy-undermining injustices. Anderson and Honneth (2005) ask us to consider in this light institutional practices that

> threaten individuals' own self-esteem by making it much harder (and, in limit cases, even impossible) to think of oneself as worthwhile. . . . It is, of course, psychologically possible to sustain a sense of self-worth in the face of denigrating and humiliating attitudes, but it is harder to do so, and there are significant costs associated with having to shield oneself from these negative

> attitudes and having to find subcultures for support. And so even if one's effort . . . is successful, the question of justice is whether the burden is fair.
>
> (p. 131)

All aspects of social justice are important for dealing with our growing inequality, but the third aspect is especially relevant to the realm of difference. It is hardly news that we need to create spaces for public conversations, relationship building, and change-oriented action across social divides, as well as the professionals who can bring together people from across such divides. When Self-Other divides are reduced or even erased, the opportunities that heterogeneity holds in store become visible. They emerge especially in the context of *smart* action to address complex problems, that is, action that is well informed by gathering and taking into account all the diverse sources of knowledge about the problem. As we will see below, collective intelligence provides an interesting way to link social justice with smart action.

Pressing Social Problems

The complex problems that social partnerships are meant to address seem to be multiplying and creating a growing need for interventions. Even without considering the ongoing effects of the deep recession of 2008, there are troubling signs of increasing income inequality and declining social justice in the US. Social justice is important not just for individual well-being; it is also a necessary ingredient in sustaining democratic governance and a key to equality of opportunity. The US is commonly portrayed as a nation of freedom and equality where anyone who strives hard can make it. Narratives of civil and group-based rights and privileges accorded to those who were previously discriminated against maintain the illusion of social fairness and support a national forgetting that rights once gained can also be whittled away and removed. For its part, the ideology of rugged individualism supports tendencies to blame lack of success on the qualities of individuals rather than on structural factors (e.g., see Reason, Broido, Davis, & Evans, 2005). Data complicate the story.

A recent comparative study of distributive social justice in the countries of the Organization for Economic Co-operation and Development (OECD) looked for the presence of policies and practices that would support the fair distribution of socially valued resources such as income, education, and health care (Schraad-Tischler, 2011). The OECD includes the highly industrialized, relatively wealthy economies of Europe, Australia and New Zealand, Japan and South Korea, the US and Canada, and Mexico and Chile. The US is 27th in terms of the overall index of social justice. On one of the indicators, income inequality, the US was ranked 28th, with only Turkey, Mexico, and Chile lower on the list. The common measure here is the Gini coefficient, where perfect inequality (one person has all the income) is 1 and perfect equality is 0. For the US, it has gone from 0.35 in 1980

Social Partnerships Across Social Divides   **11**

to 0.45 in 2007 and 0.47 in 2010. As a point of comparison, Denmark and Norway stand at around 0.25, and the average for all OECD countries is 0.31 (Schraad-Tischler, 2011, p. 32, Figure 10; also see "Gini in the bottle," 2013).

An additional detail is needed to explain how these facts relate to social partnerships: it is the gradual retreat of government as the provider of a social safety net and the guarantor of a measure of equity in the distribution of resources. Since 1980, the US and other countries that rank near the bottom of the chart—England, for instance—have been following *neoliberal* economic and social policies (elaborated in Chapter 3), that claim the superiority of relatively unregulated private markets over the work of public entities and thus argue for limiting the role and size of government. Social partnerships, including nongovernmental organizations (NGOs) have been urged to fill the vacuum left by the state, but doing so with the available resources, in the context of increasing inequality, is an improbable task.

Pressures to Contribute to the 'Real World'

As should be clear by now, pressures on higher education for relevance and attention to real-world conditions come from a number of different though often interconnected sources. First, sources that favor the ascendancy and domination of private markets tend to translate the quest for relevance with reference to knowledge as a marketable commodity and thus press for its utility to businesses and for practical applications in various fields. Second, as public support for higher education comes under attack, institutions are pressed to prove their usefulness by aggressively pursuing market alternatives to public funding and contributing their resources—including students as volunteers and service providers—to solve social problems. Third, from the perspective of democratic engagement, the shrinking of the public sphere, including the translation of citizenship and freedom into the customer's ability to choose among marketable commodities, is itself a problem: contributing to the real world here means using resources for the public good and not only for personal and private gain and renewing democratic life by creating processes and spaces for democratic work in communities. Harry Boyte (2003) captures this task:

> [we need bold, savvy, and above all *political* citizens and civic institutions if we are to tame a technological, manipulative state, to transform an increasingly materialistic and competitive culture, and to address effectively the mounting practical challenges of a turbulent and interconnected world.]
>
> (p. 1)

Thus the press for relevance and real-world connections can assume vastly different meanings depending on one's framework and perspective about the role and functions of higher education in society and an emphasis on its private or public purposes. What is incontrovertible is that the pressure is real and a harbinger of change.

Given the interconnectedness of the world, it is becoming increasingly difficult to escape awareness that our responsibilities to others and others' rights extend well beyond the political boundaries of the nation. Democratic engagement in the global age and in the age of difference thus requires an expanded notion of citizenship that involves social rights and responsibilities as well as political ones and expands from the nation state to the global 'community.' It thus needs to incorporate multiculturalism and global citizenship, which are about human rights, social justice, and an ethical responsibility to others on the basis of our common humanity and the recognition of our interdependence (Keith, 2005; Taylor et al., 1994).

The following is a summary of the trends that favor social partnerships constructed along democratic lines:

- The current era favors networks rather than traditionally hierarchical and bureaucratic organizations. Networks may come together around particular problems that require various kinds of expertise and information and can be reformed quickly when new and different problems emerge. Social partnerships are networked organizational forms.
- Networks arise at least in part because of the speed of change and the need for organizations to be smart and nimble. Complexity also increases the need for collective intelligence gathered from diverse sources.
- The 'messy' social problems that partnerships generally address are increasing; complexity or scale is partly the cause, the other part being (neoliberal) policies that favor the retreat of government and put pressure on the intervention of citizens and civil society actors such as NGOs.
- Increasing diversity can present opportunities for us to collaborate by creating democratic spaces and processes that support social justice and the best use of the rich information available from all sources and realms of society.

All the above make it increasingly important to learn to collaborate in social partnerships that cross social divides. We are urgently called, from all sides, to work together at the very time that our divisions dampen our hope, constrict our will, and prevent us from sharing our knowledge and acting in consort. The call is to tap into and turn to constructive use those emotional and political energies that now find outlets in apathy, incivility, destructive ideologies, isolation, and social selfishness. In this context, we need not only new administrators and managers, but also new types of professionals who can use diversity as a resource, helping people with different social histories and from different social locations bring their experiences and perspectives to bear on any given problem and forge them into a collective intelligence, constructing workable and creative answers to the pressing issues we face in common.

Needed: A New Kind of Professional

Who or what is a professional? Readers may answer that it is someone who is a specialist in a given discipline, has expert (technical) knowledge and knows how to apply it to a given field or set of problems or issues. Given the context of this book, there are two immediate difficulties with this construction: first, expert knowledge can be used in ways that create borders and work against the horizontal sharing of power and knowledge; second, there is (as yet) no discipline or field that prepares professionals for the work advanced in this book. As I argue here and as fully discussed in Chapter 5, this is so because engaging in partnerships across social divides is less about applying technical knowledge than it is about being a wise practitioner.

The new kind of professional that is the subject of this book draws from a number of alternative constructions and is elaborated in Chapter 4. For the time being, I will use the construct of democratic civic professionalism, with the understanding that it is inclusive of the issues mentioned above: networks and collaboration, social justice, and difference. The subsections below introduce this new professionalism and three of its important tasks or practices: interrupting oppressive normalcies, Self-Other transformation, and developing collective intelligence to address social and community problems.

Democratic Civic Professionalism

The academic professional who possesses specialized technical knowledge is a creation of the modern age and especially the early 20th century; our times call instead for a democratic civic professional or wise practitioner. Boyte and Fretz (2010) provide a succinct explanation of the difference: instead of "practitioners applying a technical emphasis, civic professionals are those who work *with* citizens, rather than acting *on* them." Unlike to the expert who comes into a community as the knower and problem solver, the civic professional acts from the premise that "the greatest untapped resource for improving health and social well-being is the knowledge, wisdom, and energy of individuals, families, and communities who face challenging issues in their everyday lives" (p. 84). These are the themes of Self-Other transformation and collective intelligence.

Boyte and Fretz give as an example the Citizen Professional Center at the University of Minnesota, whose work is guided by core principles that conform quite closely to the self-determination and recognition aspects of social justice outlined above. Among them are the notion that professionals should see themselves as partners and not just as service providers, look to the resources of families and communities and not only to their own, and ensure that citizens drive programs instead of creating programs to serve citizens. Like all professionals, civic professionals rely on a body of knowledge and skills; included here are also understanding the sociopolitical and public aspects of personal problems and being able to facilitate public conversations and actions pertaining to these problems. A major focus is on identity:

> seeing oneself first as a citizen with special expertise working alongside other citizens with their own special expertise in order to solve community problems that require everyone's effort. This not just an idealistic self-image but comes from a grounded realization that the really big problems . . . — sometimes known as "wicked problems"—cannot be solved by professionals working alone, nor by government action alone. We will not make headway against the tide unless we all row together.
> ("The Citizen Professional Idea," n.d.)

What this means is that the civic professional is transformed from a technical expert and service provider into a facilitator of partnerships and networks that bring manifold resources to bear on solving community and public problems. The professional does have valuable knowledge, attributes, orientation, and capabilities, which are especially evident in the ways he or she exercises leadership and facilitates the work. These include awareness of normal ways of being that are oppressive and ways to interrupt them, an orientation to working equitably, democratically and inclusively in all types of social settings (termed Self-Other transformation), and the capacity to draw out people's understandings and knowledge, or collective intelligence. The next section briefly explains these three ways of practicing.

Practices for the Democratic Civic Professional

Disturbing and Interrupting the Normal

The very essence of normalcy is that it is taken for granted and hardly questioned. If we notice it, especially if we are on the dominant side of a divide, we might simply feel comfortable: it is how things are supposed to be. But, as discussed in Chapter 2, what is felt as normal is produced through what Foucault terms technologies of power, which find expression through language and habits of thought, heart, and action. For example, it may seem quite normal for academics to see and represent themselves as expert knowers and problem solvers and feel good in doing so; in turn, members of a community that is being helped by those academics and other expert professionals might feel powerless to help themselves and genuinely desire and appreciate the outside help. But even in this best case scenario, the helper-helped relationship serves the recognitive interests of the academics, enhancing their self-esteem while sabotaging the self-esteem of those who are 'helped.' These dynamics are at times quite subtle and thus the democratic civic professional needs, first, to become aware of these tendencies inside him or herself, and second, to *unlearn* the attitudes and behaviors that support them. The interruption comes through the actions of a developmental leader who understands the importance of leadership practices that encourage and cultivate capacities for action in others, even if the others are resistant to seeing themselves and acting as responsible agents.

Self-Other Transformation

If we think about Self and Other through the shortcut of dominant and oppressed, Self-Other transformation means changing a relation of dominant (or privileged, advantaged) and oppressed (or subordinate, dis-advantaged) to an equitable one, where neither party dominates or oppresses the other and respect and recognition are accorded mutually. Oppression takes many forms, such as silencing, marginalization, and exploitation, which have economic, cultural, social, and psychic aspects. One of the ways to think of it is as the absence of social justice as discussed above (see also Young, 2011). Thinking with difference rather than binary opposites means undoing and unlearning ways of being and relating that are deeply embodied in our identities and part of the normal workings of our institutions. It is thus not enough to try to change oneself—even if it were possible to do so—because Self-Other is a social relation that is maintained by both parties and is not just inherent in individuals: our very language, for instance, has metaphors of light and dark that consciously and unconsciously influence how we think of ourselves and relate as raced persons.

Engaging in social partnerships democratically calls for a transformation of this divide by reducing the capacity of Self to define and supporting the capacity of Others to define themselves: these are important aspects of power sharing and of an orientation to democracy that is about social justice as recognition. As we will see especially in Chapter 8, what is involved is more than the goodwill of the professional. Those whom Self defines as Others are definitely not puppets who simply accept being so defined: they do have agency, which is often exercised through various forms of resistance and rebellion that block pathways to collaboration.

Collective Intelligence

Sharing information from multiple perspectives typically enables groups to develop new, more complex and creative understandings of a problem or situation. Solutions thus emerge that are generally more viable than is the case when planning and decision making are either expert-driven or not informed by multiple perspectives. The literature refers to this sharing of information as collective intelligence, a fast-growing practice that is based on the evolving model of the learning organization and on complexity theory (Boud, Cressey, & Docherty, 2006). The central idea is that collective intelligence is essential for dealing with problems in environments marked by rapid change and complexity and that those who are on the ground, experiencing a problem firsthand, constitute a vital source of information. Page's (2007) cutting-edge research demonstrates the superior outcomes produced by diverse groups.

Exchanging information is qualitatively different from co-constructing knowledge, which is much less frequent and considerably more difficult to achieve. A collective is not necessarily intelligent and might be overly conformist. Collective intelligence requires bringing together groups that include as much diversity as possible—of opinion, capacities, knowledge base—and enabling participants to engage in collective reflection and dialogue that valorizes [ascribes] the value understandings and experiences each brings to the table and leads to a creative and productive synergy (Levy, 1995; Rojzman, 2009). Self-Other transformation must thus be part of the process of creating collective intelligence.

A key question then centers on how groups across social divides, which are often separated by prejudices and Self-Other binaries can come to share information openly and truthfully, generating collective intelligence through their exchange. If these groups are to work together to address social problems, and if the democratic civic professional is one who (among other things) facilitates this process, how is this done? What capacities are needed? Answering these questions is, in large part, what the book is about.

Notes

1. Some "toolkits" and resources that identify and explain activities that may be undertaken toward these ends are provided in various endnotes. However, the book is not primarily about applying what others have developed, but thinking constructively and reflectively with others and working collaboratively with them to create appropriate practices.
2. Chapter 3 discusses neoliberal 'managerialism.' Well-respected figures propose widely different alternatives: Wheatley (2010) locates leadership and organizational change in the context of a relational, participative universe while Senge, Scharmer, Jaworski, and Flowers (2004) write about collective learning and 'presence.'

2

DIFFERENT LENSES FOR UNDERSTANDING PARTNERSHIPS

Learning from the Addams-Lincoln Family Center Case

We can learn a great deal when things don't go well, if we are willing to engage in reflection. And so I begin with an interorganizational project that accomplished its tangible goal of creating a school-based family center but failed, in most respects, as a partnership. The narrative is a composite drawn from a number of attempted collaborations, creating a teaching case that will generate questions and ideas to be explored in this and other chapters. The case also includes selective data, created in the same fashion, such as would be culled from documents, observations, and interviews with participants. Details are provided in part so that readers can engage in their own search for additional insights about the case.

The chapter includes a brief review of the partnership literature. I explore what the case has to teach us by examining it through different lenses. First comes the literature on partnerships and collaboration, including basic processes such as shared purpose and open communication. The second pertains to enablers and barriers identified through a search of the literature on university-community partnerships, such as building relationships, addressing power inequities, participatory processes, and respect. The barriers often fall in the gray area of unexamined assumptions that accord power to university partners in ways that often escape them, such as what constitutes legitimate roles, knowledge, and actions. The very fact of having legitimacy goes along with what I term the power of the normal.

This point leads to the third lens, *thinking tools*, which is about using theories and concepts to reflect on deeper sources of the problem and consider normal and alternative practices. An important way to cultivate democratic civic professionals is to examine and interrupt oppressive normalcies and hegemonic assumptions that create borders. Reflecting with thinking tools helps illuminate aspects of the case that are not generally addressed in the literature. It also illustrates the approach I take to engaging in partnerships: in contexts where partnerships cross social divides, democratic engagement can only begin when we are willing to look at the borders that divide us and commit to bridging them.

If you are tempted to question the credibility of the case that follows, I assure you that events such as those described here do actually happen. I often use this case as a role play in a course on university-school-community partnerships, and find that it deepens our understanding of the issues and sparks discussion about alternative practices.

Case Narrative

The Story: Brief Summary

Two organizations and their respective leaders are the main actors in this interorganizational partnership: Lincoln School, an inner-city 7th- to 12th-grade school where the new family center is to be located, and its principal, Jerome Harris; and the Jane Addams Center for Social and Economic Justice, an entity that is part of the College of Social Work at nearby Urban University, with Dr. Vince Cantril as director. The Jane Addams Center has a long history of sponsoring programs and activities in the surrounding neighborhood and placing social work interns in neighboring schools including, lately, Lincoln. A strong and well-respected principal, Mr. Harris has made significant improvements in the school and established excellent relationships with the local community.

The collaboration began in earnest when the center and school submitted a joint grant proposal for a three-year program that would create a family center at Lincoln. The Jane Addams Center, as the lead agency, was awarded the grant. The vision was that educators, social service workers, community members, and families would join in a partnership that would provide needed supports for students, caregivers, and community members, thus creating a circle of care around the students and providing a fulcrum that would lift the whole community (Dryfoos, Quinn, & Barkin, 2005; Epstein, Coates, Sanders, & Simon, 1997). The grant was received at the end of June. An advisory board representing all major stakeholders was quickly created and charged with reviewing the vision, mission, and goals of the family center and advise partnership leaders (Dr. Cantril and Mr. Harris) on the structure for implementation and the hiring of a director. All of this had to be accomplished by September, the start of the school year.

The board began meeting in July. It is now late August. The assigned tasks have been completed and candidates for the director position have been interviewed. The board has advanced two candidates with strong credentials but also important differences. Carol Davis (ranked first) is the director of a neighborhood organization that engages in youth advocacy and community organizing and is well known and respected by locals. Nancy Green (ranked second) has held responsible administrative positions in social service organizations in similar neighborhoods and is currently assistant director of an agency that serves diverse at-risk youth and families in a nearby suburb. Davis is African American and Green is white.

Let me fast-forward to a crisis that clearly revealed serious fault lines in the collaboration. A meeting of the Family Center Advisory Board is in progress. As you approach the meeting room, you catch snippets of the conversation.

- The experience of either candidate is not in question. What is in question here is the voice of the community. We believed we were entrusted with selecting the best candidate to run the family center. But you just disregarded us!
- Why does your boss think he knows best and can make a unilateral decision?
- The director did meet both candidates; he interviewed them.
- This Jane Addams Center for Social Justice has been meddling in our community, with their "we want to help you" for years, and now that they've actually asked for our input, they're just going to ignore it?
- This makes me sad. We picked Nancy Green as one of our candidates, but now you don't trust her because she's not from the community? She has a lot of experience in similar communities and she has another great asset, a solid track record at getting funding, which the family center will need!
- I call a vote on whether we should continue this partnership!
- We need to think of the families and students. Where will we get the money for a new start?
- In the best interest of the students, we should accept Nancy Green. She's not a complete outsider. We will need more clarity, good bylaws for our future work together; we'll need to build trust. But now we need to move on.
- We had the perfect person in Carol Davis, someone we know and trust, someone with excellent credentials plus lots of experience and a strong record of achievements right here in this community. The principal and the community will never go along with the decision to hire Nancy Green.

The meeting goes on. In the end, a bare majority carries a vote in support of continuing to jointly develop the family center with Nancy Green as director. You ask around and piece together the main contours of the story.

The Actors

The Jane Addams Center for Social and Economic Justice (JAC) has been in existence for over 30 years. Higher education centers must support themselves through outside funding, especially in our current times of reduced funding for public education, and JAC is no exception. The university provides the space and a minimal operating budget and pays the director's salary, while outside grants support ongoing activities as well as new initiatives. When a state agency announced a request for proposals (RFP) for service integration projects that involved service agencies and schools, it was easy to set the wheels in motion.

The grant fit the priorities and capabilities of JAC perfectly: the proposal had to be submitted by a consortium of organizations including educational and social services, which would work collaboratively on an integrated, systems approach to meeting the academic, social, and emotional needs of at-risk youth. The RFP required the lead agency to demonstrate extensive prior experience in providing technical assistance for program integration, including training and professional development to promote cross-systems collaboration, and JAC had an excellent track record in all aspects of the RFP. The social work interns at Lincoln School could already claim some accomplishments, which had been duly documented as initial evidence of successful collaboration. Social work teams had supported the work of the teachers and school staff and facilitated access to social services for students and families, through the network of service agencies that had long-established connections with JAC.

Dr. Vince Cantril, JAC's director, has come to his position in part because he is good at getting grants—he enjoys the work and the projects created through such funding give him a sense of accomplishment. A white man in his late forties, he has held this position for the past seven years. Under his leadership, the Center's projects have grown and are now reaching across the underserved areas of the city, while the staff has almost doubled in size. Dr. Cantril was born into a professional family that strongly valued education and, with a little sacrifice, managed to send him to excellent schools. He attended Jesuit institutions of higher education that instilled in him a strong ethic of public service and commitment to the poor. When he received his doctorate 10 years ago, he was already on the faculty at the School of Social Work, and when the leadership of the Center became available he jumped at the opportunity. His philosophy is in line with the Center's mission, which is captured by its name: Jane Addams was a founder of the Settlement House Movement in Chicago. The settlement house she created, Hull House, catered to the poor immigrants in the neighborhood, providing an array of programs that included night school for adults, clubs for children and youth, skill training, cultural activities, gym facilities, and a coffee house and meeting place. An ardent activist for empowered immigrant and poor communities, women and peace, Jane Addams won the Nobel Peace Prize in 1931.

While Vince Cantril still does some teaching, the Center is his real passion: he is dedicated to community advancement and considers himself a community advocate. His accomplishments are well regarded in the university and his mentor, a departmental colleague, has advised him to start preparing a dossier for promotion to full professor. Interviews with staff confirm that he is generally well liked and respected. Many professionals and administrators of service agencies in the city were trained by the College of Social Work and have maintained good working relationships with the college and with him personally. They continue to provide internship sites for current students and are frequent collaborators on grant-funded projects.

Lincoln School (LS) is a small school with roots in the neighborhood. Its student body of around 450 is almost entirely African American and most of the students qualify for free or reduced-price meals.[1] Its 27 teachers are about evenly divided between African Americans and whites and about two-thirds are women. The school is able to keep on site students who would otherwise be referred to disciplinary schools because, through the efforts of Principal Harris, it has received special outside funding for two youth workers who provide additional supports and handle the tougher discipline cases. The motto painted on the school entrance, "Each One, Teach One," is an African American saying that calls on the community to take responsibility for everyone's learning: one of the youth workers who is from the neighborhood is charged with family and community involvement.

Jerome Harris, the principal of Lincoln School, is an African American man in his late fifties who strongly identifies with the school and community. This is the neighborhood in which he grew up and where his parents, both retired educators, still live. Having attended a public, college-preparatory high school in the city, he was one of the few local young people to be admitted to Urban University, from which he received a B.A. in Community Development, with a teaching certificate in Social Studies, and a Master's of Education with a principal's certificate. Mr. Harris has been principal of LS for the past 12 years. Prior to his tenure, principals came and went, but he chose this tough school and neighborhood and decided to stay.

Mr. Harris considers education the central civil rights issue of our times (Moses, Perry, Delpit, & Cortes, 2008). He is deeply troubled by the high drop-out rate in urban schools, especially that of young African American and Latino men, and is proud of his accomplishments as principal. He is passionate as he explains his philosophy of education: "This is a place of last resort for our students. They've been failed by the system over and over again, and if we fail them too, it's the school-to-prison pipeline.[2] We're losing our youth, especially our boys. We have to save them. That's what this is about." As part of the program that funds the youth workers, he has instituted a modified version of a zero-tolerance policy that has reduced the need for harsh discipline and contributed to feelings of "school as community" for both students and teachers. Teacher attrition has vastly declined; the student drop-out rate decreased by almost 40% during his first 8 years and has since stabilized at around 25%; 70% of the graduates have gone on to regular employment, community college, or some form of postsecondary education.

An Urgent Need

While these are impressive achievements for this school and neighborhood, the students who leave before graduating trouble Principal Harris deeply. He has done everything possible to keep the students and community engaged and ensure that teachers attend to students' social and emotional needs as well as to their academic work (Catalano, Berglund, Ryan, Lonczak, & Hawkins, 2004; Durlak, Weissberg, Dymnicki, Taylor, & Schellinger, 2011). Graduates keep in touch and many come back to mentor the young people and participate in rite-of-passage ceremonies. Nonetheless, LS seems to have reached an impasse.

A Promising Partnership?

The connection to JAC and Vince Cantril came out of this need and a fortuitous meeting with one of Lincoln's graduates, Takisha Jones, who had received a social work degree from Urban University and was now working at a local service agency. Knowing of his dream to turn Lincoln into a community school, Takisha introduced Harris to Cantril about a year ago; they agreed on a common purpose that focused on community development and a process that would begin with obtaining funding for a family center. In the meantime, JAC began placing social work interns in the school. Prior to this collaboration, Mr. Harris had little to do with the university, which he views as having mostly extracted resources from the community rather than contributing to it: his experiences as a student at Urban University did nothing to change this view (Swim, Hyer, Cohen, Fitzgerald, & Bylsma, 2003), and in fact he agrees with many in the neighborhood that the community has been under siege by the university for decades.

The research team routinely asks about the factors needed to ensure the success of the project and what might cause it to falter or fail. The question reveals each partner's understanding of project dynamics, as well as any unspoken fears or concerns that may influence how the partners will interpret their own roles and events. During the interview, Vince Cantril talks about the project with assurance: he has developed a relationship with Jerome Harris over the past year, they have shared ideas about the family center, and they are on the same page. He is convinced that the project is sound and will benefit all involved. He hesitates briefly about any potential problems:

> We want to be community oriented, and the community advisory board is an important aspect of this. But things can sometimes get messy with community members, you have to tread a fine line between doing things the right way and being political, doing what will win over support. But we've been at this for a long time, and understand how to deal with community politics.

His concerns relate to the unpredictability of the community and its micropolitics and the importance of professionally trained leadership for the family center, especially to plan and manage expectations for services. "In a community like this one—he points out—we could easily be overwhelmed with requests for services and find ourselves unable to deliver. The Mayor's office will be important there in keeping politics out of our process and the selection of the director will also play a part."

Answering the same question, Jerome Harris emphasizes that the family center must have a strong, empowering connection to the community. The director needs to be someone who has their full trust, understands the young people's lives, and can be their advocate. Being able to work with all the different stakeholders is also important, which may make the position hard to fill. But he has an excellent person in mind, who has the right credentials and experience, understands the system, and knows how to push for services while also maintaining good relations with the agencies, the city, and the university.

Harris also mentions a general concern about working with the university on such an important project: his belief that "they don't get it" and so can never be completely trusted. He would much rather be fully in charge and be the one to deal with the service agencies, rather than being, as he puts it, "a sort of co-director along with Cantril." To a question about how he sees Cantril, Jerome Harris smiles and replies: "I need him and he needs me." He adds that Cantril "can connect with some resources better than I can, they trust him, because he speaks their language, he's one of them. So we work together. He's not a bad guy, he even says he's for community empowerment. But he's not one of us." To the next question about what would make Cantril "one of them" and how that might come about, Harris replies:

> He could try to get to know us, see things from our perspective. He'd need to know that there's a lot he doesn't know. But he comes in as the one with the resources and the skills and the know-how—you know, come teach us how to do things right. Honestly, I don't even think he realizes he does that. So in partnering with him, we're going out on a limb. But this is a really important initiative, we've worked so hard for it, we just have to make it work.

Understanding What Happened: Three *Moments*

The narrative features three *moments* that brought to light barriers to collaboration that are particularly salient when attempting to create partnerships across social borders. As the case analysis begins to reveal and subsequent chapters develop further, many of these barriers pertain to things that are taken for granted or are unspoken, unseen, and unattended, until, as happened here, there is a crisis. In the first moment we look at the beginning and the grant funding process. The second moment is structured around the personnel decision highlighted above. The decision conformed with university rather than community practice and priorities and brought to light misunderstandings and disagreements about the vision and purposes of the family center that were not aired previously. The third moment revolves around the board meeting following the personnel decision: the decision stood and the center came into being, but the deep divisions unearthed by the decision continued to fester just beneath the surface and were never resolved.

The First Moment: A Grant Made for Us

The opportunity came via the RFP described above. Announced in April, fairly close to the end of the fiscal year, the short timeline improved funding odds and JAC was awarded a three-year grant totaling $376,000. A memo from Cantril to Harris, dated April 22, conveys the partners' agreement on the purpose of their collaboration and the process for writing and submitting the grant proposal. I have summarized the most important points:

Family Center Purpose:

- Provide access to comprehensive services for students, families, and community members.
- Reduce discipline problems and enhance student engagement and academic success by: introducing positive youth development and social and emotional learning programs; enhancing teacher effectiveness through collaboration with social service professional staff; providing outside referrals for the most serious student problems; offering preventive services aimed at reducing at-risk behaviors in the school and community.
- The family center is the first step toward creating a comprehensive community school in the Jane Addams tradition.

Process for writing and submitting the grant by the June 1 deadline:

- JAC will undertake most of the writing; LS will have the opportunity to review and ask for revisions.
- LS will provide background data on students and the community and a narrative about the school, its mission, goals, and achievements. JAC will fill in any information gaps.
- LS will consult with community organizations on needs, vision, and ideas for the family center; provide a list of such organizations; and solicit letters of support from community leaders.
- JAC will draft the grant proposal, including the implementation plan and budget and obtain letters of support from collaborating social service agencies.
- JAC will provide LS a final draft for review by May 20; comments, questions, and any revisions to be returned by May 25, leaving a few days for final revisions and obtaining the required signatures inside the university.
- JAC will be the fiscal agent. Per university rules, only employees can be named Principal Investigator (PI) on a grant: Dr. Cantril will have that

formal role. University rules also do not allow any nonemployee to be listed as a Co-PI: Mr. Harris will be listed as Director of School-Based Services and Project Associate. School district rules are even more cumbersome than the university's, making this the best possible approach.
- Informally, both Cantril and Harris will be coleaders for grant-related activities.
- Once the grant is received, Cantril will assign his assistant director, Blanche Simmons, to work on the project half time, staffing the advisory board, conducting needed research on best practices, and generally ensuring a good start for the family center.

Second Moment: Searching for a Well-Qualified Director

Once the grant was received, Cantril and Harris immediately set the advisory board in place. Informal contacts with prospective board members during the application process made the task easier. The 13-member board would report to them directly, primarily through their respective assistant director and assistant principal, who would be board members. The board included, in addition, two members of the school staff (a youth worker/counselor and a teacher); one student, an alumna who was also a social service professional (Takisha); two community members (the Parent-Teacher Organization [PTO] chair, who was also a parent, and a community influential); representatives of three stakeholder agencies (social services, corrections, and youth services); the mayor's education officer; and an education faculty member with expertise in evaluation. Given the tight deadline, board members quickly selected Blanche Simmons, JAC assistant director, as board chair and agreed to meet weekly during July and August.

The board moved almost immediately to advertise the director's position, deciding on the qualifications at its second meeting, after a visioning exercise at the half-day retreat that constituted the formal beginning of planning. Harris and Cantril concurred and board members were encouraged to recruit suitable applicants. The position announcement established the following credentials:

> Required: Master's of Social Work or equivalent degree; seven years in progressively more responsible positions in school-based family and youth services. Desirable: Experience with inter-agency collaboration in service of at-risk families and youth; demonstrated capacity to work with the Center's client groups a strong plus.

A round of interviews produced our two finalists. Both met the basic and desirable requirements for the position. However, an additional issue that emerged during the interviews generated considerable discussion: should the candidate be familiar with the local neighborhood and community and, in particular, would it be desirable if the candidate had prior experience with African American urban youth?

School and community representatives favored Carol Davis. Several board members explained that, in addition to her excellent qualifications, she had demonstrated a strong commitment to local youth and families and had a strong record of securing services for them. Other members were concerned about her community organizing strategies, which were deemed too confrontational and adversarial, although they did agree that these strategies had worked well for her and the community (Shirley, 1997). The other finalist, Nancy Green, had graduated from a social policy program at an Ivy League university and her strengths were in participatory program evaluation and research-based practice. At her current job she was known for her progressive views and had spearheaded successful programs informed by the theory and practice of positive youth development and civic engagement. She had also secured a number of large grants. As is common practice, the board was asked to submit two names to the project leaders. The board was not required to rank the candidates but did so, which generated considerable discussion and a bare majority decision. Mr. Harris indicated his agreement with the board's recommendation and Dr. Cantril was to make the official job offer.

The Decision

Dr. Cantril reversed the rank order and offered the job to Nancy Green, who accepted it. Prior to making the decision, he had conferred with his university colleague and mentor. He called Jerome Harris to let him know before the official announcement was made.

The Aftermath

Board members received a letter from Cantril informing them of his decision. He thanked them for their devotion and hard work and for submitting the names of two outstanding candidates. He explained that, based on his experience and after careful deliberation, he believed that Nancy Green was the better candidate to set the family center on a sound footing. Making the decision had been difficult but it was part of his responsibility. He trusted that they would welcome Nancy Green and support her as she started work on fulfilling the vision they all shared for the family center.

Various board members had heard other details via the rumor mill: that the hiring decision was reversed not by Cantril but by top university administrators who deemed it too risky given current tensions with the local neighborhood; that there had been strong words from Harris to Cantril, with Harris accusing him of double-dealing and betrayal and implicitly accusing him of racism by saying, "this is not your plantation." Cantril had stood his ground: Nancy Green was the better person for interfacing between the community and the agencies; Carol

Davis had significant accomplishments but was considered too confrontational and potentially damaging to relationships with agency partners and university insiders. Harris was shocked: Nancy Green would not be able to connect with the community; without Carol Davis, the family center was finished. The word was that Cantril was quite shaken by the exchange and taken aback by Harris's reaction; that Harris was still fuming; and that both had subsequently reached out to supporters about the decision. A board meeting was coming up, and there were concerns and strong feelings about what would and should happen there.

Third Moment: The Board Meeting

As in the past, the meeting was chaired by Blanche Simmons. She began by acknowledging the disagreements raised by the hiring decision, noting that they needed to be aired: the decision was the only item on the agenda, a fact that signaled the importance of the upcoming discussion. She invited especially those members who took issue with the decision to speak. After initial hesitation, the discussion got quite heated and two main issues emerged: differences about the most important requirements of the position and the decision-making process. Members who spoke in favor of Carol Davis stressed her ongoing relationships with the community: Nancy Green's skills at organizational development and fundraising were important but not as valuable: she had worked with *similar* populations, but did not know the culture, history, assets, and needs of this particular community.

The decision-making process evoked strong feelings. Community-oriented members argued that the lack of transparency made it seem especially arbitrary and in line with the university's ongoing lack of respect for the community. Anger was followed by concerns about the disempowering effects of a process that seemed to promise democratic involvement and then, at a crucial point, reverted to hierarchical decision making: how could the university ever be trusted again? There was some recognition that Dr. Cantril had the formal authority to make the decision, but he had not been expected to overturn the board's ranking.

A motion to sever the partnership and seek alternate funding for the family center was made and seconded; however, discussion revealed that most board members were unwilling to start anew, especially given a lack of appropriate resources in the community and concerns about missing the opportunity to actualize the project. Furthermore, board members representing service agencies had favored Nancy Green from the start, so defeating the motion required only a small number to switch sides. Discomfort and questions remained, but a subsequent motion to accept Cantril's decision received a majority vote.

The discussion then turned to the future: how to prevent similar occurrences from recurring and how to organize the family center's leadership so as to address issues raised at the meeting, especially the inclusion of the voices of community and school members. It was decided to proceed quickly to draft bylaws that would clarify responsibilities and establish appropriate procedures, and to call an open forum for the purpose of explaining the board's concurrence with the hiring decision and soliciting community ideas on how best to ensure the inclusion of all stakeholders in family center projects and decisions.

The meeting ended on a note of uncertainty about Mr. Harris's reaction. The school counselor, a community representative, and Takisha volunteered to meet with him and attempt to obtain his agreement with the board's decision. At the meeting, rather than agreeing, Harris simply acquiesced: he had no choice but to go along with the decision for the time being, but he would work on his own and with people he trusted to obtain funding for initiatives that would meet priorities the family center was not likely to emphasize, in light of its leadership. Beyond that, he would continue to pursue his dream of working with the community toward creating a community school. He no longer had much hope or a vested interest in the family center.

The Literature on Partnerships: Initial Case Analysis

This section examines the case, searching for answers to the overall question of what went wrong and whether the problem could have been anticipated and the crisis avoided. As mentioned above, I use three analytical lenses. The first two rely on research and theory on partnerships and collaborations that are drawn from (a) general literature on the topic and (b) the more specialized literature on partnerships across social borders, especially those that feature campus-community and school-university partnerships. The third lens introduces an alternative way of examining the case, introducing some *thinking tools* that will reappear in other chapters: social justice and power, especially the power of the normal.

Partnership Basics: The General Literature

Partnership and collaboration have become catchall terms for just about any type of interorganizational endeavors that involve working together. For instance, Gajda (2004) provides a nonexhaustive list that includes "joint ventures, consolidations, partnerships, coalitions, collaboratives, alliances, consortiums, associations, conglomerates, councils, task forces, and groups" (p. 68). Let me start with a definitional exercise.

Defining Collaboration

Drawing from both research and conceptual work, Thomson, Perry, and Miller (2009) provide the following definition:

> Collaboration is a process in which autonomous or semi-autonomous actors interact through formal and informal negotiation, jointly creating rules and

structures governing their relationships and ways to act or decide on the issues that brought them together; it is a process involving shared norms and mutually beneficial interactions.

(p. 26)

This definition alerts us to two key issues. First, collaboration is about process. This simple point tends to be overlooked: planning may emphasize producing shared visions and missions, targets and deliverables, while the process of getting there remains invisible. Second, process involves negotiation and the joint creation of the rules and structures that will govern interaction, decision making, and collaborative activities. Table 2.1, discussed below, presents relevant factors identified through an extensive review of the literature conducted by Emerson, Nabatchi, and Balogh (2012).

As Gajda (2004) explains, not every interorganizational alliance is a collaboration. She offers a continuum of low to high integration between the partners, suggesting that no practice is automatically the best and that the partners must carefully consider and negotiate a suitable position on the continuum. Starting with informal networking, the increasingly more integrated structures move on to cooperation (sharing information and mutual support), coordination (common tasks and compatible goals), collaboration (integrated strategies and collective purpose) and, finally, "coadunation" (unified structure and combined cultures, with the formation of a new, inclusive entity). Each step along the continuum puts heavier demands on the interorganizational support structures and the organizations themselves. Collaboration entails joint planning, agreement on mission and goals, equal sharing of power, and interdependence. It thus requires each organization to forgo a rather high degree of autonomy. Based on Gajda's model, we can describe the Addams-Lincoln project, with regard to the eventual partnership structure, as a collaboration. As such, it carried a significant load.[3]

Boundary Spanning

The Addams-Lincoln Family Center project brought together several organizations, each with its rules, structures, processes, and cultures governing interaction inside the organization, plus a loosely defined local 'community' organized in part through community-based and school-based entities such as the PTO and churches. Such alliances typically take place through what are termed boundary-spanning or cross-boundary mechanisms—the advisory board, in our case; coordinating committees, task forces, or less formal periodic meetings such as monthly networking events may also serve the same function, depending on the partnership structure selected. Boundaries are lines of demarcation that maintain the separate identity and integrity of organisms, groups, and organizations and identify the tasks and roles they properly assign to themselves. Cross-boundary mechanisms or structures are thus organizational forms that

Cross-boundary mechanisms facilitate interorganizational or intergroup linkages: for instance, they may make the boundaries of participating organizations more porous, creating openings that allow the sharing of information and resources.

As Peter M. Miller (2007) points out, some organizations' boundaries are more or less porous than others. Thinking about routine organizational processes and structures in light of boundary spanning mechanisms helps us see that the university and school district boundaries are not porous with respect to sharing funds, and the funding organization's rules did not provide alternatives: even though the grant was designed to foster interorganizational collaboration, the funds were directed to one of the partnering organizations, whose rules prevented outside partners from sharing the formal responsibilities assigned to the person in charge of the grant (the PI). In addition, since the recipient of funds becomes the fiscal agent with accounting responsibility, it would not be possible for it (here, the university) to reassign the funds to a third, boundary-spanning organization. Readers may counter with a list of valid reasons supporting the status quo, which does not invalidate the obstacles inherent in such routine practices: if it had been possible to create and fund a third, boundary-spanning organization, Dr. Cantril would not have been the official decision maker, which opened him to pressure to decide on the basis of the interests and perspectives of his profession and of the university and did not force him to engage the partners, whether democratically or otherwise.

The structures and processes of the advisory board and community and stakeholder input and decision making also follow routine practice but are not of the same order as the first. Like the first, they reflect *normalized* practice; the difference is that in the latter instances more suitable alternatives could easily be used, if the routine and normal were questioned. It is common knowledge that boundary-spanning mechanisms, unlike formal organizations, involve a great deal of ambiguity in roles and responsibilities (Miller, 2007). If these issues are quickly resolved, as was the case in the Addams-Lincoln Advisory Board (e.g., decisions about chairing and how to run meetings), it may be because rules and roles are borrowed from the partnering organizations whereas they should be negotiated and created anew.

Recalling that social partnerships generally operate through the logic of networks, while the dominant organizational form even in the network age typically follows the hierarchical logic of bureaucracy can add weight to this point: what if we saw the advisory board as an information node where the various entities in a network meet? At the very least, it would increase awareness and explain the importance of being intentional in fostering appropriate processes and practices.

Routine and Alternative Practices

If boundary-spanning entities considered how to engage in collaboration as much as what outcomes were desired, the processes, rules, and roles so negotiated would likely be recognizably new and different from the usual routine. We can assume that the advisory board routinely engaged in agenda setting and discussion and, when needed, made use of Robert's Rules of Order, as we saw in the third moment. These routine practices are known to favor selective participation and lead to decisions that fail to use the knowledge of all participants and fully consider the consequences of proposed actions. The purpose of Robert's Rules, a parliamentary procedure that dates to 1877, was to restrain individuals for the sake of majority rule. In addition to inhibiting participation by those unfamiliar with them, the Rules reduce the flow of information, inhibit collective intelligence, and easily lead, as we saw in the case, to bare majority decisions that may leave participants frustrated and angry.

What alternatives are there? The democratic engagement literature frequently mentions two practices that also appear in the collaboration framework in Table 2.1: deliberation and consensus decision making.[4] To deliberate, as David Mathews (2004) writes, is "to weigh the possible consequences of various approaches to a problem against all that we consider truly valuable" (p. 8). Its advantage is that, by including a careful assessment of the costs and benefits of various courses of action, it fosters reflective public judgment rather than hasty decisions based on impressionistic and partial views. In the Addams-Lincoln case, there was some consideration of the possible consequences of actions (namely rejecting the grant) during the "third-moment" board meeting, but it came on the heels of Cantril's one-sided decision that was based not on deliberation but on standard university practice and politics. Deliberation is not without its critics, who argue that its reliance on reasoned and persuasive argument ignores the ways race, class, and gender intersect with power. The play of power is discussed later in the chapter.

Let me now turn to consensus decision making. Those who have not experienced the process may think the requirements of consensus are too onerous, making it unrealistic. An immediate correction is that consensus does not require unanimous agreement. As Susskind (1999) explains, it entails

> a good-faith effort to meet the interests of all stakeholders. The key indicator of whether or not a consensus has been reached is that *everyone agrees they can live with the final proposal . . . after every effort has been made to meet any outstanding interests.*
>
> ("Definitions, Consensus," emphasis in original)

Interests refer to the needs that underlie the positions people take on an issue and the demands they make. This distinction is well known in negotiation and conflict resolution practice. In our case, the candidate list forwarded to Dr. Cantril was an expression of positions rather than interests: such transmittals would not typically include information about any needs and interests advisory board members may have expressed in meetings. Dr. Cantril's hiring decision also pushed the parties into the positions of being for or against his selection for director. The discussion during the third moment begins to reveal underlying interests: for instance, the community's voice should be heard and participants should feel respected and well regarded; there was an interest in the ongoing sustainability of the center, which took form as a position that the director should be skilled in bringing outside funding into the center. However, there was no process for exploring underlying interests and forging them into proposals that might lead to consensus.

We catch a glimpse of the process through the questions Susskind would have a facilitator ask after some deliberation of a proposal that attempted to address all interests voiced by participants:

- "Is there anyone who can't live with the last version of what has been proposed?"
- "If so, what improvement or modification can you suggest that will make it more acceptable to you, while continuing to meet the interests of everyone else with a stake in the issue?"

These and other democratic practices discussed by Mathews (2004) are designed to support *engaged citizens* in exercising their capacity for judgment and thus reach toward practical wisdom rather than leaving knowledge creation to the experts. We will meet these ideas again in Chapter 5, which also looks at action research for practitioner-oriented planning and evaluation.

Collaborative Dynamics

The above are just a small sampling of the issues in the case that point to alternative practices for cross-boundary collaboration. A model for a collaborative governance regime (CGR) by Emerson and colleagues (2012) provides an excellent integrative synthesis on the topic. Based on a wide-ranging search of the conceptual and empirical literature on cross-sector collaboration, collaborative public management and planning, collaborative processes, environmental governance, and conflict resolution, the model includes a discussion of collaborative dynamics from which Table 2.1 is drawn. The three basic processes are principled engagement, shared motivation, and capacity for joint action. As the authors point out, they are interactive and should be visualized as cycles and not as linear and sequential processes. The quality of the interaction among elements determines overall effectiveness and the interaction of all processes produces a collaborative synergy.

Principled engagement draws especially from public administration and the deliberative democracy movement and entails "fair and civil discourse, open and inclusive communication, balanced by representation of 'all relevant and significant different interests . . . and informed by the perspectives and knowledge of all participants'" (Emerson et al., 2012, p. 11). As the authors point out with regard

TABLE 2.1 Collaborative Dynamics

Basic Processes	Process Elements		
Principled engagement	*Discovery:* Identifying shared interests, concerns, values. Fact-finding and analyzing relevant information.	*Definition:* Ongoing effort to build shared meanings and common purposes. Agreeing on terminology; setting tasks, expectations, and criteria to assess alternatives.	*Deliberation:* Candid and reasoned communication. Create safe space for listening, 'hard' conversations, and meaningful voice—leading to wise judgments (collective intelligence) about the public good.	*Determination:* Making procedural and substantive decisions (e.g., final recommendations). Better/fairer determinations are made through strong engagement processes (e.g., consensus building).
Shared motivation	*Mutual trust:* Pivotal initial element that supports others in motivation cycle. Come to see one another as reasonable, predictable, dependable.	*Mutual understanding:* See and appreciate differences; able to be open, truthful, and authentic; understand and respect others' positions and interests.	*Internal legitimacy:* Ongoing collaboration supported by sense that effort and participants are trustworthy and credible and interests are compatible and interdependent; interpersonal validation.	*Shared commitment:* Norms of trust and reciprocity reinforce sense that collaboration is legitimate and effective; create bonds of shared commitment to collaborative work and process.
Capacity for joint action	*Procedural/institutional arrangements:* Process protocols and structures for interacting; informal (norms) or formal (rules, bylaws, scope, and authority); at both intra- and interorganizational levels.	*Leadership:* Need multiple opportunities and roles (convener, facilitator, rep, advocate); different roles important at different times.	*Knowledge:* The 'currency' of collaboration; reaches toward complete, balanced knowledge; combines analysis, reframing, and new, shared knowledge; becomes social capital through integration of values and judgments of all participants.	*Resources:* May include funds, time, supports, skills, expertise; it is important to fairly redistribute/share unequally distributed resources, including power.

Source: Adapted from Emerson et al., 2012, pp. 7, 10–16.

to representation, it is important for both normative and instrumental reasons to have the right people at the table, being aware that participants come with their personal values, interests, attitudes, knowledge, as well as those of the profession, organization, or other groups with which they identify.

Shared motivation pertains to "the interpersonal and relational elements of the collaborative dynamics" (Emerson et al., 2012, p. 13). It is closely associated with social capital, or the nonphysical resources that flow through social networks and accrue from repeated reciprocal social exchanges. Chief among them is trust, also described as the glue that creates ties of sociality or social bonds that transcend families and friends and thus builds communities of people who can live and work together. Trust, in turn, supports communication and actions that build mutual understanding and the trustworthiness and legitimacy of collaborative work. Information is another important resource that flows through social networks and is part of social capital.

Finally, 'capacity for joint action' is about being able to work together toward something that participants cannot achieve separately. Therefore, the process must "enhance the capacity of both self and others to achieve a common purpose" (Emerson et al., 2012, p. 14). It is obvious that all the elements of the collaborative dynamics are geared to such outcomes, but here the focus is especially on formal and informal enablers such as structures for interacting, leadership, shared knowledge (or collective intelligence—as social capital), and other necessary resources, including funding and expertise. Power is an important resource but, in what constitutes a key difference between networks and hierarchical organizations, it must be distributed in ways that enable rather than stifle collaboration. This is an important topic to which I return below.

The model is useful for thinking through the case. Some of the elements in the table stand out immediately for their absence. The earlier discussion on meeting dynamics and consensus building already alerts us to issues pertaining to principled engagement. In addition, the board meeting appeared organized to gain consensus on a decision that was already made, but this was not given as its clear purpose. The same is true for the subsequent meetings that are proposed, which are thus not exercises in public deliberation but are the normalcy in what passes for community involvement, as exemplified by public comment sessions of policy boards, where rules are designed to control and minimize participation rather than invite it. Here the university partner has the upper hand and the community can choose to continue participating or to exit. The crisis does not result in new insights and actions: a decision that does not respect one of the partners will stand, as the impasse is resolved through power politics rather than collaborative dynamics. Yet, as we saw, there are negative results nonetheless.

Concerning shared motivation, we can see that its principal element, trust, was also an issue in the case. Table 2.1 lists qualities that make someone trustworthy: he or she will be reasonable, predictable, and dependable. The research also identifies three dimensions on the basis of which people may be trusted: their capacity, integrity, and benevolence (Lewicki & Tomlinson, 2003). According to Tschannen-Moran (2004), trust also entails a "willingness to be vulnerable to another based on confidence that the other is benevolent, honest, open, reliable, and competent" (p. 17). Above, I alluded to lack of trust by school and community members with reference to Cantril's decision, which led to questioning his integrity and benevolence. The lack of trust was felt on both sides, however, as revealed especially in the separate preproject interviews with Harris and Cantril (see case narrative, above). Applying the framework in Table 2.1, this problem affects the entire cycle of shared motivations and the process of deliberation. Cantril was concerned that Harris, as a carrier of community interests and its micropolitics, might forsake the dictates of rational decision making and act unpredictably. For Harris, Cantril's professional posture was oppressive, even more so as he seemed unaware of his privilege and presented himself as community- and social justice–oriented. Cantril's approach is doubly problematic, as the discussion below will reveal, because it is not dialogical: according to Harris, he does not ask the questions and engage in the listening that might enable him to learn and change. He presents himself as the (benevolent) expert who knows.

The case also illustrates the connection between these basic processes: had deliberation and consensus building been used for the advisory board meeting in the third moment, especially with a trained facilitator, it may have initiated a process of trust repair that the review of procedural arrangements alone, suggested by advisory board members, would not have accomplished. And yet, could that have taken place without subjecting the authoritarian move by Dr. Cantril to the truth-telling of deliberation?

Similarly problematic was also the state of all the elements of the third basic process, capacity for joint action. With regard to leadership, Peter M. Miller (2007) adds the important role of boundary-spanning leader, whom he describes also as network coordinator, internal networker, liaison, process facilitator, environmental manager, bridge person, and chief worrier. According to Firestone and Fisler (cited in Miller, 2007), an important function of boundary-spanning leadership is to negotiate concerns about trust, power sharing, and participation, which may be unspoken. Wood and Gray (1991) also note that the convener needs to have a kind of enabling power that conveys legitimacy to the project, has vision, is good at creating relationships, and is skilled with regard to process. Along with Gajda (2004), they emphasize that different skills may be needed to address whatever issues are salient in a given collaboration: for instance, if legitimacy is an issue, fairness and trustworthiness are essential, since participants would need to trust that the convener's authority will not be used arbitrarily. Finally, Miller and Hafner (2008) also alert us to the importance of both supportive and strategic leadership, from within each organization and not only inside the boundary-spanning mechanism. Leadership thus emerges as an essential resource that addresses all the processes in Table 2.1—one that was also lacking in the Addams-Lincoln case, as no one took up these functions.

While the issues that trouble Cantril and Harris are easily visible through Table 2.1, the deeper sources of the problems only emerge through the lens of recognitive social justice and the community partner's perspective. References to mistrust, lack of awareness of privilege, power sharing, and leadership take us to a literature that addresses *border crossing* rather than *boundary* spanning.

The Literature on Collaboration Across Borders

The general literature, as evidenced by Table 2.1, tends to assume that there are no special obstacles to achieving mutual trust and power sharing. With some 60% of US higher education institutions located in urban areas, thus implicated in long histories of problematic 'town-gown' relations and the usual disparities in physical, social, and political resources, we must assume the existence of borders and the disrespect, violence (everyday and structural) and unacknowledged privilege that characterize Self-Other relations. As Jerome Harris reminded us, local residents may see the university as an arrogant colonizer rather than accepting its construction of itself as a well-meaning benefactor. Feeling that one is routinely approached through a deficit lens and for the purpose of extraction makes mutuality challenging: how can the university offer a partnership unless its representatives genuinely feel that the community partners are potentially their equals? A crucial challenge for leaders and participants is to create relationships and processes that begin to redress such inequities, which includes consideration of the attitudes and dispositions that are embodied as normal ways of connecting across borders.

A summary of the characteristics of a quality partnership from the perspective of community partners resonates strongly with the tenets of social justice presented in Chapter 1, especially recognitive social justice, or according recognition, respect, and a sense of common humanity to partners whom power holders have routinely constructed as *Others*. Although views vary, community participants generally prize partnerships that redress imbalances in power, resources, and outcomes. They see relationships as foundational, placing a strong emphasis on ones that communicate respect, transparency, openness, and mutuality (Hoyt, 2010; Sandy & Holland, 2006). These relationships are nurtured through empathy, preserving the integrity of each partner, seeing the partner as having capacities, different kinds of 'credentials' and knowledge, valuing what each brings to the table, knowing the partner's identity, culture, and history—or being open to listening and learning (Bringle & Hatcher, 2002; Dreese, Dutton, Neumeier, & Wilkey, 2008; Korza, Schaffer Bacon, & del Vecchio, 2008; Stoecker, Tryon, & Hilgendorf, 2009).

Quality processes are those that acknowledge and address power asymmetries and privilege in the relationship between campus and community. These include seeking and developing community assets and capacities and promoting shared ownership. They entail not only the equitable integration of resources but also the elimination of expert approaches that are patronizing and intimidating—though when mutuality and respect are present, expert knowledge has its place (Sandy & Holland, 2006; White, 2010). Such actions flow from understanding poverty and social problems from a socioeconomic and systemic vantage point and not only as personal and community deficits.

One important way to achieve the desired equity, according to Miller and Hafner (2008), is to conceptualize collaboration as dialogue, incorporating in it elements of Paulo Freire's dialogical framework: for the higher education partner who is no longer positioned as the expert, dialogue involves "humility, faith in the people, hope, and critical thinking" (p. 75). It calls for willingness to step out of one's comfort zone, be uncomfortable and be changed. Dreese and colleagues (2008) add that "the whole point of community engagement on the part of universities (students and faculty) is to be in a genuine, mutual dialogue with community folks so that all are transformed by the interaction" (p. 150). Finally, sustained engagement, an ethical commitment to social transformation for the community, and an orientation to social justice lead to meaningful outcomes that benefit the community and tangible, transformative change in the partners and the institution (CCPH, 2007).

Writings by Musil (2009, 2011) and others connected with the Association of American Colleges and Universities (AAC&U) and the recent "call to action" by the National Task Force on Civic Learning and Democratic Engagement (NTFCLDE) (2012; see Chapter 3) point to a parallel movement inside higher education that is converging around these ideas. The concepts of social justice, justice, recognition, and community, which are central to the diversity movement, are being incorporated in programs of civic engagement in higher education. These also resonate with emphases in global and globalization studies on redressing global inequalities, promoting human rights, and documenting postcolonial struggles around people's full worth and dignity and political and social citizenship. There is thus, as Musil asserts, a potential for wide cross-cutting collaboration inside higher education around these issues, which are captured by an increasingly influential construct, the Civic Learning Spiral (see Chapter 4).

It should be evident by now that the desired framework for cross-border collaborations goes beyond the tenets identified by Emerson and colleagues. It encompasses Self-Other transformation, where respect accorded to the Other comes with a new identity, as the erstwhile [former] privileged higher education professional takes on the role of a civic professional and commits to enacting, as Hoyt (2010) puts it, an "epistemology of reciprocal knowledge, realized through a two-way network of human relationships, [that] allows faculty, students, civic leaders, and residents to experiment as they learn the norms and develop the values of democracy through sustained city-campus partnerships" (p. 86).

Using Thinking Tools to Understand the Addams-Lincoln Case

This section looks at the case through the lenses of social justice and power. For community partners, social justice as recognition is a central factor in collaborations. Examining the case through this lens helps us consider whether higher education and community partners might have different orientations to social justice. Power is also a central factor and power sharing has implications for the legitimacy of a project and for building trust.

Considering which thinking tools to apply to a particular case involves searching for its major themes, a process that is both objective and subjective. Part of the answer will come from the case itself: which tools have more explanatory power, or shed light on its key dynamics? However, each case can be understood through numerous lenses and thus it is important to consider our own interests and the particular questions we want to explore at a given time. I decided to use these particular tools not only because they address underlying themes in the case but also because they illuminate what I believe are central dynamics in many cross-border collaborations.

Social Justice as a Lens

Chapter 1 briefly presented three aspects of social justice founded on the principles of redistribution, self-determination, and recognition. Looking at the crisis in the Addams-Lincoln case through these three aspects sheds light on two questions. First, were the Jane Addams Center and its leadership committed to social justice, as they claimed to be? Second, was there any legitimacy to Jerome Harris's accusation of racism? Addressing these questions will highlight fundamental misunderstandings and miscommunication between the partners.

Which Social Justice?

In developing the family center, the higher education partners seemed to focus mainly on the redistributive aspect of social justice: the center would support educational opportunity and bring needed resources into the community. However, the advisory board and decision-making processes breached other aspects of social justice, namely the principles of self-determination and recognition.

Social Justice as Self-Determination

Self-determination entails conditions and processes for inclusion that permit people to participate meaningfully and equally in decisions that impact their lives. As process and practice, the advisory board did not conform to this principle. It is true that faculty, employees, community members, and similarly placed persons are often happy for the opportunity to exert influence through an advisory process. In certain contexts, the legitimacy of power holders may be so normative that there is prestige in being accorded an advisory role; however, the legitimacy of an advisory rather than a decision-making role does not necessarily make it socially just and may, in fact, hide a power play by the more powerful partner.

Case data strongly suggest that school and community representatives on the board felt that their participation had not been meaningful or equal. Based on Table 2.1, the basic process of principled engagement and especially the element of determination suggest that decision making in sound collaborations would generally follow the tenets of self-determination. Would the scenario in the second moment have been entertained in a boundary-spanning collaboration in which the partners were relatively equal? The question of an appropriate process for self-determination, including communication and voice, was not explored in this partnership, as routine practices were adopted without considering their implications for social justice. Resolving the problem through a majority vote hardly addressed social justice, especially in light of community memory of past injustices by the university and the current circumstances in which the university had budgetary control.

Recognitive Social Justice

The second and third moments also breached the principles of recognition in a number of ways. The knowledge and contributions of the community were devalued and participants were humiliated, while their sense of self-respect and self-worth was undermined. When Cantril and Simmons reiterate that "their" candidate has worked with similar at-risk populations it devalues and silences an emergent understanding of advisory board members—that knowledge of and experience with this particular community matters and can, in some circumstances, overshadow the more abstract, categorical knowledge of the expert. In addition, the at-risk label is a deficit-based perspective that constructs young people in this neighborhood in terms of what they lack as compared to normative ways of being. The point is not that there are no needs, but that labels such as *at-risk* essentialize the deficiencies at the expense of any capacities, leading even well-meaning professionals to see inner-city neighborhoods and their residents as nothing but dilapidated housing, crime, and strings of failures (Swadener & Lubeck, 1995). The point also is that the failure to be responsive to these other facets of social justice invalidates the entire collaboration, turning a potential partnership into the provision of services and charity.

We may suppose that some of these issues underlie the reactions of some board members and Jerome Harris, reactions that Cantril interprets as evidence of a dangerous irrationality. Let me now turn to the final lens: power.

The Multiple Lenses of Power

People often see power as a force that is possessed by some, who use it to make others comply with their will. This is power as coercion, or "power over." There are other ways to understand and use power: as mentioned above in the discussion on leadership, it can be a productive or enabling force ("power to"), which is simply the capacity to make things happen; or it can refer to the capacities that are put into play when we work together—collaborative power, or "power with." It is important for us to see collaboration as a positive form of power, but for the moment let me stay with its negative aspects because they point to obstacles to collaboration.

Coercive power shades into domination when it is exercised invisibly: for instance, a meeting agenda may be manipulated so that some choices are not possible, potential conflicts are suppressed, or change that is not in the interest of a dominant group is removed from the debate. In a classic political science text, Lukes (1974/2005) terms this the second face of power, to which he adds a third: the shaping of thoughts through ideology, the manipulation of opinion and legitimizing authority, in ways that are not observable so that some things are rendered invisible and unthinkable. Thus when we think of coercive power we need to consider not only its most visible form, which is exercised through decisions, rules, or policies that some consider undesirable, but also the myriad forms that escape our awareness.

We can recognize in the above previously discussed aspects of the case, such as the (possibly unconscious) manipulation of meeting agendas and the legitimation of advisory roles. Also present, especially in the first moment, are enabling and collaborative aspects of power. Dr. Cantril seems well meaning and genuinely interested in collaboration: he is setting the stage, giving directions, and organizing tasks, apparently exercising leadership as an enabler and facilitator. The discussion that follows will briefly problematize this understanding of Dr. Cantril's power, asking whether there are any mechanisms of power as domination in what seem like routine and standard facilitative practices.

The Power of the Normal

French social thinker Michel Foucault (1984) helps us grasp dimensions of power that are further removed from view than those identified by Lukes. For Foucault, power is neither negative nor positive: it is simply the way we become *normal* persons who enact practices that are also normal (or *normalized*) for a given historical time and place. Normalization occurs mainly through discourses, or systems of thought and logical habits that circumscribe what is thinkable and unthinkable and what can be said, and provide specific ways to understand and know the world. Thus if we consider knowledge to be objective and true, this is so not on account of its inherent properties but because it is part of a discourse that makes it *true*. A dominant discourse, for instance, proclaims the scientific method as the foundation of truth. In this view, the logic Cantril uses to support his selection of Nancy Green as director of the family center is no more than a dominant discourse that maintains the superiority of the academy and academic and professional knowledge. Yet these mechanisms are largely invisible to us as a result of what Foucault terms the 'normalization of the power of normalization.'

Interrupting and Disrupting the Normal

There are nonetheless cracks in the surface of the normal, and alternative and oppositional discourses may emerge especially in the context of the histories, life stories, and narratives of those for whom dominant normalcies are oppressive. Like all discourses, oppositional ones are not the carriers of objective truth. They are ways that members of subordinated groups make sense of their reality, often through themes of struggle with coercive power and a sense of oppression and victimization; they also typically include a good measure of silencing and oppression of in-group members, through classic patterns of in-group/out-group formation. Nonetheless, through these narratives and other social and personal crises that disrupt the normal we can catch glimpses of the workings of power both inside and around us. New possibilities may thus emerge that use power to forge less oppressive and more liberating structures and identities. These same possibilities can be created in structured learning situations that offer both challenges that interrupt the normal and supports that nurture its liberatory possibilities.

One of the main ways I conceptualize these spaces is through the notion of borders and borderlands. These become metaphors for spaces where different cultures, languages, and identities meet and intersect, doing so in ways that do not erase privilege and oppression and may in fact perpetuate discrimination, racism, and the like. Nonetheless, encounters with differences and ambiguities in these undefined spaces also make them more open to disruptions of normal ways of being.

Normalcy and Its Disruption in the Case

The RFP process is an example of normalization whereby power shapes Dr. Cantril's actions but the process is invisible to him until a crisis disrupts it. The RFP itself involves technologies of power that *discipline* how we think about a given project: it provides the structure in which the project is required to fit, including the definition of the problem, regardless of local circumstances and needs. The grant administration is a further instance of normalization. The idea that one of the organizations involved (here, the university center) should be the fiscal agent is not openly questioned, nor is the role of the PI (principal investigator), which makes Cantril the official decision maker, or the role of Blanche Simmons as board chair. A dominant discourse that no one seems to challenge until the crisis, constructs Cantril, Simmons, and the university as the ones with the knowledge, skills, and resources and thus as reliable managers of the project. Indeed, the whole first moment can be seen as normalization while the process that makes it normal is partly visible through Harris's concerns but does not enter the conversation as a challenge.

What adds to the ambiguity is that the partnership work spans multiple organizations but is ruled by the university. Metaphorically, we are in a borderland that is a colonial outpost of the university, that is, the territory is outside the borders of the colonizing state but is governed by its laws, policies, and worldview. Through this discursive lens, it is interesting to consider Jerome Harris's outburst that the family center project is not Cantril's plantation. The plantation draws from the historical memory, enshrined in everyday conversation, of distinctions between the house Negro and the field Negro: in a plantation, the house Negro ("Uncle Tom") could be counted on to smile and act in a servile manner, confirming the Master's illusory paternalism. The field Negro was more dangerous, unpredictable—*irrational*—more likely to stand up to power either through revolt or subterfuge [deceipt]. No wonder, also, that *service* may carry an altogether different connotation in African American communities than in higher education institutions that are informed by an ethic of service.

This discourse explains not only Harris's language but also his emotions surrounding the incident. As Harris sees it, he is standing up to power and here the power has decidedly racist overtones. In what is termed everyday racism, it is not the singular act that counts as racist, but the single act in the context of a multidimensional experience. Philomena Essed (2002) explains that "one event triggers memories of other, similar incidents, of the beliefs surrounding the event. . . . In other words, each instantiation of everyday racism has meaning only in relation to the whole complex of relations and practices" (p. 207).

For the moment, we are faced with a seeming impasse: on one side is the expert-manager technocrat steeped in a discourse of rationality and efficiency that is deeply embedded in the university's culture and epistemology. On the other side is an Other who sees coercive power through the cracks, as his memory, experience, worldview—discourse—has taught him to question such practices. Is one of them right? For Foucault and postmodern writers in general there is no single Truth but only partial, local truths: the answer is to be found in dialogue on the ground or through social action that changes the power dynamics and the discourse.

The next chapter attempts to gain a broader perspective on these discourses by locating them and higher education engagement in a historical sweep: we may think of Cantril as a carrier of modernity and Harris as a carrier of counter-discourses that carry the voices of Others. The democratic engagement movement that advances higher education partnerships as grounds for the development of socially just and democratic practices must contend with old patterns that are deeply rooted in modernity as well as more recent ones emerging from market-oriented policies designed to remake higher education *for* the knowledge economy and in the image of smart and nimble businesses. Prospective civic professionals must learn to recognize these different orientations influencing social partnerships.

Notes

1. This statistic is a common indicator of level of poverty. Eligibility is based on federal poverty guidelines: households can qualify for free meals or reduced-price meals (family income below 130% and 185% of the poverty level, respectively). For 2013–2014, these figures were $23,550 and $43,568 for 4-person households, respectively (Federal Register/Vol. 78, No 58/Friday, March 22, 2013/Notices. Retrieved from www.fns.usda.gov/sites/default/files/IEG_Notice-032213.pdf).
2. For background on the "school-to-prison pipeline" and mandatory "zero-tolerance" school discipline policies see Michelle Alexander (2010) and the ACLU Racial Justice Program (http://www.aclu.org/racial-justice/school-prison-pipeline).
3. Following Gajda (2004), I will refer to cooperation, coordination, and collaboration as partnerships. As she notes, "collaboration is increasingly considered the means by which student, school, and community level outcomes will be obtained" (p. 66). This is also evidenced by the frequency of RFPs for integrated collaborative approaches to social problems.
4. Claiming that typical evaluations prevent participants from realizing what they have learned, the Kettering Foundation also proposes alternative approaches to evaluation that can turn it into a process to further civic learning and initiate civic deliberation about future actions. See Mathews (2004) for the alternative. For traditional evaluation research methods see http://www.socialresearchmethods.net/kb/intreval.php; http://evaluationtoolbox.net.au/.

3

DEMOCRATIC ENGAGEMENT IN HIGHER EDUCATION

Between Modernity and Neoliberalism

> We dare not be passive about increasing our nation's civic capacity any more than we are passive about revitalizing its economy.
> (National Task Force on Civic Learning and Democratic Engagement [NTFCLDE], 2012, p. 69)

> The ascendancy of neoliberalism . . . has produced a fundamental shift in the way universities and other institutions of higher education have defined and justified their institutional existence. . . . Universities are seen as a key driver in the knowledge economy.
> (Peters & Olssen, 2011, p. 42)

One of the questions this book asks is how projects such as the Addams-Lincoln Family Center might become grounds for the development of democratic practices in campus-community partnerships. The question locates this project in the arena of higher education democratic engagement whose goal, as alluded in the first epigraph, is to use the power of higher education to foster civic capacity and a more participatory democracy. The case falls short of this goal, as it typifies instead the modality of outreach or activity-and-place engagement, which utilizes the knowledge and resources of experts in the academy to address real-world problems but involves nonexperts only as the recipients of service. Outreach of this kind can comport with the trend to which the second epigraph refers—neoliberalism—which is pressing higher education to turn its information and knowledge resources into marketable commodities. This chapter considers these different modalities of engagement in light of the larger sociopolitical and historical trends with which democratic engagement must contend.

In *To Serve a Larger Purpose* (Saltmarsh & Hartley, 2011), Derek Barker, a program officer with the Kettering Foundation, presents a view common among proponents of democratic engagement that while engagement defined in terms of activity and place has flourished in higher education over the past 20 years, its sense of purpose has waned. The Kettering Foundation is a research institution devoted to promoting democracy, civic learning, and the democratic mission of education. Supporting the strong view that we need a transformation of higher education and its relationship to the real world, Barker proposes that civic engagement be replaced with democratic engagement, which "requires something more—a larger sense of purpose and distinct processes to strengthen our communities and to build a participatory democracy" (pp. 9–10).

There is cause for some optimism. The national report cited above, commissioned by the US Department of Education on the heels of extensive and ongoing advocacy, has issued a call to action to reinsert democratic engagement in a national agenda for higher education.[1] As the two epigraphs suggest, however, the road ahead is steep and the engagement movement needs to contend with increasingly pervasive, exclusively economic discourses and practices in education. The 1980s saw both the creation of Campus Compact, with its emphasis on higher education's civic mission, and the Reagan administration's national education report, *A Nation at Risk* (National Commission on Excellence in Education, 1983), which initiated a 30-year shift in education policy that privileged its economic functions. Current and future engagement initiatives will have to navigate the tensions between these two orientations.

The chapter will show that the inroads of economic discourses in education compound other obstacles on the path of democratizing higher education. As the authors of *A Crucible Moment* aver, universities have gained their legitimacy through organizational forms and approaches to knowledge that include a high degree of compartmentalization and specialization. And while these have "produced a great deal of new knowledge, [they have] . . . also produced a technocracy that places certain kinds of expertise above all others" (NTFCLDE, 2012, p. 6). Fragmentation also means that the engagement movement has been somewhat disconnected from potentially allied initiatives such as those that stress diversity, although this may be changing (Banks, 2008).[2]

The chapter in divided into four sections. The first section provides a brief account of the engaged university movement (see Table 3.1). The second and third sections look at broad historical trends—modernity and neoliberalism—and their influence on higher education. Included here is the voice of Others—understandings and epistemologies that dominant modern and neoliberal trends marginalize, which reemerge through democratic practices that center on diversity as multivocality. The fourth section concludes the chapter by presenting different ways of framing partnerships and professionals' work that are drawn from the discussion in this chapter and the previous one. These frames, captured in Table 3.2, identify major differences, obstacles, and supports for democratic engagement. The main focus here and elsewhere continues to be on what actors inside the university need to understand and do in order to become possible partners. I take this approach not to privilege the view from the university but to look for the ways this privilege is maintained and how it is challenged and addressed. As Chapter 2 details, community partners themselves have raised these issues.

The Engaged University: Movement and Institutionalization

The earliest examples of what would become the engagement movement feature young people involved in various forms of experiential learning, social action, and work in communities, which were eventually institutionalized in higher education as service- and community-based learning (Stanton, Giles, & Cruz, 1999). A second stage involved the faculty, as engagement required reconsidering the tripartite division of their work—teaching, scholarship, and service (Boyer, 1990, 1996). Questions about the larger purpose and mission of higher education, present all along, finally crystallized in 2006, when community engagement was incorporated into the Carnegie classification that provides the nomenclature for the higher education sector. Professional organizations, journals, and foundations provided additional supports. This means that we can talk about a movement that dates back to the 1960s and its gradual institutionalization starting from the 1980s to the present.

Chronology and Main Events

A long-standing tradition in American higher education holds that colleges and universities should contribute to society: the outreach functions of land-grant institutions are just one example of a broader pragmatic and democratizing—though not uncontested—ethos that is an important aspect of American life (Bonnen, 1997). The engagement movement claims their legacy, while also inserting new meanings to strengthen higher education's contribution to democratic life. Table 3.1 captures the main actors, events and wide scope of the movement, which has addressed the following:

- mission and internal practices of institutions (including tenure and promotion)
- academic identities: students and faculty as engaged citizens
- supports: new organizations and publications, compacts, declarations, funding and research opportunities, work of discipline-based and professional associations
- government: legislation and policy initiatives

Starting with Students

Formal beginnings can be dated to 1984, with the foundation of the Campus Opportunity Outreach League (COOL) by Wayne Meisel, a social activist and Harvard graduate who took a 1,500-mile walk through East Coast campuses to

TABLE 3.1 Timeline and Road Markers in University Engagement

1984	Founding of student-based Campus Opportunity Outreach League (COOL)
1985	Presidents of Brown, Georgetown, Stanford & Education Commission of the States create Campus Compact
1990	Office of National Service (ONS) and Points of Light Institute created to support volunteering & service-learning. ONS later renamed Corporation for National and Community Service.
	Ernest Boyer, *Scholarship Reconsidered*
1993	(Federal) Corporation for National and Community Service created, supporting AmeriCorps, Learn and Serve America, Senior Corps
1994	First issue of the *Michigan Journal of Community Service Learning* is published.
1996	Ernest Boyer, *The Scholarship of Engagement*
	First issue of *Journal of Higher Education for Outreach and Engagement* (originally *Journal of Public Service and Outreach*)
1998	Community-Campus Partnerships for Health is created; begins publication of its peer-refereed journal, *Partnership Perspectives*
1999	Boyte & Hollander, *Wingspread Declaration on Renewing the Civic Mission of the American Research University*. To date, signed by 565 college and university presidents
	Presidents' Declaration on the Civic Responsibility of Higher Education
	Kellogg Commission on the Future of State and Land Grant Universities. *Returning to Our Roots: The Engaged Institution* (1999).
2002	American Political Science Association creates Standing Committee on Civic Education and Engagement. Two-year study results in *Democracy at Risk: How Political Choices Undermine Citizen Participation and What We Can Do About It* (Macedo et al., 2005).
September 2005	Talloires Network (international association) is created, with Tisch College of Citizenship and Public Service, Tufts University, at the center. Initial signatories: 29 university leaders from 23 countries.
Fall 2005	Scholars from engaged research universities convened by Campus Compact and Tisch College, Tufts University. First report: *New Times Demand New Scholarship: Research Universities and Civic Engagement—A Leadership Agenda* (Gibson, 2006).
June 2006	International network spearheaded by Council of Europe. Higher education leaders issue declaration and call to action: *Higher Education and Democratic Culture: Citizenship, Human Rights and Civic Responsibility* (Huber & Harkavy, 2007).
2006	Wingspread Conference, *Achieving the Promise of Authentic Community-Higher Education Partnerships: A Community Partner Summit*, April 24–26 (CCPH, 2007). Formation of HENCE (Higher Education Network for Community Engagement) follows.
	Carnegie announces new "community engagement" classification. By 2010, 311 higher education institutions receive the classification; 190 others begin application process. Next round: 2013, for 2015 classification.

(Continued)

TABLE 3.1 (Continued)

2007	*New Times Demand New Scholarship II: Research Universities and Civic Engagement—Opportunities and Challenges* (second report; Stanton, 2008).
2007–present	American Association of Colleges and Universities (AAC&U) sponsorship of student learning outcomes and assessment rubrics related to student civic engagement (for review, see Hatcher, 2011).
2008	Research University Civic Engagement Network (TRUCEN) created; develops Research University Engaged Scholarship Toolkit (Tim Stanton & Jeffrey Howard) (Campus Compact, TRUCEN).
May 11, 2009	President Obama launches federal Office of Public Engagement (previously Office of Public Liaison). Goal to make "government inclusive, transparent, accountable, and responsive." Website includes a blog that calls for direct dialogue, ensures all can participate, & bring new voices to the table.
2012	*A Crucible Moment.* Report of National Task Force on Civic Learning and Democratic Engagement (NTFCLDE, 2012). Sponsored by AAC&U, the Global Perspective Institute, & US Department of Education.
	Creation of American Commonwealth Partnership (ACP), an alliance of K–16 educational institutions. Includes a President's Advisory Council and regular consultation with the US Department of Education.

raise awareness about student engagement (Ross, 2002). An entirely volunteer organization, COOL quickly established a presence on some 450 campuses and held successful annual conferences that have continued to this day, under different names. In 1985, the presidents of Brown, Georgetown, and Stanford Universities joined with the president of the Education Commission of the States (ECS) to create Campus Compact, a campus-based organization that would advocate for and support the civic engagement of college students through service-learning and related activities. Almost three decades later, with a membership of nearly 1,200 campuses ranging from community colleges to Research I universities, Campus Compact now includes some 25% of institutions across the American higher education sector and has broadened its focus to all aspects of institutional life.

Back in the 1960s, new orientations to citizenship and civic learning were in the air, coming on the heels of federal government programs such as the Peace Corps and Volunteers in Service to America (VISTA), and the social activism of the civil rights, antiwar, women's, and social justice movements of the 1960s and 1970s (Markoff, 1996). Citizenship was being reenvisioned as involving responsibilities as well as rights. Collectively, these fostered young people's active participation and strong sense of responsibility regarding social issues both locally and in the larger society and world, in line with what Harry Boyte (2004) terms democratic public work. A central theme revolved on integrating into academics the work that college students had been doing in and with communities, as volunteers and social change activists. Drawing on the theories of John Dewey (Giles & Eyler, 1994) and Paulo Freire (Deans, 1999), the new pedagogy of service-learning would encourage reflection on experiences in light of academic knowledge, helping students connect service in the community to larger social issues (see Chapter 6).

The general premise of the new pedagogy was that it would promote deeper, more meaningful and more connected learning, personal development, more accepting orientations toward *Others*, and civic engagement. The meaning of the latter varied according to framework one adopted. It ranged from latent (or weak) forms such as being attentive to issues and active in associations, and participating in electoral politics, to strong democratic citizenship that embraces social responsibility and social justice activism (see Battistoni, 2013; Ekman & Amnå, 2009). Marginalized and excluded groups took a critical stance, questioning the implied association of citizenship with assimilation and sense of belonging to a unified nation and emphasizing instead cultural forms of citizenship in solidarity with one's racial or ethnic group, whether at home or in the world (Ladson-Billings, 2004). Interrogating the meanings of service, proponents drew important early distinctions between service as charity and service as social justice, where the latter entailed critical analysis of power involved in the server-served relationship and the unjust social structures and practices that created needs in the first place (Mitchell, 2007; Rhoads, 1997). In addition to these divisions, service-learning did not have a disciplinary basis: Campus Compact responded by developing extensive guides for service-learning in the disciplines.

The 1980s and 1990s saw a drop in conventional political participation and activism by young people. Academic and civic leaders grew concerned, while also recognizing a point made most visibly by Wayne Meisel, COOL's founder, that different forms of engagement were emerging that shunned formal political processes (Boyte & Hollander, 1999; Ross, 2002). Students who participated in a 2001 Wingspread conference convened by Campus Compact described themselves as disillusioned with conventional politics, but not disengaged; they claimed to be "deeply involved in civic issues through non-traditional forms of engagement" (Long, 2002, p. 1), enacting their sense of social responsibility by working on problems locally and globally more than at the national level. They stressed personal forms of participation and the notion of "building a movement one person at a time" (p. 3), by developing relationships and through decentralized and nonhierarchical social networks. A general definition developed by a well-regarded proponent, Thomas Ehrlich (in Hatcher, 2011) also stressed the importance of community work that was not formally political:

> Civic engagement is working to make a difference in the civic life of our communities and developing the combination of knowledge, skills, values, and motivation to make that difference. It means promoting the quality of life in a community, through both political and non-political processes.
>
> (p. 82)

The definition that, as Braskamp (2011) remarks, "incorporates . . . one's head, heart, and hands" (p. 3), was later adopted as the conceptual framework for the AAC&U's (n.d.) *Civic Engagement VALUE Rubric*. Others provide working definitions that are more explicitly connected to diversity and global education (see Jacoby, 2009; Musil, 2009). They emphasize a heightened sense of personal and social responsibility to one's communities and to the world, civic work that addresses identity and community, and becoming change agents who promote all forms of social justice in local and global communities.

These concerns brought to attention relationships with community organizations, where the priorities of engagement called for shifting away from practices that addressed people as service recipients and promoting the ideal of equitable and mutually beneficial collaborations and partnerships. Here the service-learning field contributed by enunciating the principles of meeting *authentic* community needs, striving for *reciprocal* gains rather than one-directional activities, *interdependence*, and *sustained*, change-oriented action (Honnet & Poulson, 1994; Keith, 2005). Authenticity referred to the importance of community voice, especially in identifying local needs rather than having them determined by expert opinion. Community voice had practical as well as ethical and democratic implications: a genuine partnership would require involvement and commitment on both sides—something that, as we saw in Chapter 2, was not likely with expert-driven approaches.

An Engaged Faculty

The second important effort involved reframing the work of the faculty by validating their community engagement in the context of renewing the mission of higher education. Central here was the work of Ernest Boyer, then president of the Carnegie Foundation for the Advancement of Teaching. His influential report, *Scholarship Reconsidered* (Boyer, 1990), called for broadening the mission and social purpose of higher education: what counted as scholarship had been unduly narrowed, especially with regard to faculty reward systems that saw basic research as "the first and most essential form of scholarly activity, with other functions flowing from it . . . [but not being] considered a part of it" (p. 15). He proposed a fourfold typology for scholarship that is now well known: discovery (traditional research producing new knowledge), integration (putting existing knowledge in larger contexts), application (using knowledge to address real-world problems) and teaching (passing knowledge to others). Application and engagement were closely connected:

> The third element, the *application* of knowledge, moves toward engagement as the scholar asks, "How can knowledge be responsibly applied to consequential problems? How can it be helpful to individuals as well as institutions?" And further, "Can social problems *themselves* define an agenda for scholarly investigation?"
>
> (p. 21)

In 1996, another piece by Boyer appeared in the inaugural issue of the *Journal of Public Service and Outreach* (later renamed the *Journal of Higher Education Outreach and Engagement*). In it, he makes a stronger call for a commitment to searching for answers to social, economic, civic, and ethical problems. These are important extensions, as engagement here is not any kind of applied knowledge but knowledge that is put to the service of the common good: these activities should "serve a larger purpose: to participate in the building of a more just society and to make the nation more civil and secure" (p. 13). Universities could no longer afford to be islands of affluence and beauty amid the squalor and despair of American cities. In so doing, Boyer clearly joined in the call for social justice, including the democratic process of self-determination.

The Engaged Campus

Finally, 2006 saw the institution of the new Carnegie classification of community engagement (Carnegie Foundation, n.d.). Campuses applying for the voluntary classification are now directed to provide supportive information in two areas that were initially separate: (a) curriculum and (b) outreach and partnerships. Curricular engagement is defined as teaching, learning, and scholarship that "engage faculty, students, and community in mutually beneficial and respectful collaboration. Their interactions address community-identified needs, deepen students' civic and academic learning, enhance community well-being, and enrich the scholarship of the institution" (Carnegie Foundation, n.d., "Curricular Engagement"). Service- and community-based learning are clearly the focus here. The 'outreach and partnerships' category requires institutions to demonstrate the use of one or both approaches, defined as follows:

> Outreach focuses on the application and provision of institutional resources for community use with benefits to both campus and community. Partnerships focuses on collaborative interactions with community and related scholarship for the mutually beneficial exchange, exploration, and application of knowledge, information, and resources (research, capacity building, economic development, etc.).
> (Carnegie Foundation, n.d., "Outreach & Partnerships")

The key difference between outreach and partnerships is the collaborative nature of the latter. The democratic engagement movement continues to push for partnerships: while many proponents agree at least partly with Bonnen (1997) that outreach has had democratizing effects, they also see it as a continuation of expert-driven approaches. Nonetheless, the classification was a significant step toward achieving the long-term goal of the movement: locating engagement at the very heart of institutions of higher education—their mission. The way was now open for stronger institutional supports for what had been up to then, with regard to the curriculum and co-curriculum, largely self-initiated activities by faculty, staff, or students, and with regard to the provision of resources, largely outreach. In particular, community engaged campuses were more likely to create campus-wide centers, conduct stronger and more sustained efforts to engage community partnerships, and count 'engaged' activities in the all-important decisions on faculty tenure and promotion. Some 500 higher education institutions are now classified as 'community engaged' or have applied for the classification.[3]

The movement continues to be supported by a national and international organizational network that has often benefited from meetings convened at Wingspread, the conference center of the Johnson Foundation, and from strong support by the Kettering Foundation, the W. Kellogg Foundation, the Tisch College of Citizenship and Public Service at Tufts University, Campus Compact, the Bonner Foundation, and others. Professional associations have also contributed, especially in the field of public health, through Community-Campus Partnerships for Health (CCPH). Support has also come from federal, state, and local governments, though volunteering and community service have been promoted more often than change- and social justice–oriented varieties of engagement. Especially notable is the Corporation for National and Community Service (CNCS). With a mission "to improve lives, strengthen communities, and foster civic engagement through service and volunteering" (CNCS, n.d.), the corporation has promoted service-learning in K–12 and higher education, especially through the program *Learn and Serve America*. Volunteering and service opportunities are now available through a single government portal, United We Serve.

The Multifaceted Meanings of Engagement

This chronology and subsequent discussion reveal the magnitude of activities supporting the desired transformation. In the 30 years since the beginning of the timeline in Table 3.1, terms such as community, civic, or public engagement and engaged scholarship have become part of the lexicon inside and outside higher education, and the number of engaged students, faculty, courses, and institutions has grown extensively. At the same time, what falls under engagement varies widely (see Ostrander, 2004; Sandmann, Thornton, & Jaeger, 2009). Confronted by a dazzling array of practices, Ostrander terms engagement a 'definitional anarchy,' while Berger (2009) claims that so much 'conceptual stretch' has occurred that engagement is now just a buzzword. Somewhat more sanguine, Saltmarsh and Hartley (2011) remark that "engagement defined by activity and place has provided a vitally important foundation for the civic engagement movement" (pp. 9–10). Nonetheless, concerns about drift abound and have been a major driver behind the *Crucible Moment* report and the formation of the American Commonwealth Partnership (ACP).

Similar challenges face both strands of the Carnegie "community engaged" classification, curricular and outreach/partnerships. An ongoing major struggle for service-learning, a key practice of curricular engagement, has been between students providing a service in the spirit of charity or volunteerism and an orientation to working *with* communities toward transformative change and social justice. Outreach and partnerships, in the second strand, display the same divergent orientations. Some academics construct these orientations as a continuum (see Beere, Votruba, & Wells, 2011) with one-directional service provision (outreach) at one end and public engagement at the other; the latter is about a "mutually beneficial two-way interaction between the university and some [other] entity" (pp. 13–14).

Considering the gulf between academic identity as Cantril embodies it and the perspective and desires of community partners (Chapter 2), moving toward the democratic end of the continuum is no small feat. Every academic is not Dr. Cantril, but if academic normalcies support his enactment of professional identity, a profound shift in orientation is needed. Currently, dominant discourses normalize the campus and its representatives as active agents and the community as passive recipients. What is required to transform these discourses and the attendant relationships into collaborations, where university experts act as civic professionals and the erstwhile recipients and consumers of their services become partners who have (and are seen as having) assets and local knowledge? This is one of the key questions the book explores.

Given these contradictory pressures and shifting meanings, it is worth asking what exactly is being institutionalized on campuses. A research project conducted by the National Collaborative for the Study of University Engagement at Michigan State University partly addresses the question (Glass, Doberneck, & Schweitzer, 2011). The authors developed a typology of engaged activities reported by faculty applying for tenure and promotion and used it to analyze faculty engagement. The typology follows the usual tripartite division (research and creative activities, instruction, and service) and adds a fourth category, publicly engaged commercialized activities. Overall, it is broadly inclusive and does make visible activities that were previously given little or no credit. Probably the most important innovations, from the perspective of the engagement movement, are the stretching of research to include activities directed at practical and community-based problems, and the stretching of instruction to include nontraditional, noncredit, and public-oriented activities. The percentage of faculty who reported these activities was fairly high, although it varied greatly by discipline. The typology for publicly engaged service activities, on the other hand, did not stray from the tradition of providing expert and technical assistance and clinical services. Although there has been a stretching of traditional boundaries, it would be hard to conclude that the transformation envisioned by Boyer and the engagement movement is on the way.

We should also consider the limits: is it possible for the academy to be driven by the values of democratic engagement? Are proponents of institutional transformation overplaying their hand, and would it be wiser to push for either incremental change or a kind of institutionalization that fits into academic disciplines and departments? Butin (2006) argues for this position with regard to institutionalizing service-learning as a transformative practice. We need to consider the political nature of educational reform and the ideological forces that are creating struggles both outside and inside institutions (see Rhoads & Liu, 2008).

I alluded to these pressures in Chapter 1. Briefly, they can be subsumed under three categories. First, there is pressure for close involvement with the market, following the business model of competitive success by being responsive to the real world of the customer or consumer. Here the reference is to the commodification of knowledge and thus the push for universities to become providers of information services in a deregulated (liberalized) market. Second, the call is for the academy to address social problems exacerbated by neoliberal practices that include reducing the scope and resources of government. Third, as institutions devoted to higher learning, universities need to shore up democracy and the vanishing democratic public sphere, by reviving the public role of *citizen* in contradistinction to the private role of *consumer*.

With regard to the long trends that influence these forces as they impinge on higher education, commentators generally point to a global shift of vast proportions that is subsumed under globalization and the knowledge economy. Less attention is paid to earlier historical orientations to academic knowledge and professions that are aligned with these global trends. I propose that to understand the current state and possibilities of the democratic engagement movement we need to look at the meta-context created by the worldviews of modernity and neoliberalism. A meta-context involves going behind what we generally see to capture broader trends. In this case, it refers to long trends that span our historical age and whose influence is invisible unless we step outside it. That is the purpose of the next section.

Modernity and Neoliberalism as Meta-context

The terms *modern* and *modernity* convey a host of ideas and practices: values and ways of life that are up-to-date, forward looking, and progressive; an early 20th century Western architectural and artistic style ("modernist"); and a period in European and North American history that began, depending on the historian, in the 15th century (the print age), the 16th and 17th centuries (Humanism and the Renaissance), or the 18th century (the Enlightenment), and lasted into the first half of the 20th century (Toulmin, 1990). I will use the term according to the last meaning: a long historical period that lasted between two and three and one half centuries, and has thus been quite formative for both our psyche and our social institutions. At its core is a worldview that is predicated on laws of certainty.

We are now in a transitional period, at the early stages of a new era that is described alternatively as high modernity, postmodernity, or the Internet and global age. Neoliberalism can be considered part of this transition: as a late stage of modernity, it extends one of its tenets, namely a calculative rationality; it does so, however, through the channels of the communication revolution that is an integral part of the Internet and global age.

Modernity

Modernity, according to Toulmin (1990) has two sources: the humanism of the Renaissance, personified in the French philosopher Michel de Montaigne and English poet William Shakespeare; and the natural philosophy of the Enlightenment, the best-known proponents of which are another French philosopher, René Descartes, and English physicist and mathematician Isaac Newton. Humanism and natural philosophy give rise to two orientations that are interwoven but remain distinct, one to freedom and democracy and the other to reason and science. There is continuity in the two periods, in the form of new understandings of human beings as endowed with the capacity to reason and to rule themselves in a universe that could be studied and understood, its movements no longer in the grip of the divine or the unfathomable forces of fate. There are also important differences. Humanism entails "respect for the rational possibilities of human experience . . . [as well as] a delicate feeling for the *limits* of human experience" (Toulmin, 1990, p. 27). Montaigne and other Renaissance writers were known for accepting all human experience: they valued reason but did not divorce it from other aspects of life, including bodily appetites.

As a creature of the Enlightenment, however, modernity constructs the world through the separation and exclusion of binary (either/or) opposites. Rather than the body, soul, and mind of Montaigne we have Descartes' mind *versus* matter—where the body, women, blacks, emotions, and nature are part of matter and thus subject to the higher realm of the intellect. What is now known as Cartesian dualism creates an epistemology in which there is no room for middle positions. Furthermore, the dominant side of the duality creates the categories that define both sides: effectively, we do not have man or woman, white or black, heterosexual or homosexual, or North or South on their own terms, but woman as non-man, black as nonwhite, and so on for all other binary constructions. This means, as we saw in Chapter 1, that the dominant side (Self, I) must find the subaltern side (not-I) deficient, wanting, or incomprehensible.[4]

This second modernity is for Toulmin a turn away from humanism, in a historic climate of high uncertainty, toward a worldview less amenable to ambiguity and tolerance, bent on establishing three pillars that would provide unshakeable supports for the new world: certainty, systematicity, and the clean slate. Certainty and systematicity can be easily grasped given the Enlightenment's penchant for science as the search for universally applicable laws suitable for predicting and controlling nature and, later, people. 'Clean slate' refers to the use of abstract, decontextualized rationality: the local, historical and experiential, traditions and passions are seen as obstacles to pure, timeless, and universal knowledge and are thus ignored, pushed aside or underground, in attempted erasure. The rational *man* of the Enlightenment is not only rational; *he* is autonomous and *unencumbered*. That is, he is *self*-defining rather than being subject to the norms and dictates of a community, tradition, or culture, creating his identity through a self-transparent consciousness.

These two starting points, the Renaissance and the Enlightenment, were enshrined in the university in the division between the humanities and the sciences, with the social sciences at times uncomfortably straddling these domains. Humanism did not simply vanish; in fact, writing in 1990, Toulmin suggested that modernity should be 'humanized': "We are not compelled to *choose between* 16th century humanism and 17th century exact science," he wrote. It was possible to assert the achievements of both eras. In fact, in our postmodern times the exclusive focus of the modern on "the written, the universal, the general, and the timeless . . . [was] being broadened to include once again the oral, the particular, the local, and the timely" (p. 186). In 2014, Toulmin's hopeful synthesis seems far off, as an emboldened neoliberalism claims that "There Is No Alternative" (the famous 'TINA' of former British Prime Minister Margaret Thatcher) to a system centered on economic man, a calculative rational chooser operating as an unencumbered individual in the private, competitive markets that increasingly rule all spheres of life (Peters, 2011). For the moment, let me turn to modernity as the story of the success of Cartesian rationality and science in dethroning humanistic understandings that had located reasonable human beings *in* the world rather than *over* it and in making progress and technology into new religions. I begin with modern *man*, and then proceed to knowledge and modern organizations.

Modern Man

In the bookstore, symbol of the print and the modern age, *literary man* sits alone, having left behind the time when he (or she) would have been part of a story circle or a theater crowd, listening to tales spun by a bard. Active, vocal interactions between players and audience—not merely polite clapping at the end—would conspire to make the play different each night. But this is no longer so when the written text enters the scene and the reader can separate himself or herself from the collectivity. The page stimulates the individual imagination: we can stop and think, go back and savor meanings, developing our own ideas and internal theater of the mind. Print also creates its own kind of order and stability: we come to expect sequence and progression, cause and effect, beginning, middle, and end. Reading and writing train us to make sense of the world in particular ways. Marshall McLuhan (1962) argued that "print exists by virtue of the static separation of functions and fosters a mentality that gradually resists any but a separative and compartmentalizing or specialist outlook" (p. 126).

From the changes that began in the print era, we proceed to Lockean individualism and the unencumbered, rational man of the liberal state, choosing self-interest and rights over traditional duties and responsibilities, preferring future possibilities over a stable and well-ordered past. As part of his well-known general theory of society, the 'father' of American sociology, Talcott Parsons, posited a developmental path from traditional to modern that applied equally to people and societies (Trevino, 2001). Becoming modern (see Inkeles, 1975) meant considering oneself the citizen of a nation rather than a member of one's local groupings; adhering to authority legitimated by legal and technical expertise rather than local custom; making judgments based on objective evidence; and accepting that rewards for work should be based on objective standards of performance. Culturally modern people appreciate innovation, are future oriented rather than fatalistic, active rather than passive, tolerant of impersonality and impartiality, and willing to be mobile in pursuit of their own goals and economic opportunities.

All human development, including that of Others, was said to follow in this man's image, whose worldview, incidentally, seems close to Cantril's. This Western-oriented evolutionary path to modernity as progress remained dominant in the decades of the 1960s and 1970s, after which postcolonial critics increasingly questioned its presumed universal validity, ascribing it instead to Western, Eurocentric, and patriarchal biases (Keith & Keith, 2010). We will find them later in more extreme forms, nonetheless, carried by the precepts of neoliberalism.

Knowledge

One of the ways to understand the limits and possibilities of modernity's dream of freedom and democracy is to consider its centerpiece: the human capacity for reason. The influential German sociologist and public intellectual Jürgen Habermas (1971) proposes that pursuits of knowledge are generally attuned to three kinds of human interests: technical/instrumental, hermeneutic or interpretive, and critical. The first, also termed means-ends rationality or know-how, is about using reason to establish the most efficient means to pursue one's goals, removing from the calculus other values such as concern for the broader common good. Hermeneutics relates to the world of understanding and interpretations, that is, the ways different people construct the meanings of actions and events, including historical ones. It is thus attuned to diversity. Critical reason interrogates systems of domination in order to understand their sources and determine the real-world actions that might reduce domination and create spaces for more freedom. Critical reason and critical hermeneutics thus ask what kind of society knowledge should help create; this is the human interest that fed into modernity's project of freedom, democracy, justice, and human development. In this chapter I focus primarily on technical/instrumental reason, which in the Enlightenment variant of modernity came to dominate all others, staking successful claims to scientificity. Chapters 4 and 5 will continue the discussion by exploring the different ways knowledge can be construed to support professional practice.

Instrumental/technical reason is most common and appropriate to the natural and physical sciences and technical tasks. The ideal approach, often termed *positivism*, is for the scientist to be an objective, neutral, and value-free observer or experimenter who tests hypotheses, measures results, looks for regularities, and reports findings in ways that allow for the accumulation of knowledge toward the development of predictive general laws. The appeal of this scientific/technical mode of thinking is in the visible results it has produced. In the pursuit of predictability and control for human behavior and the social world, human, social, and management sciences have often adopted this positivistic epistemology, which has seen a resurgence since the 1990s under the neoliberal regime. This how Max van Manen (2007), a prominent phenomenologist, puts it:

> In professional fields such as pedagogy, psychology and nursing, the dominance of technological and calculative thought is so strong that it seems well-nigh impossible to offer acceptable alternatives to the technocratic ideologies and the inherently instrumental presuppositional structures of professional practice. The roots of this technologizing of professional knowledge have grown deeply into the metaphysical sensibilities of western cultures.
>
> (p. 19)

In other words, these ways of apprehending the world have become part of the very being of the professional. The very language we use to understand our experiences is implicated. Consider, for instance, the difference between problem solving and inquiry: inquiry is an open-ended search that may complicate our understanding, while problem solving, by definition, leads to clear and definitive answers. Our everyday language is replete with problems, and we routinely use problem-solving curricula that were originally derived from engineering fields. This is but one example of the dominance of instrumental/technical approaches in areas of life where hermeneutic, phronetic, or critical approaches might be more appropriate and useful.

Modern Organizations and the Drive for Efficiency in Management

The modern organizational form par excellence is the bureaucracy. As a construct, bureaucracy includes a formal hierarchical management structure, written rules and records, organizational division along specialized tasks and functions, written job descriptions for all personnel, impartial hiring of the best qualified, and impersonal, equal treatment for everyone. Of course these are at best only approximated in real life. We are now so accustomed to equating bureaucracy with inefficiency that we fail to realize it was seen as a vast improvement over practices that conformed to the traditional side of Parsons's traditional-modern divide, such as hiring members of one's family, clan, or community rather than strangers who had demonstrated their capabilities through credentialed achievements. In the Addams-Lincoln case, Cantril's hiring decision could be seen as attuned to the modern side of this divide.

When bureaucracy and the technical/scientific propensity to measure and calculate are combined with historical changes in the economy (from craft guilds to factories and from mercantile to industrial capitalism), we get life that is regulated by the clock and the importance of "being on time," school days that last a set number of hours and minutes, with specified times when we are "off" or "on break" and thus "not working." An expert, managerial class in politics, administration, and the economy comes to control and dictate the means to which scientific innovations, discoveries, and knowledge will be put. Recalling Foucault, this happens through processes of normalization. Calculation and metrics become accepted in the quest of efficiency, which comes to mean achieving measurable goals set by experts and managers: scientific management (or Taylorism) prescribes how to achieve the most efficient forms of production, the *best* educational system (Tyack, 1974), and so on. What is more, an ordered and efficient world is said to produce more happiness: for Taylor, piecework would allow workers to freely determine the pace of their work, thus exerting control over their earnings.

In addition to being bureaucratic along these lines, educational institutions also measure and classify students, give tests and exams, and provide credentialing documents attesting that the specified number of contact hours (meaning instructional *time*) have been spent in learning. Experts in specialized institutions such as research and land-grant universities conduct research and outreach (to farmers, teachers, and other practitioners) so as to maximize the latter's productivity and efficiency. These organizations operate in accordance with instrumental reason: they set goals and timelines for accomplishing them and report quantitative results. In turn, students (and their parents) come to think of education largely in terms of its potential economic benefits: college becomes a means to a job, the worth of a job is reduced to its monetary value, and the possessor of the job is less a human being than human capital (Nussbaum, 2009). The result is a significant distortion of the humanistic vision of the first modernity.

These are some of the general trends that did not reach equally and at the same time into all social institutions. They apply fairly well to industrial factories and to working-class K–12 schools, which administrative progressives transformed into *modern* organizations in the early 1900s through the application of instrumental rationality and scientific methods (Tyack, 1974). They will also immediately sound true with respect to current trends emphasizing measurement and accountability in public education—though accountability is now measured in terms of outcomes rather than time spent in school. Because of their status as professionals protected by professional organizations, university faculties retained considerable autonomy, until recently escaping from these modern means of control, though other aspects of the bureaucratic ethos are embedded in the institutional culture.

This brief description, along with the upcoming section, should add to our understanding of the conflict between Cantril and Harris with regard to hiring the family center director. Although they both work in bureaucratic systems (a university and a school district), as a member of a minority group that often finds itself disadvantaged by supposedly neutral rules and procedures, Harris is steeped in a subculture and discourse that mistrusts and does not fully subscribe to the myths of efficiency and objectivity, including the universal validity of scientific research—at least when they are proclaimed by a university expert. In some ways, he speaks for an *Other* side of modernity.

Modernity's Other *Sides*

From both Enlightenment and humanistic perspectives, modernity can be characterized as an era of increasing democracy, freedoms, rights, and progress: witness the 18th-century French and American Revolutions and the progressive extension of civil and human rights. However, a critical humanist perspective sees these advances in the context of people's struggles against various modes of oppression including chattel slavery, colonial conquest, patriarchy, labor exploitation, and the like. The continuity of the modern narrative can only be achieved through a selective forgetting and retelling that glosses over the manifold seamy sides of the actual historical period. Modernity as an era ended in part through the rise of Others in various movements of the second half of the 20th century: movements for decolonization, civil rights, women's rights, and gay and lesbian rights that saw the start of what we now term identity politics, as demands for new, more personal freedoms including the right to define oneself and be recognized in all one's difference—reminding us of the definition of recognitive social justice. Otherness and difference convey a critique of the modernist construction, pointing to its oppressive nature for all identities—even those that are dominant. Difference opens up binaries, rendering visible in-between, third spaces: think of all the identity groups that now exist where dichotomies prevailed, claiming the right to define themselves in their own terms.

In the Addams-Lincoln case, Cantril constructed himself as measured, professional, and rational, and Harris as irrational, one who easily flies off the handle and with whom one can't reason. As this brief discussion suggests, Harris would have ample justification for countering that reason entails an exercise of power. Owing to this alternative history, Harris also had a well-developed critique at his command, in the form of a counter-discourse (or counter-stories) that enabled him to reject Cantril's attempt to construct the situation along the lines of a modern script.

This chapter began by pointing to the engagement movement as a countertrend to the neoliberal discourse that has been achieving dominance in higher education and other social institutions since the 1980s. The next section delves into the origins and meanings of neoliberalism. Based on the contents of this section, it should now be clear that neoliberalism did not come out of the blue; rather, it refashioned trends long established within modernity, from which it continues to draw strength. What is new about it are the forms of control it has developed as it adapted to the reshaped contours of globalized network society. This ascent is not uncontested, however, as modernity's humanist roots and the challenges to its oppressive tendencies, which became increasingly visible in the latter part of the 20th century, remain active.

Liberalism, Neoliberalism, and the Marketization of Higher Education

Neoliberalism entered the Anglo-American scene with the Reagan presidency in the US (1980–1988), the Thatcher government in the UK (1979–1990) and, in the Southern hemisphere, the Fourth Labour Government in New Zealand (1984–1993), which Donald Kettl (2000) termed "the most comprehensive and aggressive [neoliberal] effort in the Western world" (p. 13). All indicators point to the 1980s as a critical historical moment. As the Soviet Union and its Eastern European allies crumbled, it was the end of the Cold War that had guided and constrained the economic and foreign policies of the US, Europe, and their allies. Would the fall of the Berlin Wall be a symbolic opening for democratic engagement? Joseph Stiglitz, a Nobel laureate who was chief economist at the World Bank and chairman of the Council of Economic Advisors under President Clinton writes that it was, instead, a missed opportunity:

> The end of the Cold War opened up new opportunities to try to create a new, global economic order . . . that was based more . . . on ideas of social justice. The world had the chance to set up a level playing field. We missed that opportunity. . . . [Commercial and financial interests] wanted to seize this new opportunity to expand—to create a world that would open up new markets for themselves, for the corporations of the advanced industrial countries. And they used the US government to advance that perspective.
> (Stiglitz, 2003, para. 4)

The question now was how to forge new modes of control appropriate for the horizontal and nonhierarchical organization of network society. I begin with a brief overview of the liberal philosophical antecedents of neoliberalism, its origins and meanings, and then focus on its construction of management and human beings, leaving a discussion of knowledge for the next chapter. As in the previous section, the emphasis is on a conceptual rendering of the period more than on historical details.

Liberal Antecedents

The 'neo' in neoliberalism points to its origins in liberalism, a system of philosophical, political, and economic thought that has two historical points of reference, both within modernity: classical liberalism and social (or social welfare) liberalism. Classical liberalism, which developed in the early modern period, partakes of modernity's faith in human reason and is associated primarily with the defense of individual rights and the imposition of limits on powerful institutions to prevent them from infringing on those rights. Historically, it stood counter to the absolute rule of kings and church. It is thus mostly about negative freedom, meaning the removal of barriers that stand in the way of supposedly natural human propensities. The classic freedoms—of thought, speech, religion, assembly, and so on—go along with the classic notions of limited government and separation of church and state: people should be *free to* make themselves and follow their own conscience by being *free from* arbitrary exercises of institutionalized power (or tyranny) and traditional restraints. Classical economic liberalism extends these freedoms to the realm of economic property and market transactions. The historic context here was mercantilism, which imposed tight regulations on commercial activities through tariffs, monopolies, and legal restrictions on where and with whom one could trade. Very simply put, the liberal idea was that removing these restrictions would bring competition to the marketplace which, in turn, would result in higher quality and lower prices.

Coming after the Industrial Revolution and in the historical context of the Great Depression, social liberalism constituted a rethinking of the Enlightenment-based assumptions of liberalism: the concentration of economic power had created new constraints on human freedom, along with ideologies and social movements that resisted this oppressive power. With the spread of democratic ideals to include more than the original propertied classes, there was a new need for action to support the freedom of all citizens. In this context, social liberalism maintained that the state should do more than refrain from certain (tyrannical) actions. President Franklin D. Roosevelt's 'Four Freedoms'—of expression and of religion, plus freedom from want and fear—became the foundation in the US for liberally oriented state action in the realms of education, social welfare, worker protections, interventions against monopolies, and Keynesian economic measures to stem capitalism's economic cycles (Alterman, 2012).

Neoliberalism

Although the term is seldom defined, there is general agreement that there are two distinct orientations to neoliberalism (Boas & Gans-Morse, 2009; Peters, 2011). One was developed by the German Freiburg School of Economics and has informed Germany's policy since its post–World War II reconstruction. The Freiburg economists coined the term "social market economy" to emphasize a free-market approach in the context of supports for social equity, including a non-Keynesian, moderate approach to social welfare. It bears noting that after a half century of these policies, Germany is now the strongest economy in the European Union. It is fairly high in terms of equity, with a Gini coefficient of 0.30 in 2010 (the most recent year for which we have data); in contrast, the US stood at 0.469 in 2010 and 0.48 in 2014. As noted in Chapter 1, in the United States other indicators of social justice show a decline as well.

The second orientation, originally associated with Austrian political economists Ludwig von Mises and Friedrich Hayek, is now closely aligned with American economist and Nobel laureate Milton Friedman and the University of Chicago. Chicago School neoliberalism follows the precepts of classical liberalism in providing a comprehensive theory of society that includes a moral and political philosophy and thus a theory of human nature and governance. There are major differences, however, especially with regard to the wide reach of economic thinking, with property rights generally taking precedence over other rights. Market mechanisms should govern all spheres of social life and thus all problems that arise in private markets are seen as the result of government regulations interfering with the operation of markets.

Freedom for Milton Friedman is equated with being free to exercise market choice, which means that ideally all social goods should be turned into commodities for exchange in private markets, with competition providing quality assurance. The application of this philosophy to education, through the breaking up of the 'state monopoly' of schooling and setting up school choice and voucher programs in its stead, provides a well-known example. Government outsourcing of erstwhile public works, including prisons, roads, security, and military operations is another. In his book *What Money Can't Buy*, philosopher Michael Sandel (2012) writes about the invasion of the market into areas such as prisons (buying a cell upgrade), life insurance (companies cashing in on their employees' life insurance), and standing in line (paying a line-holder), among many others.

The Chicago School version of neoliberalism, which critics term "market fundamentalism," is being globalized. As Michael A. Peters (2011) explains, Austrian and Chicago school neoliberalism was created in the context of the Cold War, serving to advance free-market capitalism in response to what was then seen as the socialist menace of the USSR. The writings of von Mises and other theorists are explicit in this orientation. For instance, in his book, *Bureaucracy*, von Mises (1947) proclaims this organizational form a tool of state control that substitutes for free enterprise and is a harbinger of totalitarianism. Policies based on Chicago School neoliberalism were put into effect in Latin American countries before being adopted in the US and the UK and other advanced Western countries in the 1980s and beyond. Under the influence of Chicago School economists, Chile was the first country, in the 1960s, to experiment with the radical privatization of education, social security, public workers' pensions, health, and the like (see Boas & Gans-Morse, 2009). An advisor to the Chilean generals, Milton Friedman would later sit on President Reagan's Council of Economic Advisors.

I have outlined above the main tenets of Anglo-American neoliberalism. The role of government, however, requires further comment. Like classical liberalism, neoliberalism advocates a "waning of the state," but it does so only with regard to the provision of social welfare and related services, while calling for a stronger interventionist state to expand the scope of private enterprise and to shore up the free market. In other words, whereas in classical liberalism the individual and economic actors were to be freed from state interference, in modern Anglo-American neoliberalism the state is called upon to create the conditions necessary to ensure the maintenance of a neoliberal market regime.

It must do so, however, in the context of what I described in Chapter 1 as network society, whose organizational forms cannot be managed by command-and-control bureaucracies and require instead what Goldsmith and Eggers (2004) term "managing (or governing) by network." *Smart* and *nimble* organizations that are nonhierarchical and devolve operational decisions down to the team at the shop floor level or its equivalent do not give up control; they simply exercise it differently. Enter accounting processes that produce calculative selves in calculative spaces, or new technologies of control. The term coined in this context was new public management or managerialism. I will explain these terms in the context of neoliberal inroads into higher education.

The Marketization of Higher Education

Christopher Newfield (2003, 2008)—English and humanities professor, blogger for the Huffington Post, and a seemingly Renaissance man—has undertaken extensive research on the long-term relationship between economic interests, corporate culture, and American higher education. He presents historical data from the 1880s on, showing that the character of this relationship changed with the advent of the neoliberal policies of the 1980s and 1990s. The new status of knowledge as a commodity, combined with declining higher education budgets imposed by the 'smaller government' ethos of neoliberalism, shifted the balance of the relation between higher education and business: what had seemed like a two-way exchange or partnership through which the humanities influenced business culture now came close to a one-way *outreach* by business, as it asserted the dominance of its culture and practices on higher education. Newfield (2003) explains: "Firms had the recipe, they said, for transforming complicated, long-term research and teaching into major revenues. The commercialization of teaching and research would revitalize these services just as deregulated capitalism had revitalized the overall economy" (p. 6). As he sums it up: "business came to the university bearing three gifts: the management of complexity, financial control, and entrepreneurial opportunity" (p. 6). Taking their cue from what is termed the global public management revolution (Kettl, 2000), the new management emphasized productivity, accountability for results, and marketization, the use of market-style incentives to replace traditional controls.

New Public Management (NPM)

In industry, new management practices were designed to devolve decision making down to the 'shop-floor' level, enabling a firm to take advantage of knowledge at the local level. Understandably, decentralization in this context was not a move toward participatory democracy—though greater freedom was often invoked (see McGregor, 2009)—but one toward a different type of control, exercised through new measures of accountability for production and efficiency goals established higher up in the chain of command. When such practices were introduced in the public sector, they were usually justified as a means to undo unmanageable bureaucracies and their inefficiencies.

Interestingly, the new management initiatives in higher education were not initiated especially to change stifling bureaucratic practices but to exert control over self-regulating, semi-autonomous professionals: academics must become knowledge workers. The new administrative model superimposed on the modernist university involved two radically new procedures. The first took the form of a new ethos of efficiency and calculability that revolves around the smart-and-nimble metaphor. New management enacts smart and nimble precepts in higher education by drastically reducing the number of tenured faculty and employing in their place clinical faculty, adjuncts, and hourly workers—a new professional proletariat, the "flexible" workforce of the for-profit world.[5] The second procedure, coming on the heels of deregulation and market liberalization, involves standards, or *metrics*, to monitor the quality of the academic 'product' (Newfield, 2008). As I elaborate below, a new climate of accountability redefined the meaning of professional responsibility. Earlier notions of the professional as a social trustee with moral, ethical, and collective responsibilities, already weakened through the modern regime's emphasis on the self-oriented technical expert, were further eroded in a push for accountability to the utilitarian goals of neoliberal elites (Brint, 1994; Solbrekke & Englund, 2011).

New accreditation practices supported these initiatives by shifting from traditional (input) indicators of quality to outcomes assessment. As an example, scholarly journals worldwide are now assigned a quantitative measure of their reach—the impact factor—that is used to produce rankings. These and other metrics make the impact of faculty research calculable and make it possible to rank institutions globally, creating the category of world-class university. In 2003, Shanghai's Jiao Tong University began publishing an Academic Ranking of World Universities (ARWU) that listed the top 1,000 universities worldwide. In 2004, London's Times Higher Education (THE) began doing the same for the top 200 universities (Baty, 2012). Given the relatively small number of higher education institutions included in the "world-class" category, this means stiff competition for status and the attendant standardization. Implicit here is a neoliberal agenda that according to Hazelkorn (2011) uses rankings to concentrate resources on a few elite institutions because many governments see having a world class university as a "panacea for ensuring success in the global economy."

In a related development, the 1999 Bologna Accord ("Bologna for Pedestrians," 2009) created a European Higher Education Area (EHEA.info) which now includes 47 member countries that have worked to achieve coherence and common priorities among their higher education institutions. Economic concerns are paramount, as a major goal is to create and enhance a European higher education sector designed to maintain international competitiveness (also see Solbrekke & Englund, 2011). Along with the deregulation of higher education, marketing efforts began to appear in the 1980s, while research on higher education marketing made its entrance in the 1990s, drawing from business marketing theories. The authors of an extensive review of the literature (Hemsley-Brown & Oplatka, 2006) determine that higher education positioned itself as a "service sector business."

Economic Man

Using Foucault's terms, we can see how the above might become implicated in the process of normalization as new technologies of the self. As Michael A. Peters (2011) alerts us, while in classical liberalism freedom for the autonomous individual required freedom from interference by state, tradition, church, and the like, under neoliberalism public and private policy actively support the creation of free-to-choose 'economic man.' As he explains,

> In neoliberalism the state seeks to create an individual that is an enterprising and competitive entrepreneur. . . . This means that for neoliberal perspectives, the end goals of freedom, choice, consumer sovereignty, competition and individual initiative, as well as those of compliance and obedience, must be constructions of the state acting now in its positive role.
>
> (pp. 44–45)

Peter Miller (1994) provides an excellent account of how this is accomplished, as he discusses the application of managerial accounting to create calculable spaces and calculable selves. He draws on Foucault's understanding of power as a form of *disciplining* (i.e., self-imposed restraints) that becomes internalized and normalized and thus acts indirectly on people rather than being a visible form of coercion or domination. Appealing to the liberal value of freedom of choice, calculable selves are created by defining a possible field of action within which people can be free to act. For instance, people may be given certain targets, left free to determine how best to achieve them, and be held accountable for measurable results. Miller terms this *responsibilized autonomy*. In the field of education, this is achieved when the state or other controlling entity calls for results-oriented standards accompanied by appropriate assessments measures. Cost or profit centers and forms of payment that are based on performance also work in similar ways.

Miller's account helps us understand the repercussions of these practices on the self. For instance, profit centers diffuse 'profit consciousness' from command-and-control operations, making it a central value of semiautonomous centers within the organization and the newly calculative selves who inhabit these calculable spaces. One's professional life becomes immersed in planning how to achieve desired results, reporting on results, planning subsequent improvements, and so on. As each activity is infused with the same calculability, we increasingly think in terms of objectives and metrics, which begin to colonize our everyday experience, or our lifeworld: my scholarly work should be targeted to at least some high-impact journals; the project I am interested in needs to be made into a proposal that is in line with the goals and targets of potential funders; my teaching is fine, according to the number that counts the most on student evaluations; I need to do more marketing for my latest project, since I will be able to use the profit (sorry, I meant to say the budget surplus) to travel to those important conferences in Honolulu and Prague and buy the latest equipment. And so on.

If one is good at it—as Dr. Cantril definitely is—being an academic entrepreneur can open up new horizons and can be quite enjoyable and even profitable. What if, instead, one wants to criticize the system and the metrics it uses? In all likelihood, the critique will be framed as a search for more suitable alternatives, since in this academic space a discourse that does not include metrics is unthinkable. Failure is seen as a problem with a particular metric rather than with calculability itself. The beauty (should I use this word?) of such a regime is that it seeps into our consciousness whether or not we agree with it. Noncompliance is a recipe for self-marginalization and invisibility.

Conclusion

It is time to ask what this grand tour through time means with regard to the quest for higher education democratic engagement that is inclusive of difference and supports border-crossing partnerships. Returning briefly to the Addams-Lincoln case, the analysis in Chapter 2 drew first from the literature on collaborations and university-community partnerships and subsequently used the thinking tools of social justice and power. It identified power as the normalization of practices, relations of domination, and worldviews, which makes the operation of power through these practices and worldviews invisible. It is thus possible for Cantril to see his actions as legitimately falling in the domain of his professional expertise: he was the one who knew best. This analysis also helped us understand how Cantril could claim to be an advocate of social justice while failing to see those aspects of social justice that were violated by the normalized practices used to administer the project, as well as by his unilateral hiring decision. The analysis left nagging questions that touched especially on Cantril's expert mindset, suggesting deeper causes for its invisible pervasiveness. These questions point to the existence of hegemonic or paradigmatic assumptions, that is, assumptions that are very hard to see because they are creatures of deeply rooted processes through which ideas, discourses, and practices conforming to interests that are dominant in an era become normalized.

Stephen Brookfield (2011) writes about prescriptive, causal, and paradigmatic assumptions, seeing the latter as foundational because they are used "to order the world into fundamental categories" (p. 17). One of the tasks of this chapter has been to hunt for paradigmatic hegemonic assumptions. Starting with a review of the engaged university movement and the push to transform engagement as outreach into democratic engagement, this chapter has interrogated the meta-contexts of modernity and neoliberalism to make their paradigmatic assumptions visible. Their new visibility should have clarified that the orientations to knowledge, organization, and the self that characterize these eras are not normal but rather, have been *normalized* through the workings of power. As an example, the 'modern' side of the traditional-modern divide speaks to the paradigmatic assumptions of a Eurocentric/Western worldview that are constructed as valid the world over. These hegemonic assumptions are embedded in dominant discourses that constitute major obstacles to the desired transformation of the university-based expert into a civic professional able to promote democratic engagement. In particular, the binary opposites they rely on leave no room for the multivocality of dialogue and the epistemology of reciprocity. *Others* are forever consigned to the margins, as are the participatory and recognitive aspects of social justice. The knowledge, understandings and interests embodied in Jerome Harris and his community cannot contribute to collective intelligence since, according to paradigmatic assumptions, they can only count if they become instrumentally rational, calculative, and affectively neutral, and refrain from valuing the particular and the collective. The next two chapters will propose that collaboration across borders must start with difference and creating spaces that disturb binary opposites and normal approaches to knowledge, organization, and identity.

Table 3.2 presents the central ideas introduced in this chapter, conveying in summary form how the different historical meta-contexts influence our constructions and attempts to engage in social partnerships. The first column lists the broad trends, also including those discussed in Chapter 1, and related orientations to knowledge, organization, and identity. The plus signs in the next three columns signify a supportive relationship of the given aspect of the meta-context for the particular modality of engagement.

Given that the table is essentially of a summary of previously presented ideas, I won't provide an extended commentary. The aim of this exercise has been to render the context visible: obstacles to democratic engagement are not merely problems of people or organizations but of identities, social structures,

TABLE 3.2 Meta-contexts and their Supports for Modalities of Engagement and Professional Orientation

Meta-context Trends	Outreach: Expert Professional	Partnership: Civic Professional	Partnership: Border-crossing Democratic Professional
Humanistic Modernity			
• Knowledge/epistemology: hermeneutics, critical reason, free thinking, reciprocity			+
• Organization: community-based, democratic, multivocal		+	+
• Identity: free thinker, value all human experience		+	+
Enlightenment Modernity			
• Knowledge/epistemology: technical/instrumental, positivism, binary opposites	+		
• Organization: scientific management, bureaucracy, efficiency	+		
• Identity: Modern *man*, expert professional/technocrat; Self-Other binary	+	+	
Rise of Others			+
Network society	+	+	+
Neoliberalism			
• Knowledge/epistemology: technical/instrumental, positivism, measurement	+		
• Organization: new managerialism, horizontal networks, free market competition	+		
• Identity: Economic *man*, calculable selves, market relationships (consumer/client)	+		

+ Indicates supports that aspects of the meta-context provide for the given modality of engagement and professionalism and organizations that epitomize deeply embedded worldviews. The humanistic trends in Modernity, the rise of Others, and the fact that we have entered a new era that operates according to the logic of networks do create some hope for transformative change. Nonetheless, neoliberalism and its antecedent, Enlightenment Modernity, constitute daunting barriers to democratic engagement. I will take up this discussion again in the concluding chapter, while Part 3 will illustrate some of the practices that can support democratic engagement across borders. The next two chapters take up the notion of the professional practitioner and especially the democratic civic professional and the alternative epistemology of phronesis that supports this work.

Notes

1. See http://www.ed.gov/civic-learning. The report was launched at the White House on January 10, 2012, along with the US Department of Education's own Road Map. One recommendation calls for a Civic Action Corps, paralleling the ROTC (Reserve Officers' Training Corps).
2. See also *Diversity & Democracy*, a journal that has been hosted on the AAC&U website since 2013 (http://www.aacu.org/diversitydemocracy/), and the discussion of approaches such as the Civic Learning Spiral in Chapter 4.
3. After three rounds of applications, 311 institutions are now designated as "community engaged," while another 190 have applied or otherwise indicated an interest. The institutions include many large state universities and well-known private ones. A fourth round (2013–2014) will lead to additional designations in 2015. The application period has ended. The names of institutions qualifying for the classifications will be announced in 2015.
4. There is also the exotic Other, who is desired rather than hated, but is really just a projection and a fantasy, not a real human being with needs and emotions.
5. According to Marklein (2008), adjunct (part-time) and contingent faculty were 22% of the faculty in 1970, 35% in 1980, 43% in 1999, and 48% in 2005.

PART 2
Thinking About Professional Practice

4

CROSSING BORDERS

From Experts to Democratic Civic Professionals

> If higher education is to serve humane purposes, we who educate must insist that knowing is not enough, that we are not fully human until we recognize what we know and take responsibility for it.
>
> (Palmer, 2007, p. 7)

> This is my home / this thin edge of / barbwire. / But the skin of the earth is seamless. / The sea cannot be fenced, / *el mar* does not stop at borders.
>
> (Anzaldúa, 1985, p. 24)

The first three chapters have elaborated the theme of campus-community collaborations across borders, identifying supports and obstacles, including those that are embedded in the meta-contexts and hegemonic assumptions of modernity and neoliberalism. The main purpose of this chapter is to interrogate notions of the professional and profession, so as to understand what is involved in being the kind of professional who can engage in partnerships in this particular context. I term this person the (border-crossing) democratic civic professional.

In the article from which the first epigraph is drawn, Parker Palmer (2007) criticizes education for upholding the mythology of value-free knowledge, creating graduates who have knowledge but not the value commitments and discernment with which to uphold the core values of their fields. Recognizing the pathologies that social institutions often embody, he advocates for 'new' professionals who can question these institutions. He asks: "how might we prepare students to be teachers, lawyers, physicians, and clergy—to say nothing of parents and neighbors and citizens—who can help transform the institutions that dominate our lives?" (Palmer, 2007, "Educating the New Professional").

Palmer's article builds a bridge between misrecognized institutional and societal pathologies and the self-awareness and actions of professionals in everyday settings, seeing them as part of a cloth we weave collectively and through which we either participate in injustice or, acting courageously, interrupt it. Along with Palmer, I am asking how 'new professionals' can overcome normalized dominant worldviews, learn from their emotions, and be supported in becoming wise practitioners and partners who can engage with others across borders. Given current trends toward the (neoliberal) marketization of higher education and knowledge, it is especially important to reweave a purposive and ethical connection between knowledge, practice, and the practitioner, in the context of collective responsibility for maintaining this connection.

The second epigraph comes from a poem by lesbian Chicana feminist Gloria Anzaldúa (1985), who is building a different sort of bridge. She writes movingly about her experience of borders and borderlands as dangerous, lonely, wounding, and unnatural spaces. Home, a place where we expect to feel safe, loved, and accepted, should not feel like "a thin edge of barbwire"; but it does, at least at times, when one's life is lived in borderlands. The key to being in borderlands and crossing borders is in one's experience of this symbolic place as home, at the center of our being. Writing as an *Other*, Anzaldúa feels its oppressive power to fence in and expel what does not belong. But there must also be hope, a healing of the split that allows us to be "on both shores at once." "The possibilities are numerous," she adds, echoing Palmer, "once we decide to act and not react" (pp. 100–101).

What is the experience of crossing borders as a member of a dominant group and through the privilege and power conferred to one's status and identity? Members of these groups may only see the border's exotic nature rather than its dangers. They may not even readily sense its presence, because they do not experience the discomfort or if they do, they can choose to 'go back home' to the safety of their normalcy. To purposefully enter the borderlands and remain there means leaving behind the comfort and safety of the known (also, possibly, its straitjackets) and risking willingly the dangers of an unknown, entering zones of discomfort in which we may experience being not only strangers and outsiders but outcasts. Border-crossing professionals thus place themselves inside a tension: choosing to stay with the discomfort that goes with making one's home in the borderland, so as to learn about and disrupt the oppressive normalcies of their usual homes. The hope is that in this 'third space,' like Anzaldúa and oppressed people, we may also experience healing and wholeness.

The backdrop to this quest is the call for a new democratic professional that comes from the engagement movement discussed in Chapter 3. One of the points to be kept in mind in reading this chapter is this starting place for change: understanding how one embodies the hidden assumptions that surround professional identity, knowledge, and practice. For instance, if Dr. Cantril's decision, in the Addams-Lincoln case, can be taken as normative in the higher education environment that surrounds him, how do prevailing notions of the professional, professional knowledge, and professional practice normalize it and what alternative associational forms and practices could support change?

Questions about the professional and the profession frame the contents of this chapter, while the next chapter will take up specifically the question of practice and learning and being supported in this kind of practice. The first section of this chapter investigates definitions of the professional and details three constructions: expert, social trustee, and civic professional. Continuing with organizing principles from Chapter 3, I single out three factors that are implicated in these constructions: identity, knowledge, and associational context. The second section further develops the construct of the democratic civic professional, looking especially at the border-crossing aspects of university-community partnerships and the associational supports needed for this work. The third section and conclusion bring these threads together and begin to ask what is involved in bringing about the desired transformation, which is the topic of the next chapter. I return to the Addams-Lincoln case at various points, to ground the narrative.

The Professional and the Profession

There is little agreement in the academic literature on what constitutes a professional. In everyday use, a professional is someone who is knowledgeable and skilled in practice, appropriately credentialed, and receives payment for his/her services. Surveys show that for the public a profession is synonymous with an occupation and different from a job (Hamilton, 2002). It is not necessary to belong to one of the designated professions to be considered a professional: what is important is that the work is not routine but involves some judgment and the person can be trusted to do it well with little or no supervision. In addition, professionals give full-time commitment to the work, are remunerated for it, and continue to develop their knowledge and skills: this is, for instance, what separates professional boxers from their amateur counterparts.

Some social scientists agree with some of these definitions. A sociological view identifies the professional middle class simply by reference to income and education: those who earn "at least a middling income from the application of a relatively complex body of knowledge" (Brint, 1994, p. 9). In early 15th-century Europe, a 'professional' could simply declare that he or she was skilled at an occupation. Now, one needs formal credentials, a combination of skills and knowledge, and substantial control over one's work (Quigley, 2011). Historically, however, a profession was more than an occupation, as it entailed a vocation or a calling to fulfill moral and public, *higher* purposes. In fact, the etymology of profession refers to a public declaration, originally of the vows taken on entering a religious order—an orientation that nowadays is partly retained in the social trustee professional, discussed below (Solbrekke & Englund, 2011).

Personal attributes are also associated with professional status. Professionals are expected to be dependable and responsible, committed to their work, and motivated by more than financial gain. When tensions arise, they are expected to be disciplined and in control even under pressure, making carefully considered rational decisions: emotions, personal life, and personal needs must not interfere with one's work. Of course, 'female' professions include expectations for the display of appropriate emotions such as caring, or what is called emotional labor (Hochschild, 1983/2003), but the initial proviso stands. Clothing and demeanor support this affect: there's a degree of formality, a sense of comfortable command of the surrounding environment and of oneself. Often, there are symbolic garments and rituals: the white coat and stethoscope of the doctor (and in the US, the colorful scrubs of the nurses!), the business suit, academic regalia, and special languages that signify member status, are understood by insiders, and create a common identity. We can easily see here traces of the paradigmatic assumptions of modernity, including the separation of reason and the emotions in the related quest for certainty, systematicity, and the clean slate.

Belonging to a profession, as opposed to just having professional status, has additional requirements. There is an organized aspect in the form of an association that performs important functions for the professions and for society, especially in the realm of self-regulation. Traditionally, professionals were highly esteemed members of society whose work was central to its well-being. Because only a peer could understand and evaluate the work of another, professions needed to be autonomous: autonomy carries responsibility, and as part of an exchange or social contract, these professionals were called on collectively to uphold the public trust and engage in self-regulation that would ensure their responsibility and integrity (Blass, 2010; Hamilton, 2002). Associational functions include ensuring the competence and integrity of members, providing opportunities for professional development and knowledge exchange, mentoring and initiating new generations of young professionals, advocating for the profession and its interests, and responding to outside demands and requirements.

Medicine, the law, the clergy, and the professoriate were the traditional 'learned professions,' but most other professions have been granted self-regulatory status by government legislation and are empowered to monitor themselves through their associations: for instance, engineers, architects, therapists, and other professional practitioners must pass external exams typically controlled by the relevant associations before they can be registered or licensed ("board certified") to practice in their fields. At times such functions involve a mix of professional associations and state boards, but state intrusions into self-regulation tend to diminish professional status.[1] The same associations also sponsor meetings, conferences, and professional development and continuing education activities.

There are implications here for habits of mind: belonging to a profession is about more than having knowledge and skills that are relevant to a field of practice: it is about ways of seeing the world and of framing problems, assumptions, and value judgments. It is about personal dispositions, ethical postures, and more. In summary, a profession involves knowledge and skills, an identity and related attributes, and associational life. All of these are implicated in professional practice, as we will see in the next chapter. For now, let me return to internal differences within the broad category of the professional. The literature refers mainly to two orientations: the expert professional and the social trustee professional; I previously introduced a third, the civic professional. We live in the age of the expert, and other traditions have been in retreat for quite some time, but their ideas are coming back to life, as indeed the engagement movement demonstrates.

The Professional: Expert and Social Trustee

An expert is someone who has a thorough command of a knowledge base, can speak knowledgeably about issues in her/his area of expertise and apply this knowledge to problems in the field. Present-day experts generally adhere to market values, which means that their work is usually framed in terms of relationships between employer and employee, contractor and consultant, or service provider and client (Brint, 1994; Sullivan, 2005). Solbrekke and Englund (2011) summarize the trend by noting that the safe and efficient delivery of technical "services to the public has become paramount in professional practices" (pp. 849–850).

There is growing awareness, however, of the difficulties that attend narrow constructions of professional expertise, both with regard to the field of expertise and the exclusive focus on skills, techniques and technical aspects of the work: devoid of values or ethical commitments, the professional's only question pertains to whether something is technically feasible and not to its social or intrinsic worth. In his study of professionalism in American life, William Sullivan (2005) confirms these assessments, adding that the worst kind of professionalism is one that can lock people into individualistic, technical pursuits.

As discussed in Chapter 1, these views are being challenged, especially through emphases on teamwork and collaboration in fields such as business, public administration, and health. Also raised increasingly is the need for professionals to look beyond technical expertise, engaging their emotional intelligence as well as their rationality, and committing to using their knowledge in socially responsible ways. At the same time, as we saw in Chapter 3 under the headings of new public management and managerialism, the push for calculability and measurement is if anything intensified under neoliberal regimes that use metrics as new technologies of control. As I indicate below, democratic civic professionalism arises partly in response to these trends.

The notion of the social trustee professional may not be as familiar to us as that of the expert. Brint's (1994) historical research shows that it was common in the premodern era and began to be eroded through the combined forces of an individualistic, competitive economy, the autonomous liberal self of modernity, the advent of bureaucratic organizations, and the encroachment of scientific and instrumental approaches into all knowledge domains. Aspects of it have been retained, however, in professional work that is oriented to public service and advocacy, including the nonprofit world, health, social services, education, investigative journalism, and the like.

Traditionally, the social trustee professional was one who was entrusted to work with significant autonomy in areas of great importance to society as a whole *and* was imbued with a sense of service and mission. Thus social trustee professionalism entails viewing the resources to which one has access, including expert knowledge, as held in trust for the public and to be used for the public good. Here, the ethics of stewardship and service are integrated with professional ethics, carrying especially the obligation to act to protect those who are vulnerable—which nowadays may go beyond people, for instance, to endangered species and the environment.

Normatively, the social trustee is oriented primarily to community, public, or associational life, which is supposed to trump self-interest. He or she views rewards, whether monetary or honorific, as signifying professional achievement and recognition and thus as constituting more than the market value of services provided (Quigley, 2011). Returning to the case in Chapter 2, Jane Addams is a historical example of a social trustee professional, although her approach was infused with democratic practice, thus muting one of the criticisms leveled at these professionals: a paternalistic tendency to act on the belief that they understand what people need better than the people themselves. To ground these different types of professionals in real life, I take a brief historical detour providing an account of developments around the University of Chicago at the turn of the 20th century, the times of Jane Addams and John Dewey and the community-oriented Chicago School of (Urban) Sociology.

Expert, Social Trustee and Civic Professional: A Historical Interlude

In the US, both the expert and the civic professional emerged around the end of the 19th century, with the expert professional constituting the dominant trend. Large-scale urbanization, immigration, and the growth of public bureaucracies and large corporate structures gave rise to the two tendencies. The Center for Democracy and Citizenship (2012) recounts the rise of the (expert) technocratic elite:[2]

> A new generation of managers and technical specialists developed who drew their basic metaphors and language from science. . . . A culture of professionalism detached knowledge from communities and civic life in field after field, emphasizing rationality, methodical processes, and standards of "objectivity," in place of public deliberation and active citizenship. Professionals came to see themselves as coming in to *fix* problems and meet deficiencies they found in communities.
>
> (Center for Democracy and Citizenship, chapter 2)

These are the administrative progressives mentioned in Chapter 3, who stood for the application of scientific rationality in management, carrying forth the Enlightenment's torch of instrumental reason.

The countertrend of the time was the rise of the democratic progressives, whose professional homes were not in management and administration but in a budding higher education engagement movement (Harkavy & Puckett, 1994). This was the environment that supported notions of civic professionalism in the US, which Jane Addams and John Dewey demonstrated through their work in and around the University of Chicago starting in the 1890s (see also Boyte & Fretz, 2010). For them and associated colleagues, civic professionalism meant that academic and professional knowledge and practice should promote the meaningful inclusion of those who were on the margins of American life, supporting their participation in social reform efforts that addressed their needs. A core idea was working *with* people and not for or on them, for mutual teaching and learning. This approach led to an appreciation of the knowledge and capacities of the people who lived in the neighborhoods around the university and support for community education to develop additional capacities among neighborhood residents, enabling them to engage in collaborative reform-oriented work.

Like many of the American universities created around this time, the University of Chicago promoted a socially reformist ethos of service to society that included applied approaches to scholarship, research, and teaching. Aligned with the later emphasis of Ernest Boyer, the rationale advanced by university presidents was that engagement contributed to the advancement and dissemination of knowledge. Dewey, Addams, and other academic social reformers associated with the Chicago School of Sociology promoted research, teaching, and service as connected activities and as ways of being engaged with the world. An engaged research agenda involved the search for in-depth, locally grounded understandings of the causes of poverty and other social problems affecting the university's urban neighbors.

Along with engaged research, civic professionalism was associated with democratic practice in communities. Many academics made their way to Jane Addams' Hull House, where university-educated women (called the 'residents') engaged neighborhood residents and strove to become part of the local community. Hull House was not a center for the university to provide outreach services to the neighborhood and facilitate academic researchers' access to field sites; it was a site for university civic engagement that fostered border-crossing identities and practices informed by both academic and community knowledge. Enacting the three R's of the settlement movement—residence, research, and reform—the new democratic civic professionals strove to gain insider knowledge of these immigrant neighborhoods and cooperated with residents to develop community education programs that were informed by their understandings and responsive to their interests.

At its best, Hull House was about Self-Other transformation: as discussed in Chapter 1, it meant mutual learning, respectful relationships, and a new sense of recognition of the common humanity across divides. A sense of this transformation is captured by Paulo Freire's notion of dialogue versus monologue, where dialogue is an epistemological and ontological relationship that positions all parties as knowers and agents and where the previously silent (or disregarded and silenced) community members begin to believe in themselves while the privileged, higher-status academics start looking upon themselves with humility (see Deans, 1999).

Hull House residents enacting community education and community organizing practices alert us to the special place of developmental leadership and a new professional identity in the practice of democratic civic professionals: when working with those who have been relegated to social marginality, professionals need to be proactive in establishing the foundations for partnership relations. As it is only possible to reach toward partnership if one truly believes that the other has resources to bring to the table, this orientation requires a commitment to looking for, seeing, and supporting the capacities of those who are normally seen—and may see themselves—through deficit lenses (Belenky, Bond, & Weinstock, 1997; Preskill, 2005). By insisting that academics, researchers, and other professionals become neighbors of those they would normally see as research subjects and service recipients, the Hull House tradition also asserts the need for self-awareness on the part of the professional, so as to disrupt hidden normalcies and change the nature of the relationship between professionals as givers of service and community people as service recipients.

Although achievements did not always match espoused values, Jane Addams and her colleagues provide a model for democratic work across the borders between campus and community that gives prominence to social justice and Self-Other transformation. The work of Hull House and the University of Chicago thus constituted important beginnings. These included developing, as a tool to support this transformative work, an early version of action research "Chicago style," which entailed community-based research to document a social problem, followed with reform-oriented advocacy work (Harkavy & Puckett, 1994). The University of Chicago, along with other higher education institutions, retreated from this applied orientation in the 1920s, but the tradition of participatory action research was there to be revived by Lewin in the 1940s and Kemmis and Carr in the 1970s and has remained a significant trend in engaged social science (see Carr, 2006; Torre, Fine, Stoudt, & Fox, 2012).

This brief historical detour must also take cognizance of what I termed (see Chapter 3) the rise of *Others*, through the civil rights, social justice, and identity movements of the 1960s and beyond, which opened up public spaces for multiple epistemologies and resistance to dominant group constructions of Others. In the early 20th century, the legitimacy of democratic progressives among their community neighbors and the neighbors' need for allies seemed strong enough for the reformers to act as enablers of community voice and capacity building. The political and social consciousness that developed among marginalized and oppressed groups in the course of later social movements changed this relation: the civil rights movement, for instance, went from a time when white participation was invited to one when such allies were no longer sought or trusted. A frequent response of movement folks to well-intentioned but at times naïve offers of help by outsiders was to question the outsiders' motives and constructions of the community's needs and interests. The deepening of social divisions, along with the earlier self-serving retreat of higher education from interaction with outside communities (the rise of community colleges notwithstanding) and the equally self-serving expansion of urban campuses on the heels of urban renewal impacted university-community relations as well. Trust had to be rebuilt, including renewing the legitimacy of these institutions. These trends provide further insights into the emergence of the higher education engagement movement in the 1980s.

Table 4.1 summarizes the three orientations to the profession including differences in professional knowledge, identity, and associational life. The latter has not yet been discussed so the table constitutes a preview. The Addams-Lincoln case, below, provides a partial illustration.

Revisiting the Addams-Lincoln Case

Based on the above narrative, what kind of professional is Cantril and is he a good one? According to whose definition? What kind of identity does his associational life foster? Does it support ethical professional practice and if so, what is its focus? The discussion is organized according to the categories in Table 4.1, although I start with identity, and then move on to knowledge and associational life.

Considering these questions leads to a possibly surprising conclusion: Cantril seems to embody the identity, character, and many of the qualities of a good academic professional. He has a high degree of autonomy and is self-motivated, and his commitment to his work is akin to a vocation. He also seems responsible and trustworthy in his commitments, as he sought funding and followed through on the proposed collaboration with Harris. His orientation is that of an expert/ social trustee. He is the director of a center that abides by the aspirational ethic of serving the community. The staff appear to respect and trust him as a person and as a leader whose work conforms with the social justice mission of the center. Cantril takes his leadership of the center seriously: the center has grown, as he and his staff have solicited funding for various projects. Part of his motivation may come from being an academic entrepreneur, in a neoliberal sense, but if so it is not the sum total of who he is: he seems to be motivated by the rewards of his professional community and not mainly by monetary gain.

With regard to knowledge and practice, Cantril displays a modernist bias toward technocracy. He values rational, scientific knowledge and embraces the rational paradigm in professional education, as exemplified by his choice of

TABLE 4.1 Comparison of Expert, Social Trustee, and Democratic Civic Professional

	Expert Professional	Social Trustee	Democratic Civic Professional
Knowledge and its uses	Scientific rationality; modernist bias for technocracy; data oriented Accountable to client/employer	Apply knowledge and skills to achieve social/public good Accountable to public and client/employer	Cultivate knowledge from multiple sources/voices; develop collective intelligence; use it in public regarding ways Accountable to public/community
Identity (motivation and character)	*Motivation*: personal satisfaction, recognition, monetary rewards *Character*: integrity about technical use of one's knowledge; responsible, disciplined; value job well done	*Motivation*: personal satisfaction, recognition, social good; work as vocation; community-oriented *Character*: integrity about social uses of knowledge; responsible, disciplined, committed to higher purpose	*Motivation*: social justice, community uplift, healthy democracy, growth-in-connection *Character*: comfortable sharing power/authority; emotionally intelligent; teacher/learner
Work or associational life	*High degree of work autonomy* Individual or team work Professional association credentials, self-regulates, promulgates ethical codes	*High degree of work autonomy* Individual or team work Professional association credentials, self-regulates, promulgates ethical codes	*Collaborative/partner* Hull House as model Inclusive communities of practice/networks across divides Ethics of reciprocity/dialogical

Nancy Green for Family Center director. He also seems strongly imbued with a sense of responsibility to use his professional knowledge in a public-regarding way. While some may take issue with his positivistic bias, he might argue that there is room in the academy for different approaches to knowledge and professional opinions: indeed, this is an important aspect of academic freedom! He even seems to be upholding his professional knowledge in very trying circumstances, which could be seen as the essence of integrity and ethical practice: hiring someone whom he considers less capable than the candidate he selects would mean acquiescing irresponsibly to community politics.

Turning to associational life, we know that Cantril is a member of a profession that takes social justice to heart. The code of ethics of the National Association of Social Workers (1996/2008) is quite a model that stresses not only professional service but also enhancing human well-being, sensitivity to cultural and ethnic diversity, and the participation of those who are being served, "with particular attention to the needs and empowerment of people who are vulnerable, oppressed, and living in poverty" (Preamble). In this and other professions, however, a crucial question is the extent to which such statements become embedded in everyday practice and embodied the practitioner (see Chapter 5 in this book). Here, at least, this does not seem to have happened. With regard to his campus-based peer community, we know that one of its members is mentoring Cantril through the promotion process and supported him through the decision about the family center director. Beyond fitting the criteria of a good academic professional, Cantril is also an engaged professional, as understood by prevailing definitions of engagement as outreach. From inside the university, there is no problem with how he handled the hiring decision. In fact, it may enhance his chances of getting the promotion.

With regard to partnerships, however, this is the crux of the problem. From a community member's perspective, rather than constituting professional virtue Cantril's action may signify he is a team player who will protect the university's interests (and his own) above all else. His practice easily attracts critiques that are leveled at the social trustee and the expert professional. The benevolent paternalism of the social trustee that he displays may have been more acceptable in the past, but presently, and especially given the entry of Others in the field, symbolized here by Harris and members of the local community, it is recognized as the arrogance of power; it also fails in the self-determination and recognitive aspects of social justice. As an expert, Cantril's arrogance resides at the intersection of knowledge and power: his use of the scientific discourse can be seen as power disguised as rationality.

The Democratic Civic Professional

As is true for civic engagement (see Chapter 3), there are various interpretations of what constitutes the civic or civic-minded professional. The construct incorporates aspects of the social trustee tradition in the sense that the professional commits to advancing the public good through her or his knowledge and practice. I will join the terms democratic and civic, thus privileging constructions of a new professional that link civic work with democratic participation. As I use it in this book, the construct of the democratic civic professional also takes into account the reality of living in a multicultural, diverse nation and world, which puts a premium on personal and social responsibility, social justice, and practices of inclusion that move out from local communities of place and communities of identity to diverse communities across the globe. Citizenship and democratic participation here go beyond subscribing to a national identity, knowledge of government ('civics'), keeping informed about issues, and voting. Benjamin Barber (1984/2004) refers to robust versions of participation in public and community life as 'strong democracy,' while John Dewey writes about a democratic way of life (Benson, Harkavy, & Puckett, 2007). Globalism or cosmopolitanism call on us to build human connections that lead to fellow feelings and caring action for all others. As Giri (2006) argues—with support from the civic learning spiral, below—this means feeling solidarity and behaving in socially responsible ways as both citizens of the world and members of a human family.

The discussion that follows is designed to develop a construct of the professional with the knowledge, capacities, and dispositions to engage in border-crossing university-community partnerships. The next section addresses the necessary associational supports. I begin with three well-researched and influential constructs that I also examine in light of the contents of Chapter 2: the civic-minded professional (CMP), the civic-minded graduate (CMG) and the civic learning spiral (CLS). The CMP draws from philanthropic studies, philosophy, and political science. The CMG is based on the multidisciplinary literature on civic learning outcomes and a conceptual model that locates these outcomes at the intersection of identity, educational experiences, and civic experiences (Steinberg, Hatcher, & Bringle, 2011).[3] Instruments based on the CMG have been utilized extensively to assess the development of civic mindedness in higher education. The CLS is a developmental growth model that can be used to examine educational experiences from childhood to adulthood. It consists of six intertwined factors that proceed from the self outward and from knowledge, skills, and values to public action.[4] Table 4.2 provides a summary of the CMP and CMG and Table 4.3 summarizes the CLS.

Although the CMG concerns undergraduate education, it is relevant to this book inasmuch as the knowledge, skills, and habits of the civic-minded professional should ideally be developed in college and even earlier. In fact, all the cases in Part 3 focus on the development of young people as well as professionals and other adults. In addition, the fact that the engagement movement sees the civically engaged graduate as an important responsibility of higher education points to a strong base of research and writing on undergraduate experiences

TABLE 4.2 Civic-Minded Professional and Civic-Minded Graduate

FACTORS	I *Civic-Minded Professional (CMP)*	II *Civic-Minded Graduate (CMG)*
Knowledge	*Discipline*/field of expertise	A *discipline* relevant to community involvement
	Voluntary action: knowledge of organizations and opportunities for service/community work; community social networks	*Voluntary action:* know how to contribute to society through volunteering and nonprofits
	Citizenship: informed about social justice and policy issues related to own work	*Citizenship:* informed about contemporary social issues
Skills/capacities	*Consensus building:* civic skills in deliberation (listen before making decisions); ease, comfort across diverse perspectives and cross-cultural settings; connectedness to others, even if different	*Consensus building,* listening and communication *Diversity:* understanding, sensitivity and respect for those who are different from oneself based on race, class, religion, etc.
Dispositions (identity)	*Work as key aspect of identity;* dedicated to achieving the public good (civic responsibility) *Social trustee of knowledge:* to improve society, serve others, create public knowledge (democratic dispositions)	*Overall self-efficacy:* self-awareness, self-understanding *Value commitments,* including community engagement *Social trustee of knowledge*
Behavioral intentions/actions	*Politically active,* adhering to democratic values (equity, participation, community voice)	*Intention to be involved* in community service in future; desire to take action and realistic view of possible results

that supports civic mindedness. This research may also be useful in professional learning and development.

Table 4.2 easily reveals strong similarities between the CMG and CMP, making a detailed comparison unnecessary. In general, the constructs support Sullivan's (2005) and others' understanding of the democratic civic professional as someone who needs to be grounded in two main areas: the substantive knowledge and skills of her/his field; and knowledge, skills, practices, and attitudes connected with democratic work. The discussion of knowledge here is abbreviated because it is taken up fully in Chapter 5. Comparing this table with Table 2.1 suggests two complementary framings of the construct and work of the democratic civic professional. Table 2.1 is about collaborative processes while Table 4.2 focuses more on attributes and outcomes. According to extensive research, guided experiences that involve collaborative processes are linked to civic engagement outcomes. This is especially the case with border-crossing practices such as service-learning coursework, community-based learning and research, student leadership programs, and 'dialogues across difference' (Hatcher, 2011).

Bringing the two tables—and processes and outcomes—together thus allows us to see more. As an example, Table 4.2 might give the impression that knowledge and skills for democratic work are another area of expertise to be overlaid on knowledge of one's field or of a discipline related to community involvement. But seeing knowledge as a capacity for joint action (Table 2.1) clarifies the potential of democratic work to change how we approach knowledge: it is negotiated, reframed, and shared. By integrating the values and judgment of all participants, knowledge gathered collaboratively becomes social capital. Taking a second example, consensus building and listening are important democratic or civic skills in the CMP and CMG; but locating them in collaborative dynamics helps us see them as involved in the creation of an interactive space that supports shared motivations, principled engagement, and capacity for joint action (these are the three basic collaboration processes in Table 2.1). By enabling the creation of a safe space for difficult conversations, in the context of legitimacy, the processes of listening and consensus building—and in general, deliberation—help build mutual understanding and trust and lead to wise judgments and the corresponding practice.

Table 4.2 focuses on measurable outcomes in the areas of knowledge, skills and capacities, and identity, which are the traditional components of learning outcomes assessment. One advantage of this framing is that it makes visible the purposive goals toward which processes build. We need this perspective to grasp, for instance, that ethical commitment is an aspirational goal of the democratic civic professional and that it needs to be integral to his or her attributes and dispositions. Table 2.1 provides a more detailed and subtle grasp of the interconnected processes the democratic civic professional may engage in. An advantage of this framing is that it provides a conceptual basis for considering civic and democratic engagement as process. I will return to this point in the next chapter.

It is important to remember that the collaborative dynamics summarized in Table 2.1 pertain to crossing boundaries. As Anzaldúa's writings warn us, border-crossing partnerships need to overcome a sometimes profound mistrust on both sides. On the side of the professional, experiences are filtered through a lens that hides privilege, savior orientations, unexamined assumptions about community deficits, and the like. On the community side, the lens is informed by histories and experiences with social and economic injustice and racism that may create a readiness to search for the privileged partner's disrespect and deficit assumptions. Collaboration cannot begin in earnest until sufficient trust has been built, which must be one of the tasks of the democratic civic professional. In turn, building trust requires that the professional unlearn normalized dispositions, attitudes, and behaviors—habits of the head and heart—that are both personal and professional.

When the focus—as it is here—is on the civic professional and expressions of democratic citizenship, we must also consider different orientations to citizenship that come from a group's history of privilege and oppression. What, for instance, is citizenship for members of groups that were historically denied it and were subsequently relegated to second-class citizenship—African Americans, First Nation 'Native' Americans and other racialized groups? Reviewing the various influences that comprise the American worldview (including Enlightenment scientific rationality, Judeo-Christianity, and the notion of Manifest Destiny), Gloria Ladson-Billings (2004) reminds us that large segments of the American population are excluded from this narrative. As an identity that conveys membership in "a righteous, rational, powerful nation that was divinely appointed to spread its brand of democracy throughout the world" (p. 105). American citizenship (and the American nation) looks very different from the perspective of those whose experiences fit the 'melting pot' narrative and those for whom this vision meant genocide, enslavement, and racially motivated exclusion and erasure.

The point is that there are social aspects to citizenship as well as political and civil ones. Especially for scholars who focus on multiculturalism, social justice, and global citizenship, citizenship is about social identity, being recognized, having the capacity to participate in decisions that matter, belonging to larger communities, and fighting oppression wherever it occurs. In other words, it is about struggle and conflict and ethical obligations owed to those who are excluded or marginalized from full social and political citizenship in one's nation and beyond, to those with whom one shares a sense of solidarity: citizenship is thus also about identities, solidarities, and allegiances that cross national boundaries (Taylor et al., 2004).

These views complicate our understanding of democratic civic professionalism. For instance, they suggest that broadening the national narrative to include voices and histories that have been erased and privatized should be part of the task of the democratic civic professional. These broader understandings of civic and democratic professional work are in line with communicative democracy (Young, 2000) and the work of grassroots organizers who pioneered civil rights citizenship schools and change-oriented community education such as Ella Baker (Preskill, 2005), Septima Clark, Miles Horton, and Paulo Freire (Horton & Freire, 1990) and the oral history and community-arts process we will encounter in Chapter 7. With help from feminist, womanist, and radical democratic activists we thus move from orientations to the democratic civic professional that continue to draw heavily on traditions of reasoned deliberation to ones that emphasize relationships, culture, group membership, and development of capacities that include emotional intelligence and insight. The African American tradition of social uplift is especially important here, and is the notion of 'public homeplaces' (see below) that reconnect the personal, communicative, and political (Belenky et al., 1997).

The third construct mentioned above, the CLS (Musil, 2009), addresses some of these important aspects of civic work. It is especially useful for considering the border-crossing professional because it integrates insights from the movements for civic engagement, diversity and multiculturalism, and global learning as well as being attuned to border crossing and Self-Other transformation. The CLS locates civic learning in a series of concentric spirals that, like the turning of a wheel, grow outward from the self and then back to the self, illuminating increasingly complex webs of relationships and interdependencies. Musil offers a series of questions that help us grasp this concept:

- "who am I? (knowledge of self)
- who are we? (communal/collective knowledge)
- what does it feel to be them? (empathetic knowledge)
- how do we talk with one another? (intercultural process knowledge)
- how do we improve our shared lives? (applied, engaged knowledge)" (p. 57)

Returning to the beginning, as we spiral through these questions, produces new insights.

The six 'braided' elements of the CLS also proceed outward from the person and back (the self, communities, and cultures) and from knowledge, skills, and values to public action. Table 4.3 reproduces a list of outcomes that Musil and colleagues developed for each of these elements, which shows the richness of the construct. As the CLS suggests, much of the work of the democratic civic professional centers on the difficult conflicts and tensions that are at the heart of the unfinished project that is democratic life. Diversity is more than and different from something to be appreciated and celebrated: it is about recognizing that communities both include and exclude, that privilege and oppression exist, that each of us is deeply implicated in this conflicted and complex world. It is about recognizing that we are embedded in relationships, communities, and histories that create who we are but that we also have the capacity to embrace self-chosen identities and communities and to imagine more hopeful, equitable, and just futures. Democratic civic work is not about being a passive bystander "at the intersection where worlds collide" but about moving out of one's comfort zone, actively transgressing borders and at times even "negotiating traffic" in the middle of the intersection. Harry Boyte and Eric Fretz (2010) write about this new professional/practitioner operating on the tension line between 'The World As It Is' (the status quo) and 'The World As It Should Be' (the 'ought' or the good), ideas that are developed further under the rubric of phronesis in Chapter 5. Beyond knowledge and skills, and beyond abstract exercises in ethics, acting as an engaged professional in the everyday world of experience requires personal qualities of integrity, courage, empathy, caring, and resilience that help us stay

TABLE 4.3 Civic Learning Spiral: Expected Outcomes

THE SELF:
- Understanding that the self is always embedded in relationships, a social location, and a specific historic moment
- Awareness of ways one's identity is connected to inherited and self-chosen communities
- Ability to express one's voice to affect change
- Disposition to become active in what a person cares about
- Capacity to stand up for oneself and one's passionate commitments

COMMUNITIES AND CULTURES:
- Appreciation of the rich resources and accumulated wisdom of diverse communities and cultures
- Understanding how communities can also exclude, judge, and restrict
- Curiosity to learn about the diversity of groups locally and globally
- Willingness to move from the comfort zone to the contact zone by transgressing boundaries that divide
- Capacity to describe comparative civic traditions expressed within and by different cultural groups

KNOWLEDGE:
- Recognition that knowledge is dynamic, changing, and consistently reevaluated
- Understanding that knowledge is socially constructed and implicated with power
- Familiarity with key historical struggles, campaigns, and social movements to achieve the full promise of democracy
- Deep knowledge about the fundamental principles of and central arguments about democracy over time as expressed in the United States and in other countries
- Ability to describe the main civic intellectual debates within one's college major

SKILLS:
- Adeptness at critical thinking, conflict resolution, and cooperative methods
- Ability to listen eloquently and speak confidently
- Skills in deliberation, dialogue, and community building
- Development of a civic imagination
- Capacity to work well across multiple differences

VALUES:
- Serious exploration of and reflection about core animating personal values
- Examination of personal values in the context of promoting the public good
- Espousal of democratic aspirations of equality, opportunity, liberty, and justice
- Development of affective qualities of character, integrity, empathy, and hope
- Ability to negotiate traffic at the intersection where worlds collide

PUBLIC ACTION:
- Understanding of, commitment to, and ability to live in communal contexts
- Disposition to create and participate in democratic governance structures of school, college, and the community
- Disciplined civic practices that lead to constructive participation in the communities in which one lives and works
- Formulate multiple strategies for action (service, advocacy, policy change) to accomplish public ends/purposes
- Planning, carrying out, and reflecting upon public action
- Development of the moral and political courage to take risks to achieve the public good
- Determination to raise ethical issues and questions in and about public life

Source: Adapted from Musil 2009, pp. 62–63. Used with permission.

with the tensions and discomforts, take necessary risks, grow in understanding, and—like Sankofa, the mythical Akan bird—learn the lessons of our pasts and so go forward together, hopefully a little wiser.

This is a long way from the expert and social trustee professional and even the civic-minded professional as portrayed in Table 4.2. What sort of education, experiences, and supports are needed on this path? I already mentioned above educational experiences that touch the intellect and the heart and combine reflection and action, such as service- and community-based learning that is infused with social justice. But what exactly happens through these programs, and what makes them work? Many writers refer to *third spaces* or borderlands where this work takes place, and the next section will return to this topic. For now, I want to recall some powerful insights of Parker Palmer's (2007). Like the spiral, his proposal for educating 'new' professionals encompasses the self, institutions, communities, values, and knowledge. His focus is on harnessing the power of our emotions, moving outward from self-knowledge to creating communities of support for the complicated and painful but also exhilarating work of changing ourselves and changing our institutions. I have reproduced highlights of his five proposals:

- Take emotions seriously: professionalism is not about hiding emotions in order to present a face that is rational and in control.
- Examine and debunk the myth that we are the powerless victims of powerful institutions.
- Understand when painful emotions come from ourselves, our histories, and our shadows, and when they emanate from institutions that carry societal pathologies—and act on them (emotional intelligence and emotionally intelligent action).
- Form communities of discernment and support that constitute 'circles of trust.'
- Model and live undivided lives, in full awareness that we are imperfect beings in an imperfect world, challenging ourselves, colleagues, and institutions "to keep faith with [our] profession's deepest values" ("living an undivided life").

Often defined as "the ability to monitor one's own and others' feelings and emotions, to discriminate among them and to use this information to guide one's thinking and actions" (Salovey & Mayer, 1990, p. 189), emotional intelligence is usually limited to the intrapersonal and interpersonal levels. Understanding that these realms are deeply enmeshed with the social and political and with power leads to the conclusion that democratic civic work must occur at all these levels and that we need what I term critical emotional intelligence, that is, understanding the play of emotions in the context of dynamics of power. Rather than the autonomous rational selves of modernity, we are beings-in-relation. Social justice is about changing economic and social institutions but also about recognizing how we ourselves embody privilege and oppression, including in our relation to authority (see chapters in Part 2). Change must thus involve a deeply personal 'unlearning.' Bourdieu's *habitus*, a thinking tool presented in Chapter 5, will alert us that such change is disturbing and that part of the process involves accepting being uncomfortable.

The next section discusses the third component of professionalism: associational life. Earlier, I pointed to the functions of professional associations, especially with regard to the maintenance of professional autonomy through self-regulation, which includes ensuring the competence and integrity of members and supporting the development of professional identities, habits of mind, and worldviews. The main question now pertains to the kind of associational life that is likely to support the development of the border-crossing democratic civic professional.

Communities of Practice and *Third Spaces*

Different types of associations support professionals and their work. As noted in the discussion of the engagement movement, organizations such as Campus Compact, the Carnegie Foundation, Wingspread-related groups, the Association of American Colleges & Universities (AAC&U), and disciplinary associations operating mostly at the national level have done much to create supports, add to content knowledge, conduct and disseminate research, and offer appropriate policies, practices, and ethical codes (see Table 3.1). These supports have also been useful to campus-based organizations, providing, for instance, instruments for local research and models for institutionalizing engaged scholarship, teaching and research through appropriate tenure, and promotion guidelines. However, the deep changes involved in enacting democratic civic engagement, especially when crossing social borders, require additional and different kinds of associational supports.

Sociologist Thomas Sergiovanni (2005) proposes three distinct conceptual models of associational supports for change-oriented projects: formal organizations, markets, and communities. Formal organizations follow rational lines that typify a bureaucracy and emphasize hierarchy, written rules, standards, the efficient pursuit of organizational goals and objectives, formal roles, and segmented relationships. The latter means that we interact through our organizational roles rather than with our whole self. Markets rely on competition, incentives, and choice. As we saw in Chapter 3, the formal organization and market models correspond respectively to modernist and neoliberal policy and practice. Both use direct means to influence change, generally creating reform agendas around mandates, incentives, measurement of outcomes and objectives, and changes in formal rules and roles. Changing criteria for tenure and promotion fits this pattern.

Thinking about organization as community helps us see additional and different ways that change can be supported.[5] As a construct, community has been termed murky and even meaningless, but a definition by Brint (2001) provides some clarity while remaining sufficiently open: communities are "aggregates of people who share common activities and/or beliefs and who are bound together *principally* by relations of affect, loyalty, common values, and/or personal concern" (p. 8). When change focuses on creating community, the focus goes beyond the technical aspects of a project's goals to relational tasks such as building trust, fellow-feelings, and relationships, which support open communication and collective intelligence. New identities and ways of interacting, standards, norms, and rules—in general, new practices—emerge organically and the change is thus more lasting. This approach is consonant with the desires of community partners (see Chapter 2).

Three forces for change are associated with the community orientation: professional, cultural, and democratic. Professionally informed change emphasizes collegiality, standards of expertise, ethical codes, and professional norms. Democratic forces stress commitments to the common good and democratic community. Invoking culture means creating collective meanings and "norms of obligations and commitments to build covenantal community" (Sergiovanni, p. 299). I propose that the change we are seeking in enacting the new professional involves all three and that, further, it necessitates the in-depth work of addressing power asymmetries, oppressive normalcies, and related conflicts and creating a new culture.

Communities of Practice

Two related forms of association draw from the construct of community and provide suggestive ideas for campus-based groups committed to engagement through border-crossing democratic civic professionalism: community of practice and professional learning community. The term community of practice was coined by Jean Lave and Etienne Wenger in the context of studying learning in apprenticeships and organizations (Hansman, 2001; Wenger, 2006). Wenger defines communities of practice as "groups of people who share a concern or passion for something they do and learn how to do it better as they interact regularly" (What are communities of practice?). The construct has three components: (a) a domain of interest: members of the group share competence in the domain and the group is committed to it; (b) a community: people participate in discussions, share information, engage in activities together, and build relationships that help them learn from one another; and (c) a practice: members are practitioners who share stories and ways of dealing with problems and so develop a common repertoire of resources. For this to happen there needs to be sustained interaction over time. When relationships straddle professional and personal boundaries we have circles of friends (Chevannes, 2011; Palmer, 2007).

Communities of practice can be quite informal, for instance, groups may meet over lunch or coffee. They shade into professional learning communities when they are utilized more intentionally or formally in organizations, for organizational improvement through team building and professional development. Here groups develop and commit to shared visions and create practices that help achieve them, in a process that may lead them to reinvent practice and themselves as professionals (Stoll, Bolam, McMahon, Wallace, & Thomas, 2006). In educational settings, professional learning communities typically involve groups of educators who share responsibility for student learning and, in a process that at times recalls action research and Argyris's (1991) 'double-loop learning' (see Chapter 5), collaborate on collecting and acting on data in ways that promote ongoing improvement in their students' performance (DuFour, 2004).[6] Working with one's team can be enabling, as the tasks are not only instrumental but create relationships and supports that meld personal growth and educational improvements.

In the field of education, a recent report by the National Staff Development Council (Darling-Hammond, Chung Wei, Andree, Richardson, & Orphanos, 2009) claims that this approach is part of "a new paradigm of teacher professional learning" (p. 2). The new paradigm includes learning from mentors and from one another, with ample opportunities for learning "continually, collaboratively, and on the job—to address problems and crucial challenges where [people] work" (p. 2). Both constructs share an approach to learning that is sociocultural and context-dependent, which also means that beyond cognitive activities it involves the body, a social environment, and a particular context and situation in the real world. Learning in this way can help a group adapt general principles to the knowledge gathered in a setting or validate local knowledge. How would these constructs support the work of campus-community partnerships? We are moving into the third space.

Building Third Spaces

I begin by briefly exploring third spaces and how they figure in the process of creating communities of practice that are also communities of difference where the Self-Other relation is transformed. For Sergiovanni, creating new communities involves moving from the familiar to an 'empty' space and then to a new space where we build new meanings, norms, and a new cultural order. What is required is "the reconstructing of existing individual and collective mindscapes of practice . . . [which are the] implicit mental frames through which the reality of schooling and our place in it are envisioned" (p. 297). How is this process different if we conceptualize the starting place as one where we constitute ourselves and the members of our would-be community, as Self-Other? Our familiar and normal starting place is thus one in which we relate intra- and intersubjectively as dominant and subaltern, presenting our normalized roles and hiding other parts of our selves behind masks of authority, silence, polite correctness, simple-mindedness, and the like (see Chapter 8). Scott Peck (1990) terms this a pseudo-community. The other side, the community of difference, is a space where we feel free to explore, to know or not know, depending on the circumstances, to not be in control, to be vulnerable, and thus to truly listen and learn (CLS terms it, interestingly, listening "eloquently"). It is also a place of empathy and hope (again, see the CLS) because we have experienced our collective ability to reconnect across divides and share fellow-feelings. Understanding, connections, trust, and openness can never be perfect, which is why the transformation could be thought of as new relation of 'other-to-other': but we will be more accepting of complexity and difference, and thus of the unknown areas inside and between us.

As organizations or associations, third spaces could take the form of diverse and inclusive communities on the local level that support situated learning and new identities through interactions, relationships, dialogue, and joint practice. Drawing on change-oriented work with women in marginalized communities, especially by African American women leaders, Mary Belenky and colleagues (1997) describe a tradition of creating *public homeplaces* that are nurturing and inclusive and where everyone is expected to contribute to one another's development while developing the homeplace itself. Dialogue is geared to drawing out 'silenced knowers' and help them become participants in the conversation. This is not just about working at the local level: as the authors explain, "using the homeplace as a model, the members go on working to make the whole society more inclusive, nurturing, and responsive to the developmental needs of all people—but most especially of those who have been excluded and silenced" (p. 13).

Harry Boyte (2004) has spent all his life establishing the theory and practice of participatory democratic communities engaged in what he terms public work. He references the community organizing tradition of establishing 'free spaces' that span private life and public issues and that aggrieved people can own, using them to develop civic virtues—the understanding, confidence, dignity, and consciousness to become change agents rather than seeing themselves as victims of a system.[7] Boyte and Fretz (2010) recount the experience of the College of St. Catherine in creating faculty study groups through a community-organizing approach that began by focusing on their self-interests. As they explain, self-interest is about "the self among others," where organizers know how to tie individual interests to important community issues and long-term community projects. They add, further, that "the focus on values, tied to individual faculty members' stories and life experiences, rather than a narrow issues focus, proved essential as an organizing method" (p. 73). The result was the creation of "free spaces for people to work publicly with others":

> Participating faculty were challenged to perform cultural work that was collaborative, based in intellectual, symbolic work, and aimed at the development of a public project. . . . [They] thought deeply and effectively about the

public meanings and possibilities of their own *work,* bridging the customary divide in civic theory and practice alike, which have long seen civic engagement as a function of "off-hours" voluntary and associational life.

(pp. 72–73)

Boyte and Fretz conclude by commenting on the fundamental difference between this process and the instrumental and technocratic practices that are common in organizations.

Another model is presented by Hart and Wolff (2006), who use the community of practice concept for their own campus-community partnership at Brighton University in the UK. They emphasize the organic and anthropological aspects of such communities and the importance of simply creating opportunities and spaces for people to meet:

> Thinking communities of practice, helps us cut through to the relationships that need to be fostered to transcend conventional managerial and/or bureaucratic cultures and procedures. The emphasis on community allows us to highlight the way social groupings form and provide an experience of membership, belonging and identity.
>
> (p. 130)

The fuzzy boundaries of such communities create opportunities for work at the core and at the boundaries (or periphery). While an inner core develops knowledge, understanding, and commitment and cultivates the character and 'virtues' for wise practice (see Chapter 5), boundary work keeps the whole fluid and open, avoiding some of the static features of advisory boards and steering committees and fostering the capacity for renewal.

At the same time, constructs such as the professional learning community help us make room for opportunities for learning and community-building that are more formal and structured. At my university, an important core is constituted by members of the Community Learning Network (CLN), which serves as a hub for creating relationships and connecting interested faculty, staff, students, and community members.[8] But there are other hubs that provide formal learning opportunities as well. The Teaching and Learning Center (TLC) sponsors ongoing developmental activities that are open to all interested parties. The Center for Social Justice and Multicultural Education brings together a core of people who are committed to diversity work; it collaborates with the College of Education in offering a Graduate Certificate in Diversity Leadership that caters to higher education insiders and outsiders and offers ongoing activities, such as diversity dialogues, aimed at experienced facilitators as well as the newly interested who are currently at the boundaries of the work.[9] Each core is both centered and fluid and connects to different hubs that form their own cores, comprising a network.

96 Thinking About Professional Practice

Perhaps instead of a community or a center we should envision a local association that spans the campus-community divide, a series of intersecting networks or *circles of friends* whose goal is to make collegiality inclusive, extending beyond campus walls, and striving to understand what it means to be a new professional and how to put it into practice. Chapter 5 provides an illustrative example of a circle of friends.

Summary and Conclusion: Weaving a Habit for the New Professional

Figure 4.1 attempts to capture, albeit quite schematically and briefly, ideas pertaining to the border-crossing democratic civic professional found in Chapter 2 (community partners' perspectives), the historical information presented in Chapter 3 (as summarized in Table 3.2), and information presented in this chapter, both in the historical interlude and the constructs of the professional outlined in Tables 4.1, 4.2, and 4.3. Chapter 5 will provide a detailed discussion of the learning, change, and development work needed to traverse the space between the expert and the border-crossing democratic civic professional.

How can we conceptualize the in-between space we have to traverse? We now know that 'mind' and thus mindscapes and building new meanings and a new cultural order involve our whole being—the mind is more than cognition, as it is embodied, which means that our emotions, habits, and dispositions are also involved. And because we are not separate but beings-in-relation who work in organizational contexts, the reconstruction must be both collective and individual, or organizational, intersubjective and intrasubjective. Here, in the words of the CLS, "worlds collide" and what works well for us in our usual, nonhybrid spaces may create dangerous tensions. Consider, for instance, the crisis in the Addams-Lincoln case that results from Cantril and his colleagues taking normal and familiar university identities, knowledge, and practices into the space of the community advisory board. Imagine the difference it would make to see the board as a third space rather than as a university outpost for purposes of outreach. Of course, outposts feel comfortable for members of the dominant group while third spaces often feel uncomfortable and can actually be dangerous, as the struggle between old and new identities and practices brings out resistances, fears, anger, and conflicts, both in oneself and with others.

There is also room in this process for what Sergiovanni terms *empty space*, although I don't not know if this way of seeing it accords with his perspective. Here *emptiness* is akin to Buddhist, therapeutic, and dialogical notions of making ourselves empty so we can be open to the Other: it involves authentic listening that suspends judgment, feeling for emotions that hide underneath masks, listening "eloquently" for learning and understanding the Other outside us and the Other in ourselves. The next chapter delves into this transformation from the perspective of practice, asking also how it can be cultivated.

A Expert/Social Trustee Professional	B Democratic/Civic Professional (+ border crosser)
Knowledge: own field of expertise & discipline. Engagement as outreach, with reseach-validated best practices. Positivistic epistemology (e.g., management progressives; New Public Management/new managerialism)	**Knowledge:** own field + social issues & key struggles for democracy (e.g., democratic progressives); volunteer/community networks. Dialogism: epistemology of reciprocity/uncertainty/polivocality; power-knowledge nexus
Skills/capacities: careful application of best practices & techniques; set goals & metrics for calculable results	**Capacities/practices:** support civic/democratic work across differences: e.g., dialogue, deliberation, conflict, consensus, power/task sharing, community-building
Identity/dispositions/habits: "modern individual": capable, "knower," in control. Motivated by personal gain, professional recognition, satisfaction for job well done, happy customer/client. Social trustee: Knowledge used for public/larger purpose; work as vocation	**Identity/dispositions/habits:** agent for democratic change, social justice & "difference." "Self-in-relation": teacher-learner, authentic partner, developmental leader, social trustee of knowledge. Self-aware, emotionally intelligent, curious, courageous, OK outside comfort zone/cross borders, willing to change. Motivated by self & community growth & humanization.
Work/associational life: work alone or with professional team. Professional association for credentialing, prof. development & safeguard professional interests. Social trustee: professional association guarantee self-regulation & public trust.	**Work/associational life:** Jane Addams Hull House as model: create inclusive democratic community of difference (open, equal & authentic communication; trusting & caring relationships; Self-Other transformation). Collective intelligence for public work.

FIGURE 4.1 From Professional as Expert/Social Trustee to Professional as Democratic Civic Border Crosser

Notes

1. Professional self-regulation has undergone considerable reform in the recent past, moving toward greater accountability and transparency and shifting from protecting the profession from interference to protecting the public from wrongdoing (Randall, 2000). For a good review and critique of the model, see Blass (2010).
2. This trend runs across many fields. See for example Tyack (1974) on progressives who introduced scientific management in education; Benson and Harkavy (2002) and Peters (2004) on higher education.
3. The CMP is based on Hatcher's (2008) dissertation research. She is the executive director of the Center for Service and Learning at Indiana University–Purdue University Indianapolis. Bringle, a former executive director of the Center, was the main influence in the development of the CMG. See Bringle, Studer, Wilson, Clayton, and Steinberg (2011); Bringle and Hatcher (2002); Hatcher (2011); and Steinberg et al. (2011).
4. The CLS is the work of the Association of American Colleges and Universities (AAC&U) and its senior vice president, Caryn McTighe Musil, who was the lead author of the *Crucible* report (NTFCLDE, 2012). The spiral provides the conceptual model for the AAC&U's Civic Engagement Rubric (Hatcher, 2011; Musil, 2009). Sylvia Hurtado and colleagues at UCLA's Higher Education Research Institute (Hurtado, Ruiz & Whang, 2012) use the CLS framework and research instruments like the Cooperative Institutional Research Program (CIRP) to research civic learning and campus-based practices that support it.
5. 'Community' is used here as concept, which is different from the way I use 'community' elsewhere in the book (e.g., university-community partnerships, community voice, the community). The latter generally refers to informally or formally organized groups living and active in neighborhoods in which the university is also active.
6. Professional learning communities (PLCs) are used mainly in K–12 education settings. Cheryl Craig (2013) presents two models of teacher community that have implications for how knowledge and identity are constructed: (teacher) knowledge communities (organic, based on inquiry, generate personal meanings) and PLCs (administratively led and controlled, use codified formal knowledge). DuFour advocates the latter approach, of which proponents of the first are critical (e.g., Cochran-Smith & Lytle, 2009).
7. Boyte (2004) describes the Jane Addams School for Democracy in St. Paul, Minnesota, as such a space. Created in 1996, it is a partnership between residents of a largely immigrant neighborhood in St. Paul and students and faculty from St. Catherine University, Augsburg College, Macalester College, and the University of Minnesota. Inspired by Hull House, it has a nonhierarchical and nonbureaucratic structure where "everyone is a teacher." See http://inside.augsburg.edu/janeaddams/.
8. The CLN no longer exists. Through the combined effect of different priorities by a new university administration and neoliberal-style budget cuts by the Pennsylvania legislature, its funding was removed at the start of the 2013 fiscal year.
9. See http://www.cln.temple.edu for the Community Learning Network; http://www.temple.edu/tlc/ for the Teaching and Learning Center; and http://www.temple.edu/ideal/CertificateinDiversityLeadership.html for the Center for Social Justice and Multicultural Education and the Graduate Certificate in Diversity Leadership.

5
TOWARD WISE PRACTICE FOR UNIVERSITY-COMMUNITY COLLABORATIONS

> Our mind is capable of passing beyond the dividing line we have drawn for it. Beyond the pairs of opposites of which the world consists, other, new insights begin.
>
> (Hesse, 1973, p. 263)

The last chapter developed the construct of the border-crossing democratic civic professional as distinguished from the normative understanding of the professional as expert and, to a lesser degree, as social trustee. It also described community-oriented associational structures that, constructed with care, could support this new type of professional, such as a cross-border community of practice, professional development community, network, or circle of friends. This chapter offers a framework that deepens our understanding of the new professional's practice and ways to cultivate it. It is divided into three parts. The first part problematizes the meanings of practice and reviews traditional and alternative constructions of practice and learning for professional practice. The second part develops an alternative drawn in part from the neo-Aristotelian notion of phronesis. The third part delves into the process of becoming a wise practitioner and illustrates it through practical examples and a mini-case.

Phronesis, also termed practical wisdom, common sense, or *prudence*, stands at the center of a recent movement to refashion social science and knowledge for professional practice. An authoritative translator of Aristotle, Runes, describes practical wisdom as "knowledge of the proper ends of conduct and of the means of attaining them" (in Ellett, 2012, p. 15). An influential early proponent, Bent Flyvbjerg (2001), terms it reflective thought aimed at ethical action. Broadly, phronesis brings forth the vision of *wise* practitioners who help people move toward collectively constructed notions of the good, which is about people living lives worthy of human dignity. The orientation to practice and the dispositions of the wise practitioner comport well with those of the border-crossing democratic civic professional which, as announced in the epigraph, move from binary opposites to difference.

What Is Practice?

On a level that only seems simple, practice is about action, whether in the everyday or the professional world.[1] The old saying that "practice makes perfect" urges us to do something repeatedly until it becomes routine, so ingrained that we can do it without effort. Think about driving a car, speaking a foreign language, or playing a musical instrument: a great deal of attention and effort is needed at the beginning; then, with observation, feedback, and repetition, the initial laboriousness becomes not only unnecessary but downright counterproductive, an obstacle to the flawless performance that is a new normal. Practice has become habitual action. A second meaning of practice is conveyed by such phrases as religious or common practice, which refer to customary actions. There is repetition here as well, but it is not about using techniques to learn a skill; rather, actions are repeated because they have acquired symbolic or ritualistic meanings through custom or tradition or because they signify an identity. People practice their religion not in order to improve their performance of it but because that is who they are, whether through family tradition, habit, or conscious choice.

Does professional practice partake of these meanings, and if so, to what extent? Professional learning has traditionally been construed as becoming familiar with a professional knowledge base, observing professionals in action, and 'doing,' which—with enough mentoring, feedback, and repetition—leads from the first hesitant steps of the novice to the comfortable routine of the competent professional. Similarly, professional identity is affirmed through symbols and rituals. We might therefore be tempted to answer affirmatively on both counts, but it would be only partly true. Referencing the 'practice turn' and practice-based studies (PBS) as a new orientation to professional development, Silvia Gherardi (2009) explains that "the term 'practice' is an in-between concept which relates on the one hand to the semantic domain of habit and of habitual action . . . and on the other, to the domain of deliberate action" (p. 119).

The manifold contexts in which action occurs are also part and parcel of practice. Stephen Kemmis (2010) writes of an ecology of professional practice that includes (a) the perspectives of the practitioner and the client, (b) the practitioner's community of practice—which may include professional bodies, associations, and institutions that carry forth the knowledge and traditions of the profession and regulate its members, (c) the client's family, community, and any other social connections, and (d) physical and material factors (also see Hager, Lee, & Reich, 2012). These interact and play out differently in each practice situation, which all parties enter with previous sets of expectations and learned behaviors (dispositions and orientations), while policies, practice protocols, organizational requirements, and material and social circumstances provide additional structures that delineate the field of possible action. Enacting professional practice is clearly becoming more complicated than the practitioner applying professional knowledge.

Before proceeding further, let me elaborate on orientation and dispositions, which will become especially important in the later discussions of phronesis and professional development that disturbs our *normal* orientations and dispositions, or our habitus. Both are embodied and thus go beyond cognitive processes and capacities. Orientation refers to spatial direction, often relative to the points of the compass, or an introduction to the main aspects of a field or site. When we are properly oriented we feel comfortable and know the lay of the land; the opposite is true of dis-orientation, which feels uncomfortable, like losing one's bearings. The expert or the civic professional constitute different orientations to professionalism, with different ways of being and framing reality. Dispositions refer to tendencies or inclinations to think, act, and feel that are felt as natural. Psychologist Gavriel Salomon defines (thinking) dispositions as "a cluster of preferences, attitudes, and intentions, plus a set of capabilities that allow the preferences to become realized in a particular way" (in Tishman & Andrade, 1995, "How are thinking dispositions defined?"). The fact that changes in orientation and dispositions are involved in moving from the expert to the border-crossing civic professional should alert us that the shift requires, in part, a willingness to stay in the attendant discomfort.

This way of thinking about professional practice and learning for practice is quite different from traditional approaches that are imbued with the assumptions of modernity, Enlightenment thinking, and positivistic science. The difference is captured by two heuristics developed by educational researcher Thomas Schwandt (2005), which he terms Model 1 and Model 2. Both models include five interconnected and mutually interactive areas: inquiry, practice, learning, knowledge, and normative expectations about the process of learning for and in practice. Model 1 is the default that constitutes the traditional taken for granted in higher education and elsewhere. Model 2 is in line with phronesis, practice theory and post-Cartesian views that reject dualisms that separate knowledge and practice, mind and body, reason and emotions, and so on.

The Quest for Certainty: Practice as Scientific Problem Solving

Modernist constructions see practice largely as the application of a scientific knowledge base and scientific methods. Schwandt's Model 1 captures the process and its assumptions:

- Inquiry as scientific assessment to enlighten and improve practice
- Practice as instrumental, scientifically managed, and socially efficient

- Learning as principally a cognitive matter [that] takes place in the mind
- Knowledge is propositional [and] declarative, to be applied in practice
- Certainty, lack of ambiguity, order, etc. are normative (Figure 1, p. 316, text only).

On this view, knowledge creation is largely held separate from the everyday world of practice and the goals of practice are given by those of higher status and power, while the practitioner is tasked with implementing strategies determined to be effective in reaching the goals. Application may involve intermediaries—often the educators of professionals—whose role is to translate the research and knowledge base into action-oriented guides and guidelines, manuals, strategies, and techniques that the practitioner can use with minimal adaptation. The guidance may continue from the higher education classroom to the field, where the learner is mentored by the educator or a more experienced practitioner. Familiarity with and sound application of best practices or 'what works,' as determined by valid research methods, are the marks of excellent practice.[2] Higher-status practitioners have greater discretion in determining how to translate theory into practice, with the understanding that their training has made them well versed in analytical thinking and, as appropriate, the scientific method.

Michelle Allen, a writing teacher in an inner-city school, will serve as an example. Having just completed a master's degree in which she learned about action research, Miss Allen wants to use her new knowledge to increase her students' test scores, which the principal considers essential to the school's continued well-being. She contacts her professor, who reminds her about the extensive research base on teacher feedback and student learning and suggests she check the *What Works Clearinghouse* website. Armed with this knowledge, Miss Allen writes a hypothesis: students' success on written assignments (dependent variable) will vary by (a) number of assignments completed, (b) type of instructor feedback, and (c) students' responsiveness to corrective feedback (independent variables). She ensures her research variables are operationalized and methods of data collection are valid. Data analysis reveals statistically significant differences between the experimental and control groups, and Miss Allen accordingly makes changes in her student feedback methods.

One of the notable aspects in this example is the separation of knowledge from practice. In the Model 1 world, practice-based knowledge that is not validated by research is normatively suspect: as Schwandt comments, "everyday ways of judging and interpreting are thought to be primitive, underdeveloped and often irrational" (p. 319). Other assumptions evident in Miss Allen's habitual orientation are that priorities should be determined through the administrative chain of command and that practice is the property of the professional: students participate only as subjects who benefit from the researcher's and practitioner's knowledge. This approach gives control to the professional—although the control and related certainty may be illusory. The quest for certainty means that the teacher has gained some knowledge in one narrow area of practice but has possibly sacrificed the deeper understanding to be gained by including her students' knowledge and experiences and the community context. All of these may be quite relevant for generating lasting improvements. Let me now turn to the alternative, which has been gaining ground since the 1990s, and to Schwandt's Model 2.

A Contested Terrain: Professional Knowledge and Practice

Criticisms have been mounting against positivistic epistemology, the individualistic and rationalist modern paradigm, and their institutional carriers. Often aligned with the practice turn, critics represent many fields and include higher education insiders.[3] Donald Schön's (1990) well-regarded work on the reflective practitioner puts the practitioner at the center of knowledge creation. A past president of the Carnegie Foundation for the Advancement of Teaching, Lee Shulman, proposed along with colleagues that the Education Doctorate focus on the wisdom of practice.[4] Others have advocated for scholarship that is relational and validates practitioner knowledge, with Estela Bensimon (2007, p. 457) calling expressly for phronesis "as the necessary basis for doing social science that is praxis and action oriented," fosters equity-mindedness, and is attentive to issues of power, including the inequitable institutional practices in which one may be implicated. According to Lee, Dunston, and Fowler (2012), much of the field of health education and health professions (nursing in particular) is headed in the direction of partnership forms of practice. The idea of co-construction rather than transmission of knowledge has gained ground in many professional programs in higher education, although less so, according to Webster-Wright (2009), in training and professional development fields.

Schwandt's Model 2 captures the main points of this critique. It uses the same five areas as Model 1 but constructs them quite differently. I present only the headings here, incorporating a discussion in the upcoming section on phronesis. Practice here is akin to the Greek term praxis that links theory and action; it is "a form of human activity concerned with the conduct of one's life as a member of society" (p. 321).

1. "*Inquiry supports practical deliberation of means [and] ends.*"
2. "*Practice is contingent, socially enacted, constitutive of self [and] other.*"
3. "*Learning is situated, activist, constructionist.*"
4. "*Knowledge is embodied in action and wise judgement.*"
5. "*Disorder, ambiguity, uncertainty are normative.*"

The next section explores this territory through the lens of phronesis.

Phronesis as an Alternative Guide for Professional Practice

As is true for us today, the prevailing cultural orientation in ancient Athens was instrumental and technocratic. As a corrective, Aristotle argued that one's approach to the pursuit of knowledge should be guided by the purposes for which it is sought (Gadamer, in McGee, 1998).[5] He proposed three different interconnected orientations to knowledge, or intellectual virtues: episteme, techne, and phronesis. *Episteme* pertains to the search for knowledge that is certain and context independent. For Aristotle this meant a quest for perennial truths (Ellett, 2012). In our times, episteme is usually connected with the modernist approach to scientific study, including formal logic, mathematical calculation, and analytical exploration about causes, or 'know-why.' Stephen Toulmin (1996) terms the latter theoretical grasp, meaning theory building through positivistic methods. *Techne*, which reminds us appropriately of technique, refers to craft and instrumental knowledge that is used to produce things, or 'know-how.'

Before engaging in a full discussion of phronesis, let me review some key ways it is different from professional practice seen as technique that is informed by scientific knowledge. On the first count, technique can be perfected but does not have to be relearned, while phronesis has to be invented all the time, since what was wise today may not be so in different circumstances.[6] On the second count, all practice expresses values and is thus implicitly directed toward visions of the good; when practice is seen instrumentally, the good is envisioned only as the most efficient means to reach preset goals. In addition, the formal logic of episteme is not appropriate for practice situations, which need to be exposed to *practical* reason and attuned to context- and situation-based understandings. Finally, the severing of knowledge, action, and the actor misses the point that the character, understandings, and values of actors are implicated in the ongoing process of making sense of and acting in the particular situation. I trust that the connections between Schwandt's Model 2 and phronesis are now becoming clearer.

According to Jana Noel (1999), there exist multiple varieties of phronesis, in part because of the selective attention different disciplines have paid to emphases and nuances in translations of Aristotle's work. Accordingly, inquiries have explored three interconnected areas: moral character and ethical conduct, situational perception and discernment, and practical rationality. These are reflected in the three headings below: embodying the virtues, making sense of the (practice) situation, and constructing and enacting the good.

Embodying the Virtues

First, what are virtues? The following definition of phronesis suggests their meaning and role in the framework: it is a "true and reasoned state of capacity to act with regard to the things that are good or bad for man," and these capacities are the mark "of a man of discernment" (in Noel, pp. 272–273). These capacities comport with virtue ethics rather than rule-oriented morality, which stresses duty, responsibility, and obligation and is often expressed as the classic 'thou shalt' and 'thou shalt not.' In her excellent introduction to virtue ethics, Rosalind Hursthouse (1999) clarifies that the ethical precept of 'living well' carries the notion of "the sort of happiness worth having" (p. 10). The wise practitioner's virtues are thus capacities and ways of being that are directed at reaching toward such collective 'happiness.'

As is true of everything that pertains to practice, there are no universals: the specific situation will suggest what capacities are relevant and how they should be enacted. Furthermore, virtues should not be equated with what is noble or even worthy of note; for instance, for Aristotle, congeniality and a good sense of humor are virtues. Writing in the context of business ethics, Robert Solomon (1992) agrees: virtues have to do with "striv[ing] to excel [and] bring out what is best in ourselves and our shared enterprise" (p. 322). He thus adds a further dimension: virtues are not about individual talents and specialized skills but epitomize exemplary ways "of getting along with other people, a way of manifesting in one's own thoughts, feelings and actions the ideals and aims of the entire community" (p. 331). Again, a happiness "worth having."

Acting wisely involves both moral virtues, which pertain specifically to one's character, and intellectual ones, which relate to qualities that support understanding and the construction of knowledge. In practice, these are often hard to disentangle. Philosopher of education John Dewey, whose work on experience and learning from experience is well known, identified key qualities needed for reflective inquiry on practice. As discussed by Carol Rodgers (2002), they encompass the intellectual and affective domains:

- Wholeheartedness: genuine commitment to understanding and ethical practice, which includes overcoming any fears involved in evaluating one's practice;
- Directness: perceiving the situation without interference from anxiety about oneself and one's performance and self-absorption. Presence. When there is no directness something comes between oneself and the situation and deflects attention from the reality of the situation;
- Open-mindedness: 'hospitality' to new ways of seeing; the desire to listen and willingness to be self-critical, challenge one's (and others') assumptions, prejudices, and ideologies, and consider new evidence even if it goes against one's desires. Open-mindedness is not 'empty-mindedness'; it calls for intelligent critique rather than blind acceptance;
- Responsibility: careful evaluation of one's actions and the integrity to own their consequences, both positive and negative.

Others have elaborated or added complementary virtues. The wise practitioner brings to the table the ability to negotiate any tensions between the demands of different virtues, self-awareness and openness to leading an examined life, and *prudence*—a balanced approach to examining possibilities for action, which means being deliberate, not jumping to conclusions, and being willing to reconsider. Rodgers notes the importance of curiosity and desire for growth. Dunne and Pendlebury (2003), Ellett (2012), and Küpers (2013) add that the wise practitioner must be tolerant of ambiguity, open to a situation and the full experience of it, willing to doubt himself or herself and the moral rightness of one's position, have an eye for what to attend to in the situation, and desire to be creative and deliberate in one's judgments and decisions. The combined virtues make it possible to engage consciously and reflectively in experience and, in conjunction with an orientation toward finding the good in the situation, reach toward wise choices and actions. For instance, openness and directness are essential to initiate learning and movement toward wise practice and wholeheartedness and responsibility are needed to keep one going, especially when situations become difficult, dis-orienting, or unpleasant.

Unlike skills, virtues are not learned: they are cultivated in social settings and become embodied as orientations and dispositions—an inner compass that guides our perceptions, understandings, and actions. For Aristotle, the wise practitioner (*phronimos*) cannot *act* wisely without *being* wise and the separation of doing and being creates the technocrat, who may be highly skilled, clever, and able to find his or her way out of every situation, but has no ethical compass (Gadamer, 1989). Following this thinking, scholars may refer to all virtues as habits—of mind, heart, and action (Howard, Berkowitz, & Schaeffer, 2004). Recalling the earlier discussion of practice, there is intentionality in virtue and not only habitual action: one intends to do good rather than stumbling over it or 'toeing the line' (Solomon, 1992, 2008). Excellence is thus about expressing virtues that are cultivated through practice in appropriate settings and are summoned as needed in a situation (Lockwood, 2013).

With these provisos, what virtues might be helpful in border-crossing partnerships? 'Small' virtues might help ease the discomfort of awkward situations, including a genuinely friendly and caring affect and a disposition to listen well and perceive the other's capacities as well as needs. Included here may be qualities that community partners want to experience in their higher education counterparts (see Chapter 2), such as integrity, respect, truthfulness, empathy, safeguarding the other's dignity, and openness to learning with and from the community. Dispositions that favor dialogue and participatory practices are also important virtues in this context, since we should expect contestation and dialogue about what matters and what it should look like in practice. Finally, although the more privileged partner has a special responsibility to enact these and other virtues, community partners also need to cultivate the qualities that support living well; both parties, for instance, will need to take some risks, communicating more openly than is usual across borders, so as to develop trust.

This description of the virtues of the wise practitioner could be quite challenging if we did not see the process as developmental and situational. As Derek

Sellman (2012) puts it, "the *professional phronimos* . . . continually strives to be the best practitioner she or he can be given the constraints under which practice occurs" (p. 116). In a later section I will discuss this process and especially the practitioner-situation interaction, considering how certain ecologies of practice and practice situations may support the practitioner's continuous striving to enact virtuous practice or constitute obstacles to the cultivation of virtues. Let me now turn to the situation and what is involved in making sense of it from the perspective of phronesis.

Making Sense of the Situation

I begin by problematizing the two terms in the heading, starting with situation and differentiating it from a similar term, context. Situation and context both refer to the setting for an event, action, or practice, which have a bearing on how we understand it and its possibilities for action. Context typically refers to background factors occurring at any level (macro, meso, and micro) that influence the practice. For instance, we need to consider actions in their social, cultural, or historical context or, closer to the actor, in the context of specific settings such as the classroom, campus, family, or a community organization. Chapter 3 in this book lays out a context for understanding the engaged university movement and its prospects. Conversely, when something is said to be context-free, knowledge about it is considered relevant for any setting.

A theater analogy suggests the difference between context and situation. Context is like the genre and entire play, while situation is like the scene played by actors, with their props, dispositions, orientations, histories, and relationships. At the risk of stating the obvious, a *situation* is "the ultimate particular" (Aristotle, in Noel, 1999), and the richness of its particularity yields a multiplicity of possible narratives that the practitioner must 'read' and consider with regard to the actions that can unfold. Contexts influence many situations, but each situation is unique. Thus this analogy only takes us so far; as noted earlier, practice situations are co-constructed and, unlike the typical play, involve improvisation and multiple authorial voices.

Let me now turn to sensemaking. It is about open-ended inquiry—a process that Weick, Sutcliffe, and Obstfeld (2005) describe as "being thrown into an ongoing, unknowable, unpredictable streaming of experience in search of answers to the question 'what's the story?'" (p. 410). Situations are thus *talked* into existence, which happens especially when the *normal* flow of experience is interrupted by something—Shotter (2012) calls it a disquiet—that prompts a search for meaning and, for the wise practitioner, a search for possibilities to enact the good.

The search for meaning may involve one or many and include multiple ways of knowing besides the cognitive, such as a 'felt sense,' embodied feelings, or intuition. The process is similar to ethnography, where the researcher is in a setting that seems strange and incomprehensible and stays with the confusion, avoiding easy and premature conclusions, until patterns begin to emerge. Thus the linearity of analysis, evaluation, and decision making is replaced by a recursive interplay of experiencing, interpreting, and acting. Sensemaking combines habits of mind and of the heart with creativity and deliberation that integrate character and intellect, cognition and affect, and habitual and deliberate action (Kinsella & Pitman, 2012).

Two processes are central to sensemaking: situational perception and insight (Noel, 1999). The main quality in situational perception is discernment, which Dunne and Pendlebury (2003) define as "finely tuned habits of salient focusing" (p. 207) or a fine grasp of what matters in the particular situation. For Wiggins (in Noel, 1999) the practitioner "brings to bear upon a situation the greatest number of genuinely pertinent concerns and genuinely relevant considerations" (p. 280). Wise practitioners identify what is salient and pertinent through their orientation to the good and their embodied virtues and this is how they fine-tune their perception. This point is clarified in the next section and the later mini-case drawn from the Change from Within Programme. Discernment can also be glimpsed in the consensus building process in Chapter 2, as the capacity to hear, through the disparate voices in a conversation, underlying interests, values, and concerns that may form the basis of a collective interest and thus support the building of collective intelligence, the motivation to engage in collective action, and the creativity to see resources where others may only see deficits. As discussed in Chapter 4 these are also the qualities (or virtues) of the developmental leader.

Insight alludes to a seemingly intuitive understanding of key aspects of a situation that allows one to catch apparently obscure cues. For Flyvbjerg (2001) there is nothing mysterious about it: having innumerable concrete cases on which to draw makes some aspects of a particular situation just stand out. This wealth of experience gives the *virtuoso* performer an eye for the intricacies of a situation, its narrative meanings, and its possibilities. Wise practitioners may see more because, as Shulman remarked, the range and variance of their concrete experiences (rather than the median) create possible frameworks for interpretation and action. Other writers put a stress on metaphors, creativity, and imaginative leaps—which Boyte and Fretz (2010) caution must remain grounded in reality rather than be about free-floating fantasy: Martha Nussbaum (2009) offers narrative imagination as an aid to empathy and understanding others' lived realities and histories, while novelist Chimamanda Adichie (2009) counsels us to look for multiple stories rather than a single story.[7]

Considering these questions brings to mind some of the service learning students with whom I have worked in Jamaica over the years. These are US college students who cross geographic, social, and cultural borders to work with Jamaican community partners in a 5-week summer program. Let me personify them as a fictitious student, Aimee. What made me see her as perceptive and insightful? She seemed to know herself fairly well and was aware of and questioned her own reactions, which allowed her to accept feedback and return to the situation with new eyes, probing further. Like everyone else, she got frustrated and felt despairing and defeated at times by the immensity of needs, the pervasiveness and complexity of problems, her seeming insignificance, and the shortness of time. But through talking and listening, searching inwardly and outwardly, she managed to gather personal and collective resources, discovering capacities she did not know she had. While another student may have stuck with initial judgments and other-directed blame, Aimee dealt with her grief, anxiety, and vulnerability, went beyond initial assumptions and impressions, developed empathy for other participants, and cultivated relationships that expanded possibilities for understanding and action.

Aimee was thoughtful and creative in weaving a narrative that was open to revision as new information and insights emerged. Her narrative was well informed, subtle, complex, and reflected clarity of mind and depth of heart and the virtues of open-mindedness, directness, and wholeheartedness. If being or becoming Aimee seems a daunting challenge, I can assure you that she is one of the many rather than the few. There were dispositions and orientations that Aimee already embodied as she entered the situation, but it is also important that she did not do this work alone. Returning to the situation as a scene in an improvisational play, there were actors, props, and coaches—onstage, offstage, and in the audience—who played important supportive roles. Thus we should think of discernment and insight not only as personal capacities, qualities, or virtues but as collective ones, cultivated in and through a collaborative community.

Constructing and Enacting the Good

Embodying the good, sensemaking, and constructing and enacting the good are an integral whole. At times the whole will seem like a seamless flow, as when the practitioner engages in Schön's reflection-in-action or Flyvbjerg's virtuoso practice, while at other times it will be more measured, take place over time, and include individual and group sensemaking through reflection, research, dialogue, and deliberation. Shotter (2012) constructs these approaches as the difference between *resolving* on a line of action and *deciding* on a course of action by selecting from a number of clear alternatives. More fluid, the first process entails:

> moving around within a landscape of possibilities, and in so doing, being spontaneously responsive to the consequences of each move, and judging which one (or combination of moves) seems best in resolving the initial tension aroused in one's initial confusion—*judgment* is involved because . . . we are operating here only in the realm of possibilities, not that of actualities that can be named and formalized.
>
> (p. 253)

The second approach encompasses deliberation, which Pruitt and Thomas (2007) describe as a "process of carefully considering and weighing the options required to make tough decisions that have significant implications and in which, ultimately, values play a major role" (p. 22). The reasoning used in deliberation, including the reasons given for one's preferences and decisions, is substantive, meaning that it is appropriate to the demands of the situation (Toulmin, 2003). Reflection, deliberation, judgment, and resolution are all situated and thus located in the realm of practical reason. Deliberation should thus be seen not as a neutral and expert-driven technique but as a community practice that is "self-regulating and community-defined" (Barker et al., 2011, p. 20); on this view, a circle of elders or circle of friends (in the mini-case below) is no different and no less legitimate than the governing body of a formal organization.

Regardless of how it occurs, the process is about enacting the good in the particular situation and thus falls in the realm of situational ethics, rather than the broadly stated principles and goals of universal ethics. When organizations promulgate ethical codes of conduct they seldom consider this distinction, leading to a gap between ethical statement and actual practice. Nyberg (2008, p. 588) makes the valid point that "adherence to ethical codes or rules can limit ethical awareness, since ethical codes can lull people into the false belief that as long as they follow the code, they are acting ethically." Robert Solomon (1992), a well-respected business ethicist, adds that the everyday practice of most managers (and professionals) is about routine decisions that may involve "conflicts of duties, mixed messages, crossed loyalties . . . [and] implementing policies not of our own making and often against our better judgement . . . knowing that even such decisions are nevertheless one's own to live with" (p. 323). Clearly, ethical codes cannot encompass the complexities and emergent nature of everyday practice.

Returning to the example of our teacher, Miss Allen, her decision to prioritize the students' test scores and thus match her classroom and research priorities to those of the principal and policymakers erases the ethical role conflicts and crossed loyalties to which Solomon alludes. Not considering the situatedness of her students' performance, she enacts general constructions of doing well in school that are imposed by powerful entities. What if she and the principal were part of a community of practice that included spaces for dialogue, reflection, and judgment? In principle, their professional association supports educators' "belief in the worth and dignity of each human being . . . and the nurture of the democratic principles" (National Education Association, n.d.). Can we envision a different research project if a dialogue were to occur that put general principles, policy directives, and local needs on the table? Instead of such a substantive discussion, Miss Allen's main concern seems to be, as Flyvbjerg so aptly puts it (e.g., see Schram, 2012), not about what matters but only about what (research) methods.

Nyberg provides an alternative that exemplifies situational ethics and illustrates the interconnected aspects of phronesis. It involves a customer service consultant in an insurance company who decides to list as a 'qualified driver' an 85-year-old woman who does not have a license and is driven around in her own car by members of her family. The consultant takes this action, which circumvents the rules and the computer program, after deliberating with a coworker. As Nyberg remarks, this is not a 'right' decision based on following the rules; it is a 'good' decision, which expresses concern for the woman's well-being and allows her to continue being driven in an insured vehicle. By encouraging dialogue and deliberation among colleagues when such issues arise, the organization helps the consultants develop wise practice, consisting of conduct that expresses empathy, sensitivity, and moral imagination.

The discussion so far conveys how practice theory and phronesis change our understanding of professional practice. In contrast to the normative expert who applies 'what works' and uses reason in an affectively neutral technical exercise, on this alternative view practice and knowledge are situated and professional excellence means calling upon one's understanding, knowledge, skills, and embodied qualities to construct the good out of possibilities emerging within the actual situation. But how does one cultivate the qualities and capacities that help the normative expert become a wise border-crossing professional? That is the burden of the next section.

Becoming Wiser Practitioners

Previous chapters have elaborated on the notion of normalcy with respect to how it is created and becomes an invisible second nature. Chapter 4 ended with the question of how to move from *normalized* professional practice toward what we now can see as *wise* practice. The concepts, or thinking tools, of *habitus*, *field*, and *capital*, created by French social thinker Pierre Bourdieu, explain the process through which *normal* practice develops and thus will help us envision the path toward wise practice.[8] Bourdieu was concerned with practice in the general sense of human action, which includes but is not limited to professional practice. This makes his approach quite pertinent for us given that both phronesis and practice theory point to the intersection of the personal and the professional and of habitual and deliberate action. I explore the thinking tools first and then consider their use for the task at hand. Miss Allen's research project and a related thought experiment will serve as illustration.

Habitus, Field, and Capital

Bourdieu's interactive framework for making sense of practice involves the practitioner's dispositions and orientation (habitus), the settings in which they are developed and put into action (fields), and the resources the practitioner utilizes (capital) in a given field. One of the key differences between Bourdieu and Aristotle is that the more conservative Aristotle postulates a united community in which virtuous practitioners serve a common good, while Bourdieu sees social systems held together in tension, often through subtle forms of violence that operate mostly below the conscious level. The thinking tools helped him explore how structured social inequality is perpetuated and dominant groups maintain their advantage; we can also use the framework, however, to consider equitable change, as I do here.

Habitus

Bourdieu proposes that personal and group-based experiences, including collective memories, interact with social structures and become embodied in us as dispositions and orientations to practice. These comprise a background matrix that informs our tastes, the language we use, what catches our eye (our perceptions and impressions), what we make of situations, and what we consider as possible choices for action. As summarized by Reay (2004), habitus has four interrelated aspects: embodiment (a "socialized body"); agency (it both constrains and generates our actions); a compilation of collective and individual trajectories (we are both a "trace of collective history" and our personal experiences); and a complex interplay between past and present (ongoing experiences interact with relatively durable past dispositions, making it possible to transcend the social conditions that contributed to producing the habitus). Considering habitus as the "generative principle of regulated improvisation" (Bourdieu, 1977, p. 78) helps us see that we are neither entirely free nor mechanistically controlled: we are creatures of our social milieus who are capable of individual creativity and spontaneity. Crossley (2013) puts it in terms of 'dexterity': "a form of competence or mastery which affords social actors a capacity to act and react to particular types of situation" (p. 293).

Habitus is thus influenced by our affiliations with particular social groups (for instance, there is class-based habitus, professions have distinct habituses) and the particular and unique ways that each of us embodies our experiences, histories, and narratives. It draws from the emotional text of our family and early life as well as from nonpersonal realms—organizations and systems—that directly or indirectly enter our lives. Patriarchal authority relations in a family, for example, may mirror gender relations in the larger system; race, class, and gender relations in the larger system influence family and interpersonal relations; in the US, social groups are bifurcated along racial and ethnic lines, and thus intragroup habituses will also differ.

Field

This is an empirical construct, found by looking for the ways people and groups in particular social spaces form actual and symbolic networks and jostle for position in relation to others in the field. Families, professions, neighborhoods, organizations, sets of organizations, and so on may be constituted as fields that promote particular dispositions. Habitus is produced and reproduces itself in the context of these social spaces, starting with the dispositions developed in one's childhood. Importantly, while entities at the local level may be seen as fields (or perhaps as subfields), they are not autonomous and separate from overarching fields and social structures. For instance, a family as a subfield may have its own rules, but it is clearly not independent of the larger logics of family, neighborhood, the social class of its residents, systems, and so on. The rules of the game thus cannot simply be changed locally, because they go back to traditions, historical understandings, and structures that are embedded in the social fabric. There are system logics with which we interact.

Bourdieu uses the metaphor of a game to explain the field and the situated nature of the habitus. The rules of the game—the field's *logic*—become mostly second nature. This means that our practices are guided not by a rule book but by our *feel* for the game. Competing teams, composed of players who occupy different positions, accept the rules as a condition for playing. However, the rules are not geared toward fairness because teams and players have differential access to resources, or capital in the field. Some players are more skilled and resourceful than others and good players excel at improvising, being creative and inventive in how they use their resources and play the game. Habitus is always relational and oriented to position taking, which means that fields are always constituted through the use of one's capitals and the play of power.

Capital

We are familiar with economic capital but cultural and social resources, especially those that are scarce and valued in a field, are also assets—different forms of capital—in that field. Miss Allen's master's degree and her relationship with her academic mentor constituted such assets. Another asset is symbolic capital, which refers to the capacity of certain players to define what constitutes a resource and thus what has value. For example, educators and others define the capacity to speak and write standard English as an asset, thus making it into linguistic capital in the education field and other fields. People with similar amounts and kinds of capital share contiguous social spaces, can identify with one another, and develop relationships more easily because their experiences and their habituses are similar (Bourdieu, 1989).

Habitus, Field, Capital, and Phronesis

When Bourdieu's framework is located alongside the phronetic framework and their aspects are compared we can begin to perceive a path from normalized to wise practice. In each instance, Bourdieu helps us make sense of what actually exists, whereas phronesis is about what should be and, within that context, what we should try to enact in our particular practice situation. He retains the notion that human beings may strive to excel (recall that Aristotle's virtues are 'excellences'), but removes excellence from ethics and places it in the social sphere, and particularly in fields of power. The notion of field brings added understanding to (phronetic) sensemaking. When we enter a space or situation we bring along our past experiences—our embodied habitus—including our relative advantage or disadvantage, and ways of understanding the situation and acting (playing the game) that draw from the logic of the fields in which we have been accustomed to play. We also look for what constitutes capital in those fields.

There is a logic, for instance to a 'meeting' as an interactive space, that is embodied in us as a feel for this particular situation. Engaging a meeting's participants more democratically and dialogically than is customary will require more than verbal statements that change the rules. We will also need to be attuned to the embodied ways we replicate the rules of the games and positions we have played elsewhere. This is true even if we have been disadvantaged and desire to change circumstances that are felt as oppressive: there is a degree of comfort in continuing to quietly resent the ways leaders use power and authority instead of taking a position or voicing an opinion. The 'we' here is intersubjective and interactive: it takes at least two to play the game, which means that members of both 'teams' must interrupt the normalcies of the habitus while creating new logics and capitals that will reconfigure the field. They must be prepared to move through the discomfort inherent in the exercise.

With regard to the move toward wise practice, two interrelated issues emerge here and are explored further below and in Part 2. The first involves the possibility of gaining a degree of conscious awareness about our habitus and how such awareness might help us see and respond to different cues in practice situations and entertain different possible actions. Using reflection to become aware of our assumptions is standard practice in experiential pedagogy (e.g., see Brookfield, 2011); however, thinking with habitus suggests a whole new set of dimensions to be brought to awareness. The second issue involves the social setting. Bourdieu himself comments that the habitus is a fluid and *"open system of dispositions"* that is "durable but not eternal" and interacts with different situations to reveal potentialities in the one that may not have been visible in the other (Bourdieu & Wacquant, 1992, p. 133; also see Horvat & Davis, 2011). Habitus always operates in relation to a field, which means that changes in the field and what constitutes assets (capital) in it could call forth different dispositions and practices from the 'same' habitus. Thus this question: to what extent can fields (their rules and valued capitals) be changed to support dispositions of the habitus that are consonant with wise practice?

Table 5.1 offers a framework for border-crossing partnership practice that integrates practice theory, habitus-field-capital and phronesis. The three columns refer to the three aspects of phronesis, while the rows locate these aspects in the context of normalized practice (row 1), border crossing, or the space for change (row 2), and the move to wise practice and the new professional (row 3).

TABLE 5.1 Border-Crossing Partnership Framework: Practice Theory, Phronesis and Habitus-Field-Capital

Overview	Embodying the Virtues	Making Sense of the Situation	Constructing & Enacting the Good
HABITUS-FIELD-CAPITAL Moment 1: normalized assumptions about meanings and practice	Enduring and transposable dispositions, developed in 'fields of power,' that generate practice; both unconscious and reflexive. Excellence developed in 'playing the game'	Fields have a logic to which players are oriented; sensemaking uses dispositions of habitus and feel for the game. Normalcy as habitual perceptions derived from habitus-field-capital interaction	Practice involves use of capital as constituted in a field and playing by the rules of the game to create/maintain advantage and disadvantage
BORDER-CROSSING/THIRD SPACE Tension between the normal and the possible	Exploration of habitus: relevant experiences and narratives; embodied assumptions, worldviews, values, emotions; disruption and possible resistance Disturbing habits and ways of doing something well (e.g. excellence is not being good at whatever the system asks of you)	Interruption of normal flow and disquiet: what is going on here? Seeking cues to make sense of the situation differently; attending to the good in light of constraints and possibilities of the practice situation	'Capitalize' appropriate dispositions (habitus/virtues) Develop relationships that support self- and other awareness and growth/connection; provide community/field supports for wiser practice
PHRONESIS Moment 2: Move toward border-crossing democratic/civic professional	Personal dispositions (habits of mind, of heart, and of action) directed at excellence in manifesting the good—ideals cultivated through experience, guidance, life in community. Dispositions are summoned as the situation requires, to guide other-oriented ethical practice.	A wiser practitioner seeking understanding that can lead to wise action. Involves *felt* sense, empathy, insight, discernment, creativity, dialogue, and deliberation. Guided by the virtues and search for the good in the situation ('situational ethics') Dialogue/deliberation: Where are we going? Who wins/loses? What if anything should we do about it?	Resolving on a line of action (fluid process) or deliberating (more formal) in light of what is constructed as the good in the particular situation. Calling on virtues and attending to ethical role conflicts

Rather than continuing with an abstract discussion, let me return to Miss Allen and locate her in a setting that exemplifies excellence in border-crossing practice. The point is to trace her movement from the normalized habitus and practice cultivated in a typical education field to a wiser habitus and practice in this setting. An overarching theme in the table is border crossing. We tend to think of borders and Self-Other relations as constituted on the divides of race, class, gender, and identities that are valued versus those that are devalued and even stigmatized. But what fits this description here is the relationship between teachers and students that is visible in Moment 1, on which Miss Allen's old school was based. Thus it is not Miss Allen's physical move from one school to another that constitutes a border crossing, but the different quality of teacher-student relations in the two schools. Collegial relations are different as well, but the student-teacher relation is the centerpiece for the moment.

The Practitioner and the Situation: The *Change from Within Programme*

The Change from Within Programme (CFW) is a partnership between the University of the West Indies (UWI) at Mona, Jamaica, and some 55 schools that have been involved in whole-school change projects since 1992. Part of the Faculty of Humanities and Education at UWI, CFW was until recently under the leadership of Professor Pauletta Chevannes. Prior to becoming a UWI faculty member, Ms. Chevannes was the principal of one of four original CFW schools, all located in poor and 'volatile' areas in and around Jamaica's capital, Kingston. The program is founded on an alternative vision of the possibilities of education that emphasizes human development (Chevannes, 2011; Jha & Kelleher, 2006). As Chevannes puts it, "at bottom, the key is a profound belief in the power of relationships, focused on growing human capacities . . . a belief that grows from the experience with this change process, celebrated through a "circle of friends" involved in the change process itself" (p. 2).

Unlike outreach projects that transfer knowledge and practices from universities to schools, CFW began and continues to enact a partnership approach to civic engagement. UWI's then chancellor, Sir Phillip Sherlock, wanted to involve the university in addressing the problems of the wider society through education; instead of promoting university-based research, he initiated a search for schools that were successful in difficult social settings. The university would bring them together, engage with them in understanding the dynamics of their success, and provide limited assistance for ongoing development and capacity building. The effort received some grants along the way, but there were never large infusions of outside funds. When four initial schools were identified, the collaboration took the form of monthly meetings, later named Circle of Friends. True to its name, the Circle is about more than school development: it is about peer supports and relationships that straddle school identities and personal lives. As Chevannes remarks, "in any organization, if you have issues or baggage, you don't leave them home, you take your whole self with you" (Chevannes, 2011, p. 3).

Participants engage in what has become a "process of constant involvement in a search for solutions, at the local level, in each school and community" (Chevannes, 2011, p. 2). Action research at the school level has become a trademark of CFW and information about school initiatives and data tracking their effects are taken back to the Circle; the sharing and interpretation are always mixed with encouragement and celebration of successes, large and small.[9] School leaders, university staff, teachers, and other professionals (anyone can join the Circle) share and listen to stories, ideas, and the schools' best practices (meaning what has been found to work in each school's particular context); they consider needs, hopes, and possibilities and identify resources they can share or seek from other organizations. Becoming friends, they maintain their connections outside the Circle, networking, planning, and supporting one another.

In their case study of CWF, Jha and Kelleher (2006) remark on the importance of leadership as it was enacted in the program: "leadership was about dealing with a particular reality and building a process of adaptive change in relation to that reality" (p. 90). In fact, the program's name came from the principals' realization of the key to their success: each school had forged a unique path to change by finding and developing resources—"identifying the positives"—from within: within staff, teachers, students, families, communities, and within each person. Family participation and student leadership have also been strongly supported, with a student-run youth leadership camp each summer. Youth leaders are not representatives of school authorities: they have their own voice.

Placing Miss Allen in the Change from Within *Programme*

A thought experiment will place Miss Allen, a Jamaican, at Garvey Primary, an inner-city school that has been part of CFW for a few years. She accepted a position at the school because she wanted a challenge and this is early in her first trimester there. The bullets below capture the broad outlines of her experience.

Moment 1

- Miss Allen's old school, Princess Margaret, was a traditional school that served the same population as Garvey Primary. She was considered an excellent teacher there.
- While at Princess Margaret, with support from a former professor she had undertaken a successful research project that had informed changes in the ways she gave feedback to students about their writing.
- Her students' test scores improved considerably under her tutelage. However, given the large class size, she focused mainly on the good students and used strong discipline to keep the unruly 'bad' ones in check.

Border Crossing—Third Space

What she notices at Garvey Primary in comparison to Princess Margaret:

- Greater participation in school assemblies by students, parents, and service staff, including the man who guards the school gate.
- Teachers seem to maintain classroom discipline without yelling or corporal punishment.
- Little fighting among students during recess.
- No negative comments by teachers about administrators; they seem to relate well.

Her practice:

- She has been told to "look for the positives" in her students but is struggling about what to do differently.
- The students in the back of the class are becoming unruly.
- She starts feeling conflicted, anxious, and afraid the school leadership will consider her a bad teacher and her colleagues will gossip and laugh at her.

Moment 2

- On the advice of a friendly teacher, she resolves to talk to Vice Principal Grant.
- Mrs. Grant is welcoming and empathetic—a good listener. She encourages Miss Allen to learn about her unruly students and what interests them, shares information about their struggles and achievements, and invites her to the next meeting of the Circle of Friends.
- At the meeting, Miss Allen is supported in talking about the problems she has been experiencing. They laugh together, sharing vulnerabilities, as they help her reframe the situation.
- Instead of the criticism she had feared, she receives encouragement and friendly suggestions that come from participants' own trials and successes.
- Miss Allen returns to school energized: she feels the Circle "looked for the positives" in her; she now understands better what it means and is eager to try out her new ideas.

Actual cases from CFW have suggested the phronetic story line. In a rural school, boys were skipping class and congregating at the back of the school. The principal decided to find out why they preferred to be there and discovered them trying to farm. The school took the teaching (and literally, the desks) to the field, infusing the curriculum with subject matter from agriculture: as there was enough land, a school farm was created. The teachers began to see that some of the 'bad' boys were natural leaders who needed positive outlets for their talents: they changed remarkably when they were given their own plot to farm together with a team of students they selected. What about outcome measures, which are as important in Jamaica as in the US? After 8 years, the literacy rate was up from 45% to 84%; boys' attendance was at 98%, and the school had a 4-star rating (out of a possible 5) from the Ministry of Education (Chevannes, 2011).

At another school, gang violence in the community had been seeping into the school. Working with the whole school and neighborhood, the principal resolved on a line of action that included a ban on anything that might become a weapon. Metal detectors were installed as part of a broader comprehensive strategy. Teachers began to pay attention to where and with whom students were congregating, to identify the gangs, gang members, and their spaces. The school kept track of the gangs and the number of confiscated weapons—both went down—and created different uses for those spaces. Suggestions reflecting the collective intelligence of the school community were put into action. After some students died tragically, their friends agreed to receive counseling and began to perceive that one could be a man and still show his emotions (Chevannes, 2011; Jha & Kelleher, 2006). By 2009, the school had no gangs, academic performance had gone up, and ganja (marijuana) smoking had gone down.

As these examples show, action research, which was introduced by UWI and Ms. Chevannes, has been a major tool of change. The schools have made it their own, keeping careful records of their strategies and tracking performance indicators that make sense to them and fit into their ongoing improvement plans. The strategies and data are the subject of collective reflective conversations about school-level change. True to the phronetic sense that practice has to be constantly invented, Chevannes (2011) serves a reminder:

> What were the strategies you employed in order to have that shift, and are those strategies still relevant? Remember it's action research. And the same strategies you used last year may not be relevant this year: you're getting new students into the school, with a new culture, so I have to always be looking at my strategies. If I'm in this business of change, I should look at whether I should change my approach. . . . So it's always a question of looking at where you are, what you have achieved, and what should you do next.
>
> (p. 9)

Cultivating Wise Practitioners

Though the details of this mini-case are necessarily sketchy, I hope they will suggest a path toward becoming and supporting wise practitioners in border-crossing collaborations. Let me consider the main differences in how Miss Allen experienced and dealt with her classroom situation at her old school and at the beginning of the school year, as compared to what followed Mrs. Grant's intervention and the Circle of Friends' meeting. Additional thinking tools emerge from the exercise: power is a given, as it is a key element of 'new' phronetic research, Bourdieu's work, and border-crossing collaborations; leadership and trust are central to this case and to border-crossing professional practice, as the case in Chapter 2 and related discussion have already suggested. They are also central to the chapters in Part 3.

In Moment 1 (and the mini-case earlier in the chapter), Miss Allen is making sense of the situation through the professional habitus and feel for the game that guided her practice at Princess Margaret School, which constituted a normalcy for her and the field. Like Vince Cantril, her habitus is that of a good professional along the lines of the expert. She displays several qualities or virtues, or dispositions that will be part of her in the new setting, such as desire for growth and wholeheartedness, engaging in her research project out of a commitment to improve her practice and her students' learning. She desires to act in a professionally responsible manner and, as Solomon would say, she is seeking the good rather than simply stumbling over it. It is likely that her practice reflects the interaction of both personal and organizational habitus. For instance, she is comfortable with and does not seem to question authority figures such as her academic mentor and the principal. All of these would have influenced what she looked for in her practice situation and how she made sense of it.

With regard to field and capital, interrogating the logic that governs the collaboration between Miss Allen's university and Princess Margaret School leads to the conclusion that it is the logic of outreach. Here, the ruling capital is one that universities have been accumulating since modernity: knowledge as episteme. Having gained more of this capital through her master's degree, Miss Allen was gaining further advantage through her social capital that her connection with her mentor provided. Her colleagues at Princess Margaret were disadvantaged because a potential source of capital that was available to everyone in the school—knowledge from practice—was symbolically devalued. This way of understanding the situation does not make Miss Allen a self-serving opportunist; in fact, through the logic of the field and its valued capital, she could be seen as a trailblazer who, working along with the principal to improve the school, hoped to inspire others to emulate her approach. Miss Allen's focus on improving test scores may also be seen with reference to her feel for the game. Princess Margaret School is a subfield of the larger education field which is now governed by the neoliberal logic of accountability. Even if she privately questioned the *wisdom* of test scores, her feel for the game may lead her to focus her agency on what she can 'realistically' accomplish. At this point, Miss Allen was becoming an excellent professional by being creative in ways that are consonant with the field in which she was playing. Although through her actions she contributed (inadvertently) to the ongoing devaluation of local knowledge as possible capital, there was much that was virtuous in Miss Allen.

We may think of Garvey Primary School as a subfield within education that provided structures and a community whose logic and capitals would create opportunities for Miss Allen to develop potentialities in her habitus and reach toward wise practice. In the space between Moment 1 and Moment 2, she is noticing new cues, but they do not as yet suggest a line of action with regard to her professional practice. In Moment 2 she is starting to develop as a wise practitioner: in Bourdieu's terms, she is being supported for changing her practice and developing a feel for this game that, importantly, is centered on situational ethics.

Her old school is part of a larger educational field where teacher-student relations are structured around the school's need for control, which is typical of schools for children in poverty. It was thus normal to treat all students as Others: obedient ones were 'good' and those who did not conform and comply with this identity were 'bad.' This is also true in many families and thus provides supports for a personal habitus that matches this professional habitus. Miss Allen saw her students mainly through the lens of her need for girls and boys who appreciated what she had to offer and supported her sense of herself as a good teacher. Because her habitus was consistent with this field, she accepted as natural this kind of authority over the students and the practice that went with it: she excelled in authoritarian classroom management and curriculum delivery that resulted in high performance on standardized assessments.

In its broad sweep, this account simplifies a much more complex reality. Fields are replete with tensions, habitus is not merely about conforming to expectations, there is resistance and struggle, and out of these emerge possibilities for change. For Miss Allen, a possible sign of a less than perfect fit between her habitus and the field of her old school was her desire to leave. Something in her urged her on, toward new challenges and ways to pursue excellence in a school she knew would be different. Thinking with the habitus-field interaction, it is possible that her old school brought out not only the dispositions that made her comfortable and competent there, but also a desire for more. There may be similarities here with engaged academics and professionals who take the step to work with outside community groups: well-meaning and wanting to break out of a normalcy they perhaps find stifling and even unjust, they may then stumble over borders they hardly knew were there. Without supports, the border is a dangerous place. How did Miss Allen fare in this border crossing?

Let us recall that a border crossing, as the term is used here, is a disruption of Self-Other relations that puts in question what is normal inside the border; it is an entry into uncharted territory. For a dominant or advantaged identity, what is disrupted are positions in fields that conferred advantage. This can be quite disturbing and in fact a disturbed habitus, with corresponding emotions and bodily markers, is one of the signs of border crossing. The field that is captured in Moment 2 operates according to a logic that replaces authoritarian relations for developmental and democratic ones. From inside the border, Miss Allen knows she is supposed to 'find the positives' and engage the students by tailoring the curriculum and pedagogy to their needs and interests. She knows that she should 'see' the students differently, but her previous experiences have not prepared her to find such cues in her sensemaking. And the inability to be her highly competent and confident professional self, along with uncertainty and fear of failing and of being judged and punished, leave her vulnerable and emotionally drained. She will try hard to not show it, of course: like all of us, she wears masks to hide her vulnerability (R. Craig, 1994; Goffman, 1959).

Thinking about what supported Miss Allen in getting from Moment 1 to Moment 2 helps us consider what may support other professionals in this crossing. The key issue is what she will do to resolve her turmoil and this, in turn, has to do with the supports that are available to her. She is poised between two main paths: a successful border crossing or a reaffirmation of the border as normal and natural (in which case she would probably leave the school or join any marginalized disgruntled colleagues in it). The danger inherent in the latter is that it may solidify the dispositions in her habitus that resist the crossing. Supports are located in five interconnected areas: (a) the dispositions of the habitus (and, in terms of phronesis, virtues), (b) conditions in the field, (c) guided and supported reflection, (d) experiences that affirm dispositions needed in the new field and reorient the habitus, and (e) community narratives. Barriers to successful crossing tend to fall into similar categories. I start by discussing the barriers, focusing mainly on issues that pertain to the emotions and emotional habitus.

Barriers

Several potential barriers would fall in each of the above categories. For instance, one that often escapes us pertains to reflection's 'dark' side: Miss Allen could become quite aware of the negative ways her practice affects her students but be unable to deal with it emotionally and practically, and thus be left feeling even more exposed and vulnerable. My main focus here is on habitus and the habitus-field-capital interaction and the workings of two main protective mechanisms: defensiveness and distrust. At one level, they are masked by what constitutes a normalcy in Self-Other relations. It is second nature for most of us to dance around difficult topics by engaging in a superficial cordiality, equally polite denials that there is a problem of any kind, or when this is not possible, shy away from difficult subjects by refusing to engage or simply suggesting that we 'agree to disagree'. Normalcy, however, needs to be disturbed because it maintains Self-Other relations intact and undermines any possibility of real collaboration. Stripping bare these pretenses may well lead to crises such as the one in the Addams-Lincoln case, but with supports such conflicts can lead to improved relations. Beyond the power of normalcy, defensiveness and mistrust can also be dispositions of the habitus that hark back to deeper underlying issues and emotions that are at least partly buried in the subconscious.

Let me address defensiveness first. It is apparent in Moment 1 that the threat to Miss Allen's sense of professional competence is undermining her self-confidence. Here we see mainly her fears, but there are also signs of defensiveness that might prompt her to assign responsibility for the problem elsewhere: she is not to blame, it is the students and their families who are at fault, the school has left her to struggle alone and without sufficient resources, and so on. If the problem continued without a positive resolution, we could find her banding together with other disaffected teachers who would constitute a protective in-group and whose stories and experiences would affirm and strengthen her resistance to changing herself and her practice.

Research by Chris Argyris (1991), the well-known proponent of double-loop learning, is instructive because it illustrates what highly successful and advantaged professionals often do when they are faced with the possibility of failure. Working with high-level management consultants, Argyris found blind spots that were hard to dislodge because the professionals would avoid anything that might show their vulnerability, embarrass them, and make them feel incompetent. Having had little experience with failure, their reaction to it was an extreme defensiveness that kept them in denial and prevented them from learning from failure. According to Argyris, four basic values constitute a kind of 'master program' for what he sees as simply human tendencies:

> 1. To remain in unilateral control; 2. To maximize 'winning' and minimize 'losing'; 3. To suppress negative feelings; 4. To be as 'rational' as possible—by which people mean defining clear objectives and evaluating their behavior in terms of whether or not they have achieved them.
>
> (p. 103)

Confidence and other outward expressions may then be masks that even the advantaged need to wear in order to protect a vulnerable self deep within. Argyris adds that it does not help to point out others' defensiveness or try to engage them in open inquiry. He offers double-loop learning, which uses data to make visible inconsistencies between the practitioner's espoused theory of action and his/her 'theory-in-use' and supports reflective thinking that closes the loop.

Thinking with habitus, field, and capital helps us consider that, if 'master program' tendencies are indeed 'simply human,' more advantaged parties in a field may also be advantaged with regard to hiding or not seeing nor hearing what they "passionately desire to ignore." Shoshanna Felman (1982) articulates an understanding of knowledge and ignorance informed by the work of French psychoanalyst Jacques Lacan that sees ignorance as a kind of resistance:

> while learning is obviously, among other things, remembering and memorizing . . . ignorance is linked to what is *not remembered*, what will not be

memorized. But what will not be memorized is tied up with repression—the imperative to exclude from consciousness, to not admit to knowledge. Ignorance, in other words, is not a passive state of absence—a simple lack of information: it is an active dynamic of negation, an active refusal of information.

(pp. 29–30)

Psychoanalytic principles may well apply across the lines drawn by social advantage and disadvantage, but social advantage provides more ways to protect one's ignorance and forgetting, by using one's capital and the rules of the game to buttress the performance of an assured and confident self.

In a society that is built on struggle for advantage, there is also a struggle over emotional advantage. This does not mean that those who are advantaged are psychically healthier: rather, through the reverse of recognitive social justice, they may be able to obtain compliance, obedience, and respect from others that allow them to maintain their sense of self-worth and well-being. This is accomplished through a ruse and a mask, but the mask may be invisible, especially to its wearers. Resistance to repressed knowledge can take the form of placing the responsibility for failure on less advantaged parties, either at the personal or group level (here the dynamics of scapegoating come to mind). And, because the game is tacit and invisible, in an exercise of symbolic violence (meaning the violence is turned against oneself), at least some of the disadvantaged may accept responsibility and thus concur with the *rightness* of being blamed, shamed, attacked or rejected. Indeed, this is an all-too-common reaction among those who are abused, a reaction that we can now examine through the workings of habitus, field, and capital at the personal, professional, and organizational level.

Let me now turn to mistrust. Trust is defined as confidence in someone's competence, integrity, and benevolence. Any or all of these factors may be involved, depending on the person and the situation. In our case, Miss Allen needs to rebuild her trust in her competence and thus needs colleagues and administrators to trust her in that area; she also needs to trust in the benevolence of the administration and, possibly, their integrity toward her, meaning that they desire her well-being and would be fair and honest. Given the school's emphasis on relationships, the administration, in turn, needs to trust her benevolence toward the students, as well as her competence. Mistrust is not merely the absence or the opposite of trust: it is about confidently negative expectations and beliefs about the other, which means that fear and suspicion are the prevailing emotions (Lewicki & Wiethoff, 2000). Thinking with habitus and field should help us see that the histories, experiences, and collective memories can make trust or mistrust the norm across social divisions. Mistrust does not seem to be a huge obstacle in CFW, but the organizational habitus of the education field lends itself to such mistrust, and thus it is important that CFW counters it quite intentionally. It is quite likely that students who had experiences in other authoritarian schools and with authoritarian families also carry with them a disposition to mistrust teachers and authority figures, which they may carry into adulthood.

In the mini-case, we see Miss Allen struggle with fear and whether she can trust: can she reveal her concerns, thus making herself vulnerable, and ask for help without risking having her professionalism put in doubt and thus sow what might be the seeds of her own demise? Moving cautiously into the new field, she finds that she can. Here CFW departs significantly from normatively pathological institutions (see Palmer, 2007; Chapter 8) in which tensions between ethical practice and self-preservation are often the norm and thus openness and sharing one's vulnerability with authority figures can pose real dangers. Courage is one of Miss Allen's dispositions or virtues but the point here is that she is not faced with a 'lamb-to-slaughter' scenario: what helps is that the school has changed aspects of the situation in ways that make trust more likely. Wise practice is thus not about instilling character and virtue in the professional alone, but about changing relationships, rules of the game, and changing what counts as capital so as to lessen fears and danger and build safety and trust. This takes us to the topic of supports.

Supports

The Habitus and Its Dispositions

I noted above that Miss Allen's own dispositions facilitate her border crossing. For instance, leaving her old school was prompted by a desire to grow professionally and perhaps personally. Once in a new school, we see her struggling through her fears with the determination not to be defeated by the challenges. It is likely that these dispositions were involved in her professional success at the old school. She seems to have the inner strength and resilience to make it through the difficulties, including the courage to reveal her vulnerability and ask for help. Returning to the section on embodying the virtues, we can consider the qualities that support reflection according to Dewey: her strongest suit seems to be wholeheartedness, which speaks to her determination, while there are some questions regarding her directness, open-mindedness, and responsibility. But we are working with the dispositions of the habitus, including emotional dispositions, rather than the emotions of the moment. In the language of phronesis, the virtues of her character guide her as she goes through a process that includes but is not determined by the 'negative' emotions that emerge at any point in time.

Embodying any of these virtues does not mean never feeling contrary emotions but having an inner compass that will enable us to regain our balance. If we think about the case and directness, for instance, which is defined as the absence of self-absorption, Miss Allen is indeed self-absorbed in Moment 1: she is preoccupied with her performance and is unable to be open to the situation. But self-awareness and self-absorption are not necessarily immanent qualities; they are a response to the particularities of the situation. It is difficult and at times impossible to refrain from self-absorption when we feel threatened. The question is whether or not we stay there no matter what, and for Miss Allen it seems to be a temporary state. The same may be said about her open-mindedness, remembering also that dispositions or virtues interact with situations and fields: one may be open-minded in one instance, about some things and not at a different time, about others. It is also possible for conditions in a field to reveal or cultivate dispositions of the habitus that were not apparent in other fields. This takes us to the next topic.

Conditions in the Field

Supports come by the way of actions that reduce real and imaginary dangers and encourage the cultivation of virtues. Imaginary dangers are often projections of the subconscious but they feel real, and so open communication is needed to help us understand the difference. For Miss Allen, the real danger of failing professionally was reduced by the open communication and guidance from seasoned colleagues (the Circle) and superiors (the department chair, other administrators). The fact that the CFW philosophy and actual practice is about supporting positive and healthy relationships also created sufficient safety and trust: meeting and communicating with colleagues, Miss Allen experienced firsthand that her vulnerability would not become an occasion for judgment and punishment. Realizing that her fears were not founded in the reality of this particular situation (thus, they were about imaginary dangers), she was able to express dispositions of her habitus that helped her be more perceptive in her classroom and creative in her attempts to change her practice. Importantly, in suggesting that she observe her classroom rather than offering specific practices, Mrs. Grant is cultivating a virtue in Miss Allen: learning to see what her students need so they may flourish.

Other supports for border crossing in this particular field might have included clear messages (both symbolic and through action) from authority figures about what was valued (or what would accrue 'capital') and how it was supported. Perhaps there were stories, from other teachers, of instances when support, respect, and care were not withheld because one made mistakes and experienced temporary failures; capital would accrue to those who cared for students' learning and well-being, developed good relationships with them, showed the capacity to live with uncertainty and ongoing assessment and reassessment of what worked, and strove to be part of and contribute to a community of learners. Here, these would be the attributes and actions of a phronetic professional.

Reflection

As I mentioned above, the disruption of normalcy that accompanies border crossing creates the possibility for greater awareness and understanding, precisely because what was normal and taken for granted is now open to question. We make sense of our surroundings and construct the good and possible ways to enact it through various modalities of reflection: these may include inquiry, dialogue, conversations, artistic and bodily expression, working with thinking tools and data (including action research); their focus may be one's embodied sense, emotions, presuppositions, narratives, practices, organizational issues, and so on. However, disturbing the habitus may also potentially create a barrier to reflection, since it can give rise to defensiveness, anxiety, and difficult emotions that stand in the way of self-awareness and cloud one's perception of a situation. This means that the challenges of the crossing need to be accompanied by supports that reduce the anxiety and sense of danger so that reflection and learning can take place. Disturbances of the habitus and the accompanying emotions can themselves become the subject of reflection. Part 2 explores this topic further.

In the mini-case, supports are readily available no doubt because CFW is at its core a border-crossing project, a counter-story to the prevailing logic of the education field. It thus needs to be quite conscious and intentional about its orientation and practices, and the way it introduces new professionals into its fold. Thus the supports Miss Allen receives are an integral part of the institution and its habitus. The colleague who directs Miss Allen to Mrs. Grant and Mrs. Grant herself are developmental leaders who support and guide new teachers in ways that assuage fears and begin to create trust. This then frees her from the self-absorption caused by her inner turmoil and helps her direct her attention to her students. Mrs. Grant also guides and supports reflection by suggesting where she might train her attention, connecting it also to possibilities for practice, something that the Circle will further support. This tack accomplishes two things: it helps Miss Allen reframe the situation—see it differently by paying attention to different cues—and consider practice that would enact the good as it fits this particular situation.

Recalling that CFW is an example of phronetic practice can help us see that various modalities of reflective thinking and action are central to its work. Action research, as an example, is about a cycle of collective reflecting and making sense of the situation, intervening in it, collecting data, and again reflecting in a process that is ongoing. Information is gathered also through informal dialogues and conversations about what matters, conversations that are inclusive and are geared to examining practices, reflecting on problems and possible actions to address them. The wise practitioner, after all, "must always go back to school." As a result, CFW moves toward wiser practitioners and practices that benefit from collective intelligence.

Experiences That Affirm Needed Dispositions

Border-crossing practice is learned through a combination of experience and supports. But practice also requires dispositions that can be affirmed through experiences that may precede border-crossing practice and continue while it is ongoing. There is a difference between intellectual agreement with a position, say, that Others have much to contribute, are knowledgeable, and trustworthy, and thus can be valuable partners and being disposed to believe it. The disposition to believe is cultivated through experiences that, in fact, affirm it. It is through such experiences—and the surprise and amazement that often comes with them—that one may come to realize the extent of one's embodied disbelief. In fact, being *disturbed* may be a necessary part of the change process.

Let me illustrate by asking a rhetorical question: would it have helped Miss Allen if she had expressed her fears to one of her new colleagues or to Mrs. Grant and their reply had been that there was no reason to be afraid, she should just go and do such and such, adding, perhaps, "trust me, it's true" or "I've done it and it works!" My immediate reaction is that it would not, but the answer would depend on Miss Allen's state of mind, her relationship with and trust in the speaker, whether she had engaged in similar practices, and the availability of supports for engaging in the new practices. Here, she was encouraged to look for positive qualities in the 'bad' students; she might have discovered creativity and leadership where previously she only saw inappropriate behaviors. These discoveries would encourage her to experiment with practices that built on the positives she had actually experienced. The main point is that beliefs cannot be countered by telling someone not to believe; they can be countered by successful experiences. A reflective dialogue that helped Miss Allen explore her disbeliefs and fears and offered specific suggestions that addressed them might also create sufficient self-confidence for her to take some manageable steps. It might help bring to conscious awareness times when she had relevant experiences but ignored them because they did not conform to her beliefs. In turn, successful experiences should strengthen relevant dispositions to try again, expanding the options. This is the import of teaching and professional development approaches that include coaching, scaffolding, and experiential components designed expressly as challenges and supports (Baxter Magolda, 2004; Egart & Healy, 2004).

The Power of Stories

Participants in groups are frequently encouraged to share stories from their personal and/or professional lives. The rationale is typically to 'break the ice' and encourage the beginning of connections. There are other, deeper ways to understand the importance of narratives. Hearing others' experiences and understanding how they make sense of them and of the world around them brings us into the presence of real human beings. Stories and experiences convey the richness of our habitus and encourage the listener to go beyond group categorizations and begin to grasp how each of us is both a carrier of multiple group identities and also unique and different. As we discover in the chapters in Part 3, with guided facilitation, deeply felt personal stories evoke compassion and empathy: we won't necessarily agree with the other—in fact, it might set the stage for constructive conflict—but we can connect on a human level. Healthier and deeper human connections alone are not enough to transform pathological authority relations and all the 'isms' and institutionalized forms of oppression and social injustice; but they are a starting place that needs to be more prominent in our thinking about professional life.

Conclusion

This chapter has developed a two-part integrated framework for tracing and supporting the movement from the normalized practice of the expert and social trustee to the practice of the democratic civic professional. First, we have the thinking tools of habitus-field-capital, which can help us understand the starting point of a partnership: the dispositions, orientation, and capabilities of participants, including what constitutes resources and ways of being excellent in this 'game' and, generally, the logic that governs sensemaking, interactions, and actions. The realm of phronesis comes next, centered on advancing practices that support 'living well' in the particular situation. Phronesis thus transforms 'ways of being excellent' in a particular game into virtues that make situational ethics the very core of practice. This border-crossing partnership framework helps us keep in mind both the real and the possible in the particular practice situation; in fact it locates the democratic civic practitioner on the tension line between the two.

Border-crossing is a 'third' space where oppressive normalcies become visible and supports are provided for the desired transformation of the practitioner, which then also contributes to a transformed understanding of the situation and of its practice possibilities. The chapter has further developed the notion, encountered in Chapter 4, that this space requires a community or 'circle of friends.' Habitus-field-capital allow us to consider how this space can support the transformation. Habitus helps us see how self-awareness, empathy, and changes in Self-Other relations can grow by probing our discomforts, through relevant experiences that become embodied, and by storytelling that helps participants enter one another's lived realities and understandings of the situations. Field and capital train the focus on changing the rules of the game and what constitutes resources in ways that promote healthy relationships and wise practice. As empirical constructs, field and capital can also be used in a mapping exercise that enables us to visualize the given and the possible in a particular partnership.

I hope that pondering the contents of the chapter as a whole will bring home what for me has been the most important realization of all: the complex nature of knowledge for and from practice, the richness of the quest for wise practice, and the immeasurable gains that can come from unlearning our current approaches and embarking on this path. This chapter concludes Part 2 of the book. Part 3 provides illustrative cases that draw directly or indirectly from this framework.

Notes

1. 'Practice' can refer to almost anything people do. Hager, Lee, and Reich (2012) provide a conceptual framework for researching learning for/in professional practice that involves a continuum of 'more inclusive' to 'less inclusive' definitions. As used in this book, practice falls in the 'less inclusive' end of the continuum.
2. See the US Department of Education's Institute of Education Sciences, "What Works Clearinghouse" (http://ies.ed.gov/ncee/wwc/default.aspx). "Practice Guides" rate recommended practices by levels of evidence, where the highest rating ("strong evidence base") is given to strategies, programs, or practices that have "strong causal and generalizable evidence." Qualitative studies are always rated as having a "minimal evidence base," while the double-blind randomized experiment has become the gold standard for social science and education research (http://ies.ed.gov/ncee/wwc/pdf/reference_resources/wwc_procedures_v2_1_standards_handbook.pdf). For a critique, see Biesta, 2007; Lather, 2004.
3. Among them are Estela Bensimon (2007), past president of the Association for the Study of Higher Education (ASHE), Jean Bartunek (2007), past president of the Academy of Management, Linda Darling-Hammond (Darling-Hammond, Chung Wei, Andree, Richardson, & Orphanos, 2009) and Marilyn Cochran-Smith (Cochran-Smith & Lytle, 2009), two past presidents of the American Association for Educational Research (AERA).
4. See the Carnegie Project on the Education Doctorate (http://cpedinitiative.org/). Also Shulman (2004, 2007) and Shulman, Golde, Bueschel, and Garabedian (2006).
5. This discussion is based on neo-Aristotelian perspectives. Aristotle held elitist views (about women and slavery, for instance) that would be problematic for present audiences and are not aligned with my thesis.
6. Practitioners use decontextualized rules and procedures initially and rely on cases and intuitive grasp as they become more adept. See the Dreyfus and Dreyfus scale in Flyvbjerg, 2001.
7. The reductionism of single stories circumscribes our imagination and thus our ability to understand and have empathy for Others as complex human beings who are the bearers of multiple stories and possibilities.
8. Scholars agree that Bourdieu's schema draws tacitly from Aristotle, as well as others. He also infuses the whole with a *critical* flavor by locating habitus in the context of power and struggles around power. See Bourdieu, 1989; Bourdieu & Wacquant, 1992; Crossley, 2013; Leander, 2009; Reay, 2004.
9. Carr (2006) argues that conventional approaches to action research (as applied research) remain steeped in the precepts of positivism. His work contributed to an approach in the tradition of practical wisdom, started in the UK in the 1970s: instead of applying social scientific theories to practice it helped practitioners assess their own action theories. This seems to be how CFW uses action research (for practitioner-oriented resources, see Workgroup for Community Health and Development, 2013). For a critique of positivistic action research from the *critical* tradition see Torre, Fine, Stoudt, and Fox (2012).

PART 3
Learning About Professional Practice Through Cases

6

FROM NORMAL TO WISER PRACTICE IN A HIGH-SCHOOL, COMMUNITY, AND UNIVERSITY SERVICE-LEARNING PARTNERSHIP

Novella Zett Keith, with Fatima Hafiz and Jim Peterson[1]

> If you want to be a change agent you have to be prepared to change yourself.
> (Chevannes, 2011)

> Every single person has capacities, abilities and gifts, and the quality of an individual life in part depends on the extent to which these capacities are used, abilities expressed and gifts given.
> (Kretzmann & McKnight, 1997, p. 3)

This chapter builds on the framework developed in Part 1, which centers on the democratic civic professional, practice, and the constructs of the wise practitioner and wise practice or phronesis. At its heart are three critical incidents that I use to delve into this border-crossing framework as a concrete practice: I consider first the ways the incidents express *normal* ways of being, understanding, and acting by the practitioner in partnership situations and, second, the activities and interventions that supported moves toward wiser practice. A critical incident is about a crisis that shakes a person's sense of comfort, creating a dissonance between what was expected or believed and what actually happened. The incident does not have to be momentous or even visible to bystanders; what matters is that it stays with the one who experienced it—the possible sign of a submerged struggle between the desire to ignore disturbing knowledge and emotions and the desire to explore, understand, and use the situation for growth. While the experience is felt as personal, through reflection and dialogue the participant can grasp how it straddles different levels of social reality; what is disturbed is thus potentially larger because the habitus is the meeting ground between the personal and the social. In a supportive environment, critical incidents create the possibility for self-transformation and changed practice.

The incidents took place during a four-year border-crossing collaboration in which students and teachers in an inner-city high school (Upland High) and the College of Education at City University engaged in service-learning projects with members of a coalition of community-based organizations.[2] The aim was to take a partnership rather than an outreach approach to service-learning, meaning a focus on supporting capacity building in both young people and neighborhoods while pursuing an agenda that was broadly informed by social change and social justice. Service-learning philosophy and principles of practice emphasize meeting authentic community needs, mutuality in contributions and gains, and sustainability. We would use them to foster equitable relationships and guard against damaging one-sided activism. We recognized that the community would suffer if the service were to entrench potentially disempowering and disrespectful notions associated with being the recipients of charity (see McKnight, 1995); similarly, the college students would be harmed if their service work strengthened deficit constructions of Others as persons to be pitied or blamed rather than as citizens who, though disadvantaged by inequitable social arrangements, were nonetheless possible partners.

The three incidents involve, respectively, (a) instructors (as members of the college and high school leadership team), (b) students (as members of high school-college service-learning teams), and (c) an encounter between college students and community members. Each incident explores barriers and supports for wise practice starting from one of three intertwined aspects of phronesis introduced in Chapter 5. Each also taught us important lessons about situational ethics. The first incident took place early in the partnership and involved one of the coauthors, Novella, and another member of the leadership team. It serves to explore the influence of the practitioner's self on what she or he sees, the barriers emotional habitus and blind spots created for collaboration, and what supported change in my capacity to be a partner. The second incident alerted us to youth engagement as a *good* that we had not been consciously pursuing. It was brought to our attention by a comment made by Sharon, one of the teacher partners, that her students working in teams with our college students were becoming passive. The third incident, which started with college students attending a community meeting, brings all aspects of phronesis together: how the students constructed community needs (the good), how their understanding of the situation and of themselves changed through the intervention and dialogue that followed, and what they did as a result.

Before presenting the incidents, let me introduce the partnership and the partners. Located in Oakville, a metropolitan area in the US Northeast, the partnership included three entities. The first to join were the Upland Youth-Driven Service Learning Center (UYD-SLC), located in a large comprehensive high school in one of the high-poverty areas of the city, and the Community Health Collaborative (CHC), a broad coalition of local organizations, service providers, residents, and others who shared an interest in fostering healthy communities and neighborhood revitalization in the school's vicinity. Fran, a veteran English and language arts teacher at Upland and a strong service-learning advocate, was the founder-director of the Center as well as a founding member of the CHC, which was the brainchild of an activist public health physician, Deryn. The third member of the leadership team at that point was Pamela. A service-learning mover and shaker, she headed an organization that had funded the UYD-SLC and 10 other such centers across the state. Fran, Deryn, and Pamela were interested in engaging young people in empowering community-based work.

Joining a couple of years later, the third organizational partner was the College of Education at nearby City University (CU)—more specifically faculty and students in a section of a service-learning course that was part of newly instituted core requirements for teacher education majors. Novella was a member of the graduate Urban Education faculty at the college and the lead faculty for this new undergraduate course. Pamela taught one of the course's multiple sections and proposed locating it at Upland. When her organization issued a request for proposals (RFP) for higher education institutions to partner with school-based service-learning centers, the College of Education applied and became a grantee, with Novella as principal investigator.

The partnership centered on the collaboration of mixed teams of Upland and CU students on service-learning projects in the neighborhood and school. Each semester, about half or more of the class meetings of a designated section of the college's service-learning course were held in the high school, where the students worked together to conduct community-based research and plan and implement their projects. For the high school students, this work was integrated into a multidisciplinary service-learning project that fulfilled a graduation requirement. The projects were identified in collaboration with the CHC and the student teams were supported by co-instructors from the high school and university and CHC leaders. At this stage, the leadership team expanded to include Novella, a teaching assistant, Upland teachers, and CHC leaders.[3]

Embodying the Virtues: The Leadership Team

"Weren't They Wonderful?"

It was the first semester of our partnership and Fran had invited the college students and instructors to a presentation on service-learning that her students were giving in another class at the high school. With the 27 of us added to some 30 high school students and teachers in attendance, it was a large audience. The whiteness of many of us stood out, given that the student body was 100% black. The presenters were four members of the Hometeam, a core group of specially selected Upland students from the school's only college-bound small learning community. Hometeam students played an active role in many of the activities of the UYD-SLC. They maintained the website, cowrote and edited the center's publication, and were trained in service-learning, leading community focus groups to determine community needs, and doing presentations and trainings for students and teachers. Trainings focused on using a curriculum guide, *Build a House of Service*, that was coauthored by Pamela and was used in the school, region, and across the state. I was eager to see the Hometeam in action.

On this day, however, I would be disappointed. The presenters sat at the desk in the front of the class and mainly read from *Build a House of Service*. As I tried to listen carefully, I was taken aback and wondered whether this was the best that Upland could offer. The presentation itself was very basic and the delivery was not at all polished. It didn't fit the picture of Hometeam trainings I had gotten from Fran. I found myself thinking about research studies and some of the teachers I knew, who enacted culturally relevant pedagogy, believed in the students' capacities and 'pushed' the students toward high achievement. Then there were other teachers, who used the more common cultural deficit approaches characterized by low expectations rather than searching for and enhancing strengths, and whose students were less successful.[4] I knew Fran as the energetic and creative founder of the UYD-SLC, which supposedly embodied all the tenets of these valued practices—but the performance didn't match my expectations.

What was going on? Could it be an early practice run? I took some mental notes about what I might suggest to Fran we could do with the Hometeam to improve their understanding of service-learning and their delivery skills. After the presentation, Fran came up to me smiling, brimming with positive energy, and said: "Weren't they wonderful? This was so good!" I didn't know what to say, and perhaps the doubt showed in my face because she went on to explain that the students to whom they had presented were often hard to manage, but today "they were really listening, nobody got up and walked around, they were engaged, asking questions." She added: "This is the power of peer teaching."

I did not record my reply, but I remember it as something meant to be encouraging and polite. I did not tell Fran what I had been thinking. Given the drastic differences in our evaluations of the students' performance, I didn't know how to do it without coming off as the expert from the university, which was not who I wanted to be, or as someone who would criticize rather than support. The experience stayed with me in the form of a deep discomfort and many new questions. I thought I knew something that could help improve the results: how could I be supportive as well as critical without being patronizing? What could I do here with what I knew? My silence also contributed to something else: a more generalized but hidden feeling that the level of competence that Fran and others in the school accepted as "wonderful" was too low, especially as these were the star students.

Over the life of the partnership many experiences took me back to this incident and were catalysts for reflection. In particular, there was an occurrence two years later when Fatima and I first began working with Hank and his students. It was similar enough to the first experience, in the sense that Hank's students had given a brief presentation to ours, which was followed by an interaction between the two groups. All of us were pleased with the exercise; but was it also a worthwhile and successful academic learning experience, as Hank claimed? This time there was no internal struggle on my part. I asked a genuine question, Hank shared his thinking, we talked, and I think both of us learned something new. The exchange was useful in another way: it crystallized my awareness that I had changed. I could look through different eyes, getting the embodied sense of Bensimon's message that for the relation between expert and practitioner to change, the expert needs "to recognize the inadequacy of one's experience and knowledge" (2007, p. 461). I will use this situation to explore the notion of *embodying the virtues*, which shades into *sensemaking*.

Embodying the Virtues in "Weren't They Wonderful?"

The overall theme is the quality of collaboration in the leadership team; the specific focus is on how my *normal* orientation, habitus, and the qualities I embodied informed the way I made sense of the situation. I will try to capture in particular those embodied qualities that I believe limited my capacity to be a wise partner at the beginning of the partnership and how that capacity grew in ways that mattered to the collaboration. As is true for all case studies, the value of my experience and those of practitioners whose stories appear later and in other chapters is not in its applicability beyond the particular, but in the food for thought it can provide.

In Chapters 2 and 5 respectively, community partners and Dewey articulate some of the qualities (in phronetic language, virtues) that support reflection, inquiry, and collaboration. For Dewey, I emphasized directness, wholeheartedness, open-mindedness, and responsibility. Among the important qualities and practices for community partners were building relationships, addressing power inequities, an orientation to participatory processes, and respect, especially with regard to according legitimacy to community partners' knowledge and capacities. Some of these virtues seemed to be at work here but others were either not in play, absent, or needed greater supports and cultivation. Two of Dewey's qualities that stood out in this respect were directness and open-mindedness. Directness pertains to the ability to attend and be present to the reality of a situation. Defined through its opposite, it is the absence of self-absorption and concerns that cloud one's vision and deflect attention from the situation. Open-mindedness is self-explanatory except for the interesting twist that it does not mean empty-mindedness but calls for principled reaction, including critique.

A reason for considering directness is that something that should be obvious is missing from my evaluation of the students' performance: the possible effect of the audience. As both experience and research confirm, the presence of powerful onlookers suspected of biased judgment (which is a reasonable assumption here and was later confirmed by the high school partners) can create a sense of insecurity and anxiety, and thus a desire to stick to a script. This accurately describes what the Hometeam members were doing; yet my interpretation did not take into account the way we, the audience, may have contributed to the shaky performance, but focused immediately on the students' capabilities and especially on those of their teachers—as though the college representatives were not in the picture. What had clouded my vision so that I embraced a particular and biased interpretation of events? Put another way, the question is about the interaction of the habitus with aspects of a particular situation, enabling or preventing a practitioner (here, myself) from being present to it.

On one level, a different set of excellences was involved in my evaluation of the students' performance: the normal qualities that are traditionally associated with being a professional. Like the social trustee or expert, I wanted to help by identifying the problem and providing a solution. However, the core issue as I see it now pertains to how my emotional habitus interacted with the situation. In Chapter 5, I pointed to the 'passion to ignore,' a notion originating in depth psychology, warning us that knowledge and ignorance involve much more than memory or exposure to information: we tend to resist information that disrupts our beliefs about ourselves and the world and that, if taken into account, would force us to see and be in the world in new ways. On reflection, I was resisting the potentially devastating information that students and teachers might be doing the best they could with the hand that was dealt to them. Social justice as a universal principle was meeting social injustice as a reality.

Listening to the presentation, I think I didn't want to face the complexities and despair—one part of the reality—of a truly difficult school and neighborhood. I was invested in the picture of reality I had constructed from Fran's information, which was centered on capacities and positives. When I did not see them, I tried to assign blame and fell onto another ready construct: fixing the problem. The analytical orientation of the expert provides a way to distance oneself from the pain and avoid facing the reality of monumental problems, diminished possibilities, wasted talents, and the struggles and care required in such settings to produce even small victories. I think I was struggling through an emotional fog created by all kinds of vulnerabilities, including a sort of culture shock to which the college students could admit much more readily than I could. I was the one who was supposed to know: how can the professor provide guidance while also experiencing shock and powerlessness? I would have to learn. The starting place would be not to hide these emotions behind the mask of the professional (see Chapter 8) but to use them as a bridge to the college students' own shock and bewilderment, thus also opening a door of perception onto the high school students' world.

My passion to ignore had an additional side. I professed to believe in democratic, community building approaches to reducing poverty and want, approaches that emphasized people's assets, capabilities and gifts (see Asset-Based Community Development Institute, n.d.; Kretzmann & McKnight, 1997; Nussbaum & Sen, 1993); but my embodied reactions made me question whether I trusted in my community partners' capabilities and gifts. As the saying goes, did I walk the walk or just talk the talk? An interesting aspect of habitus is that it can help us grasp just how deeply we can hold onto beliefs that our intellect thinks it has jettisoned: what inconvenient truths were hidden in there? My forays into urban schools had been those of the researcher and consultant and my knowledge base drew from those activities. My personal life afforded me a partially insider view of living as a racial minority in the US, but I had class and race advantage, had never taught in a school like Upland, and had no experience about what it was like to teach and learn there. My knowledge and experiences were not inconsequential but they were certainly partial. As Hank helped me see, I had never experienced the sense of powerlessness the students felt, the loss of hope in education as a possible way out. I needed to listen to my school colleagues and learn more about their reality. If there were improvements to be made, they could only come about by working in partnership.

Self-awareness did not completely change my emotional habitus but made it easier to recognize unhelpful tendencies when they reared their head. Thinking with practice, the virtues, and habitus, I think that what was needed was not a generic open-mindedness, but a situated capacity to be open-minded in particular ways, in this place. Here, open-mindedness needed foundations such as the qualities community partners valued: humility, empathy, respect (especially for local knowledge and capabilities), self-awareness (e.g., how one's fears and vulnerabilities influence what we see), and the desire to address power inequities (especially the monopoly of legitimate knowledge). In the presence of such qualities, dialogue becomes possible and maybe even natural, as one can ask hard questions in the spirit of inquiry and as a critical friend,[5] developing wiser practice grounded in insider understandings of the situation.

Cultivating these qualities is always a work in progress. For me, this developmental process was supported by classic professional learning practices: dialogue in learning communities, with trusted partners and with students, observation, reflection, inquiry. Thinking with the virtues of wholeheartedness and responsibility, my learning was guided by a deep motivation to become a better partner and border crosser. 'Critical friend' prodding in my learning communities and through friendships such as Fatima's also helped.[6] Other incidents at the high school and in the neighborhood became embodied in me in ways that I can't imagine will ever leave me because they are part of my habitus and memories.[7] I witnessed and experienced the capacities and gifts of the high school students, teachers, and neighborhood residents. Useful insights came from reflecting with some of the thinking tools that were explored in Part 2 of the book.

One apparently simple realization was that in dealing with encounters across borders, my knowledge and past experiences did not make me immune from the kinds of reactions the white college students were having and the assumptions they were making: I began to ask myself if what I saw in them also applied to me, possibly under different guises. For instance, I and the other instructors were well aware that the college students often thought they had all the answers; but because their answers were simple and mine were more complex and informed, and because I saw myself as a well-aware border crosser, it was harder to see similar tendencies in myself.

The chapter now moves to the joint service-learning classroom and the way it was organized to support the college students in becoming wiser practitioners in their own border crossing partnerships.

Sensemaking and Constructing the Good: Working with Students

Geneva Gay's (2010) well-known book, *Culturally Responsive Teaching*, starts with the epigraph, "you can't teach what and who you don't know" (p. 1). This epigraph provides an added context for the reflection and understandings that emerged from the first incident: beyond its worth for the professional's own development, the work is essential for guiding students as they navigate this path. Self-awareness and empathy that foster understanding the reality of the students, school, and neighborhood and our own relation to that reality can help us learn what signs to look for in students, how to guide them and, at least some of the time, successfully cultivate their virtues.

Constructing the Good

Guiding students on the desired path requires instructors and facilitators (here, the leadership team) to be intentional about the *good* to be enacted through the partnership, the normalcies that thus need to be interrupted, and the tools or interventions that may interrupt problematic normalcies and support wiser practice. As discussed in Chapter 5, the phronetic framework locates the good in the realm of situational rather than universal ethics. There is a fluid, organic process where we make sense of the practice situation while exploring the possibilities of enacting a situated good through it. General ethical principles and values can be useful but only as part of an iterative process of sensemaking.

Table 6.1 provides an overview of our evolving understanding of these issues in the context of the partnership. From the start, it was clear that we should pay attention to principles of sound practice regarding service-learning and collaboration across divides. Once the partnership was ongoing, we also recognized the imperative to support youth engagement and voice and the related notion that community work and service-learning should help prepare young people for future roles as active citizens and community leaders.

The table summarizes the normalcies to be interrupted in enacting these three sets of principles and how we went about it. Since youth engagement has not been discussed previously, I should mention that a well-established literature on youth-adult partnerships emphasizes the difficulties of adults in dealing with power asymmetries vis-à-vis young people. Instead of moderating their authority

TABLE 6.1 The Good, the Normal to Be Interrupted, and Supports for Wise Practice

The Good	Campus Partner's Normalcies to Be Interrupted/Disturbed	Mechanisms to Interrupt Normalcies & Support Wiser Practice
Collaboration across divides • Value local assets (knowledge, capacities) • Difference (not Self-Other binary) • Social justice (recognition, equity, share power and resources) • Community capacity building • Authentic relationships • Developmental/democratic leadership	Expert as sole knower and problem solver Experiential/local knowledge as less than academic knowledge Technocratic orientation Fears and suspicions (masked by politeness, silence, withdrawal, and conflict avoidance) Categorization and bias/prejudice	**Structure of service-learning course** • Relationship building • Student teams • Project approach • Group work • Collective intelligence • Engaged participants in school and community • Institutional supports for partnership
Service-learning • Future teachers understand and appreciate service-learning pedagogy • Enact service-learning principles: – mutuality – meeting authentic community needs – sustainability	Traditional teaching and learning orientations Helper-helped (charity orientation) Deficit perspectives of community and its agency	• Instructors as facilitators/students as active learners and doers • Service-learning process and grading (chart) • Reflection (personal, group, written, other) • Critical incidents • Readings, ready handouts
Youth engagement • Positive youth development (capacities, active, voice) • Youth-adult partnerships (encouragement, support, developmental leadership)	Adult in charge Youth 'participates' passively; order-taker Roles, authority, and knowledge of the adults/young adults vis-à-vis the young people	• Open dialogue/reflection about college student roles, attitudes, and behaviors in teams

and providing opportunities for the young people to gradually assume more active leadership in joint endeavors, adults unwittingly contribute to silencing and disengagement (Arnold, Dolenc, & Wells, 2008). Since the two upcoming critical incidents take us into the service-learning classroom and community, I turn next to an account of service-learning pedagogy and its approach to interrupting oppressive normalcies, which are also relevant for collaboration and youth engagement across divides.

Service-Learning as a Counter-Normative Pedagogy

Research conducted by Patty Clayton and Sarah Ash (2004) reveals interesting differences in the ways students describe traditional and service-learning classrooms. The first are seen as centered on "efficiency, answer-orientation, assumption of teacher (not learner) responsibility for establishing goals, rule-constrained nature, and competitive mode" (p. 59); by contrast, the service-learning classroom is seen as inquiry guided, democratic, and collaborative (also see Howard, 1998). The right column in Table 6.1 shows the degree to which the structure of service-learning courses provides tools that can be used to interrupt these normalcies and provide supports for guiding students toward wise practice. The very openness that can immeasurably enrich the service-learning classroom disturbs normal pedagogical practice with regard to both course contents and teacher-student and student-student relationships. In terms of the first, the myriad learning opportunities the world offers cannot be easily scripted ahead of time in a syllabus. They also involve more than the cognitive realm, bringing attention to emotions, including uncertainties, fears, and resistance to knowing, and the ways our emotional habitus interacts with and influences what we see and how we make sense of it. For its part, classroom relationships shift to student as active inquirer, teacher as supportive facilitator, and peer teaching and learning. Bringing contents and instruction together means that the instructor must "see—and help . . . students see—uncertainty, confusion, insecurity, and frustration as normal, acceptable, and even beneficial dimensions of learning—as signs, in fact, that learning and growth are taking place" (Clayton & Ash, 2004, p. 61). Considering the similarity with phronetic sensemaking as described in Chapter 5—open-ended inquiry that grapples with the situation's emergent nature—reaffirms the pertinence of service-learning for cultivating wiser practice in students.

The main tools for integrating relevant experiences and academic learning are facilitated reflection, linking readings and experience, and dialogue. For the college students in this partnership, these were incorporated in the service-learning process, guiding questions, and course assignments described in Table 6.2. In line with a facilitative role, the questions along with the instructor's responses to students' reflections suggest areas for consideration, exploration, and inquiry, connections to academic contents, and questioning implicit assumptions the student may be making. Using the border-crossing partnership framework, my guidance to students would now also include comments on existing qualities (virtues) and the dispositions and orientations of the habitus, suggestions about any emergent qualities and possible cues about the good in the situation, and Bent Flyvbjerg's (2001) four questions: who wins, who loses, through what mechanisms of power, and what, if anything should be done about it?

The service-learning process began with a self-exploration and then proceeded to community-based research, identifying partners and doing a project that brought together collective gifts, interests, strengths, and concerns, all of it

TABLE 6.2 The Service-learning Process, Guiding Questions, and Course Requirements

Process	Guiding Questions	Requirements
1. Searching	Who am I and what do I really care about?	Personal statement
	How do I connect who I am with a community?	Journal entries
	Who is in this community and what holds it together?	Critical incident reflection
	What gifts do I have to contribute to this community?	
	How do I join with others to develop a project that meets our reciprocal needs?	
2. Researching	What strengths does this community have?	Community assets/needs
	What challenges does this community face?	Research report
	What's led to these strengths and challenges?	Journal entries
	How are the challenges currently being met?	
3. Identifying	What issue brings together our collective gifts and interests, and the community's strengths and concerns?	Project proposal & learning plan
	Who is doing something hopeful about this issue?	Journal entries
	What skills and content areas are being developed through this process?	
4. Collaborating/ Partnering	How do we ensure our group knows about and uses our combined assets and meets all members' needs?	Partner agreement Journal entries
	How can we establish a mutually beneficial relationship with our community partners?	Critical incident reflection
5. Planning	What precisely will our project be?	Project plan and timeline
	What tasks need to be done, when? What skills are needed?	Sustainability plan
	What do we know and need to learn?	Journal entries
	What difficulties can we expect & how will we deal with them?	
	Who will take responsibility for what?	
	Is our plan consistent with service-learning principles?	
	How could this project be sustained?	
6. Doing	Are things working out as expected?	Activities log
	What adjustments are needed in our plan?	Journal entries
	How well are we collaborating and problem solving?	Critical incident reflection
	Are we practicing service-learning principles?	

(Continued)

TABLE 6.2 (Continued)

Process	Guiding Questions	Requirements
7. **Sharing—Celebrating—Sustaining**	How can I/we best demonstrate our accomplishments, learning, and community contributions? With whom should we celebrate our achievements? How? How will the project be sustained?	Visual documentation Oral presentation Portfolio, including final reflection

culminating in a celebration at the completion of the project. Each of these components can be infused with relevant academic and practice-oriented contents. In our case, in addition to using a text on service-learning (Wade, 1997), we took special care to emphasize practices and attendant readings and reflections in the areas of self- and community-knowledge, Otherness/diversity, and building collaborative relationships among and between the college, high school students, and community partners.

We asked students to prepare and selectively share autobiographical narratives that included critical incidents about their experiences with collaboration and border crossing. We knew that we needed to break through normal processes that support bias by creating personal relationships and helping the group explore how their habitus and that of others predisposed them to make sense of situations, often through categorical thinking (that is, seeing the social category and not the person). We engaged them in classroom exercises that allowed them to explore and share their experiences and fears surrounding diversity (for examples see Chapters 7 and 8). Based on prior experience, some readings were prepared and assigned ahead of time, while others were assigned as and when needed to support learning from emerging situations. We also warned all students, from both relatively privileged and dis-advantaged positions, that the process would *disturb* and disrupt ways of thinking, feeling, and acting that felt comfortable and urged them to work through any frustrations, discomfort, and resistances: they would eventually be excited about entering this new terrain as change agents and changed persons. Words without the experience were not enough, but we would help students make the proper connections when the time came.

The second critical incident explores phronetic sensemaking in the context of student teams. Sensemaking is connected with habitus since, as we saw above, our focus as we attempt to understand situations is influenced by our dispositions, orientations, and what matters to us. In phronetic terms, it involves perception and insight in looking for the good to be enacted in the situation. The incident brings to the fore something that emerged during the second year as an unintended negative consequence of the partnership for the high school students. It is followed by an inquiry into normalcies that were not interrupted and an exploration of how to understand and support wiser practice in this context.

Making Sense of the Situation: My Students Are Becoming Passive

Before turning to the incident, let me provide some context by briefly reviewing what we saw as accomplishments between the beginning of the partnership and the end of the second year. The high school students were doing much better at moving through the steps of their service-learning projects, feeling more comfortable especially with the research requirement. They enjoyed the contact with the college students and the access these relationships had given them to the campus and to firsthand information about college. We were also pleased by what the college students were learning about service-learning pedagogy as they engaged actively in the school and neighborhood. Readings, activities done separately and together, and the instructors' increasing comfort and capacity to facilitate reflection on service-learning experiences had also changed many biased assumptions and supported the desire to connect with the neighborhood's residents and understand their history and struggles. Classroom dialogue had opened up talk about fears that white and advantaged college students frequently harbored, such as the fear of being a *minority*, of being considered racist, and of not being accepted or even hated by black people because of one's advantage and privilege; in turn, reducing ill-founded fears had made room for a growing desire to contribute and be a team member.

The critical incident, which took place during an evaluative meeting at the end of the second year, is captured in the heading as a comment made by Sharon, one of the teacher partners. Youth engagement was an important value for all of us (see Table 6.1) because we shared the sense that genuine engagement on the part of both sets of students was essential to the success of the partnership. We had all seen some obvious problems around collaboration and communication in the student teams and knew that we needed to interrupt tendencies on the part of many of the college students to arbitrarily control and limit discussion, take charge, and make one-sided decisions, which prompted various actions and reactions on the part of the high school students, including disengagement.

Many of the college students had expressed disappointment at their high school counterparts' occasional failure to come through and tended to interpret these behaviors in terms of essentialized character deficits: shirking responsibility, 'fooling around,' and a failure to take their work seriously. Sharon's insider understanding, however, lead her to make sense of these behaviors differently, in terms of relationships and dynamics inside the student teams or in terms of their interaction with the practice situation. Her naming of the problem in this way revealed the dissonance between our espoused beliefs and the actual results of our practice, turning it into a critical incident that became the focus of considerable attention.

Reflecting in light of relevant literature, this is a common phenomenon in the practice of youth engagement or youth-adult partnerships: the adults find it difficult to change their role as problem solvers and decision makers vis-à-vis the young people, who in turn fall back into youth roles of acceding to adult authority or resisting it (see Mitra, 2008; The Innovation Center et al., 2003). How much of what the college students saw as apathy or 'fooling around' might be resistance or rebellion in reaction to their practices?[8] A review of their written reflections and portfolios provides partial cues to the problem Sharon had named. The next subsection provides a sketch of how different college students made sense of their partnership work, especially the service-learning project, suggesting a connection between their perceptions and actions and the passivity Sharon saw in her students. The practice of two students, Alex and Jessica, is especially striking as it captures key aspects of what are, effectively, two modal understandings and approaches students took to their service-learning projects.

What Happened: Alex and Jessica as Partners

The first approach, typified by Alex, is a conventional or *normal* construction of leadership that focuses on the person of the leader and on a task orientation guided by the values of efficiency and goal accomplishment. The second approach (Jessica's) is person oriented and relationship oriented, and is guided by the values of participation, voice, and healthy and healing relationships. Depending on other factors, it can be described as developmental, democratic, or a combination of the two, attuned to the tenets of a 'leaderful community' that is also characterized by emotional intelligence (Barker et al., 2011). These different orientations also influence participants' understanding of the capacities required for leadership. Both Alex and Jessica mention leadership and communication as important aspects of the service-learning process, but they construct them differently.[9] Let me provide a brief summary with some supports from their written reflections.

Alex's team was larger and thus more challenging than most; it consisted of five college and four high school students. As a self-appointed leader of the team, from the very beginning Alex's focus was on the timely accomplishment of his own objectives and exercising leadership to ensure the same for the team's objectives. Personally, he was set on completing all the parts of the required course portfolio; he saw the team's objective as working efficiently to produce a quality project: painting a mural on the building of a community partner, which had been on the agenda of the CHC Beautification Subcommittee. He wrote:

> I decided that my main focus would be getting the mural finished, and that I would catch up on the paper work after it was completed. I was fortunate that some of the people in our group concentrated on the paper work, and others concentrated on completing the mural.[10] This allowed me to complete my portfolio even though the mural was finished just two days before our presentation was due. I made sure the project was done as well as possible by bringing my own brushes, rollers, paint sprayer.

In this construction, leadership means breaking down the overall task into its component parts and distributing responsibilities for completing the parts. Alex's description suggests that this was done collaboratively, that is, participants agreed on the division of labor and responsibilities—a fairly common routine in nonhierarchical groups. However, for the sake of efficiency, those who were not at the meeting were left out. This is how Alex describes planning for the final oral presentation:

> we decided to distribute each section equally among the students that were present that day. . . . We found out that two Upland students may not attend the presentation [and] . . . the presentation parts were then distributed to mostly CU students. . . . The Upland students, throughout the presentation are more than welcome to jump in and talk about any of the topics we are presenting.

Needless to say, it is not inviting to tell younger students to "jump in" when the presentation is controlled by the college students. Group processes we witnessed in the classroom suggested that it was fairly common for the college students to make such efficiency-oriented decisions and when the high school students didn't follow suit, resort to assigning tasks to those team members who were present and seemed willing to take them on. The press to get the task done was such that collaboration, when it didn't happen on its own, seemed a luxury they could not afford. Thus democratic leadership stopped at the college–high school divide. Communication was an adjunct to this construction of leadership. As Alex explains: "I also felt that communication within the group was very important. I made sure every move that I made or that we made as a group went out on the list serv. I felt that this helped keep everyone informed and on task." In other words, communication was about ensuring the open flow of information about tasks, responsibilities, and timelines. Alex does confess that he was "a little disappointed that people within the group did not give [him] much feedback through the list serv" but he does not problematize the failure of communication to flow upwards.

As opposed to this approach, the relational/developmental process typified by Jessica's orientation to the service-learning project was clearly focused on collaboration, voice, and the engagement of the Upland teammates. Working with the CHC Health Subcommittee, Jessica and her group decided to hold a fair on sexually transmitted diseases (STDs) in the school. From the beginning, she saw the work as involving both a task and a process; in fact, team building was clearly a value and a goal in her autobiographical sketch. Once her group was formed and while engaging in the second step of the service-learning process (identifying the need to be addressed), she commented: "our group is still pretty new and we haven't formed any clear roles. I feel we desperately need a facilitator, but fear that if I take on that role I will come off bossy."

There was struggle and growth around creating a genuine (young) adult-youth partnership. At the beginning, Jessica made sense of relationships through what is a common adult pitfall: wanting to give up power and authority in order to make room for the 'empowerment' of young people. She came to understand, however, that there needed to be a gradual process that engaged her creativity and judgment in inventing ways to invite the high school students in and engage their motivation. We have here many of the ingredients of wise practice through a process of sensemaking that constitutes a constant search for and movement toward the good, constructed as a task (the STD fair) and a process, becoming a team. The search is supported by other virtues that are in evidence in Jessica's work: respect, wholeheartedness, tolerance for ambiguity, empathy, care, and more.

Here, unlike Alex, Jessica deliberately stayed in a situation that she constructed as 'floundering' in order to obviate a bigger problem, acting as a 'bossy' sort of leader. Shotter (2012, chapter 5) would describe this moment as an inevitable immersion in and search through the confusion created by a disquiet. She was discouraged when the Upland team members seemed disinterested and lacking in follow-through, but she pressed on. Again thinking with Shotter, we see her resolving on a line of action directed toward enacting the good: she suggested to her CU peers that they hold preparatory meetings on their own on campus prior to the joint meetings at Upland. These preparatory meetings turned out to be key to the group becoming a team. Their focus was on both what needed to be done (a task orientation) and a process of listening and relationship and capacity building that gradually engaged the Upland team. By the end, Jessica comments:

> On the day of our project, I saw our group pull together to form a unity. . . . The group morale was high, our attitudes positive, we stuck by each other when questions were asked, as when faults were given, because we were there for one another. We were successful as a group, we met a goal that I personally had, and that was to accomplish our project as a team and not individuals. The feeling of accomplishment from this was tremendous.

Understanding Alex's and Jessica's Sensemaking

How do we understand the differences between Alex and Jessica in light of phronesis and the habitus–field–capital interchange? What stands out first is the fact that these students focused on and accomplished what they cared about while at the same time fulfilling a community need. Qualities of character or virtues were visible in the process and what they cared about did go in the direction of the good, though more so for Jessica than for Alex, whose focus on accomplishing the task, while commendable, is partial: it does not take into account the notion that 'living lives worthy of human dignity' must include both the ends (here, completing the project) and the process through which they are achieved, that is, through the engagement of the whole team. The point, though, is not to blame Alex for his partial focus but to rethink the practitioner-situation (or habitus-field-capital) interaction. The rules of the game in the field of education, institutionally enforced, are all about completing the various 'products' on which the final grade depends. Although members of the instructional team had made relevant suggestions in comments to reflections, we had not acted systematically to change the rules so as to interrupt this *normal* construction of the situation.

The desired qualities clearly resonated at the level of virtues for Jessica; her emphasis on becoming a team was unwavering, standing out even in a field that did not especially value it as capital. Jessica's process orientation had originated in her own habitus and not in our interventions. Similar virtues may have been present in Alex, though they were submerged and not called forth by the field. His comments at the end show he understood and was pained by the loss in relationships and engagement potential when the high school students were left behind. He acknowledged the artistic talent, enthusiasm, and quality work of some of the high school students and regretted not being more sensitive to what they needed. For Alex, it seemed as if the motivation to accomplish the project, with all the constraints of time and process, had interfered and won over another motivation: a desire for more, for wholeness, and for inclusive practice. Was the motivation to be a teacher a common ground that we could draw on to support the practice of youth engagement? Mary, another member of Jessica's team, expresses it this way:

> I cared so much because not only did the achievement of the [STD] fair reflect our group, but it also indicated what kind of teacher I would be. It showed that I had enough determination to make a difference . . . I felt for the first time like a teacher, even though I wasn't teaching in a traditional way with a conventional classroom.

We had engaged the students in some activities that built relationships, eased conflicts, and provided supports for sharing authority in problem solving and decision making. But what is striking in these paths through the service-learning project is that in the area of collaboration with their high school teammates, the college students acted largely through the orientation of their habitus. Their habitus seemed to include qualities that, though not *normal* in education as such, were part of their commitment to becoming teachers. After the initial anxieties and in spite of periodic and ongoing frustrations, many of the college students were quite caring, motivated and eager, enjoying this new approach to learning and teaching that expanded the classroom into this school and community and stretched them in ways that brought new qualities into play. Thus the second issue, already encountered in the Change from Within case (Chapter 5), had to do with looking for the *positives*: we had missed opportunities to support collaboration in the student teams, but the desired qualities were there and we needed to find better ways to cultivate them.

In related fashion, we had missed opportunities for building collective intelligence. The modal tendencies that Alex and Jessica expressed were present in every class. Is there any doubt that pulling together such qualities, capacities, and understandings would have made a qualitative difference for everyone? Genuinely valuing these assets would make for a rich classroom dialogue that could create a supportive community for moving toward wiser practice. There was always a fair amount of group reflection in class, but we needed to turn it into collective intelligence. This incident helped me understand, in an embodied way, the feeling-sense that in practice everything and everyone is the teacher and everyone's knowledge counts.

The next section continues to explore this incident. It moves from the current focus on understanding what prevented the high school students' engagement to a focus on hopefully wiser practice directed at supporting team collaboration and youth engagement. In phronetic terms, we move from sensemaking to enacting the good.

Enacting the Good

Service-Learning for *Youth Engagement*

Planning over the summer helped us identify several changes to be instituted in the fall, which we hoped would help enact the good as we now understood it. Some changes were simple, but they conveyed a consistent message about new rules of the game for this partnership field. For instance, in our course requirements, we gave the same number of points for collaboration as we did for completion of the project. We conveyed to the college students how all their interactions and activities, from the first relationship- and trust-building classroom sessions on campus and in the high school, to their teamwork around the project and the final celebration, fit into the service-learning process they were learning. We spoke differently about their roles: college students were neither equal partners nor teachers but should explore in-between roles, possibly as young adult allies; their desire to become teachers was important and they should try putting on their teaching 'caps' to ensure that they engaged their teammates developmentally and democratically. In our feedback to their reflections, we commented on the qualities they were developing in these regards. We continued to stress and repeat these messages until they became a common language.

Structurally, working with Hank's students rather than the Hometeam presented new opportunities. Our students were now partnering with students in his service-learning class, which was yearlong. Like ours, it was focused exclusively on the service-learning process and completion of a project. The curriculum Hank used, *Champions of Caring*, matched the emphases in the college curriculum: it focused specifically on youth engagement and youth leadership and cultivated social justice–oriented service that was grounded in deep personal commitments. We now could entertain long-term projects that Hank's students would sustain and develop from one semester to the next. Thus, although it might still be possible for a group to complete a project in one semester, it was not imperative or even desirable that they do so. Our students' project could be an interim accomplishment that was part of a longer sustained effort. We also agreed to do service-learning projects in the school, which Hank proposed because he thought they would be more engaging for his students and thus more successful. The school became a community partner, along with the CHC. Students, teachers, and staff in the school, along with CHC subcommittee chairs, identified areas of need and potential growth.

Moving to longer-term projects inside the school helped enact the good in several ways. Perhaps most important from the perspective of a border-crossing partnership, it made the high school students the most visible actors and owners of the projects. It gave them the experience of being change agents in a community that really mattered to them: their school. While the college students changed each semester, the high school students continued working on their project between semesters and into the next, providing continuity, dealing with problems that could not be resolved by previous teams, meeting with teachers and staff to share ideas and explore available resources, and generally providing leadership. Thus when the CU students arrived the following term, the Upland students served as a bridge to the new group, presenting their work, passing on stories and written records, and using their newly earned social capital to carry on the project. These assets gave the high school students a greater sense of power, making them more valuable as partners and the partnership more real and meaningful to all participants.

The change meant that the college students learned different aspects of acting as adult *allies*.[11] At the beginning of a project, they worked developmentally with the high school students to negotiate connections with community partners, including school staff, administrators, and teachers, and to identify and obtain available resources; in doing this they were still advantaged by their social skills but now worked with their teammates intentionally to cultivate their capabilities and gifts. The next set of college students would be less advantaged, since the high school students now held the keys to information, relationships, and resources about their projects. As in-school relationships became less hierarchical and more collaborative, the high school students experienced being valuable and responsible members of the community and received recognition for it. Working on projects that were visible and held in high regard in the school also created commitment and satisfaction all around. It contributed to changing the perceptions and the quality of experiences of adults in the school, who found it satisfying to work with students in these new and positive ways. Not only were several projects sustained but so were new social bonds, as several of the college students continued to go to the high school after their coursework ended. As Kate, a white college member of the *Girl Talk* team said it: "the most rewarding thing was getting to know my buddies, my *sistas*."

Even more important was the effect of this way of partnering on the high school students. Hank recounts how it instilled in some of his students the power to change, so that by making a small change in their community, they were able to transform their destiny. He will never forget a former student stopping and jumping out of his car, screaming: "I got my college degree in Criminal Justice and it was your class that made me believe it was possible!" And yet he was one whom the college students perceived as not focused.

The chapter moves next to the third critical incident and an aspect of enacting the good that has not yet been explored: the principle of meeting authentic community needs. Using a social justice framework, this principle goes beyond what *services* people in poor neighborhood might need, which is typically how needs assessments are construed, to what *assets*, along with capabilities and gifts, can support their struggle for equity and a fair share of resources.

"You People Should Get It Together"

Journeying through aspects of phronesis by the way of critical incidents now takes us from border-crossing relationships inside the leadership and student teams to an encounter between college students and neighborhood residents. The encounter takes us from the above statement that one of our college students broadcast to neighborhood residents attending a community meeting, to a project that constructed their needs differently and contributed to community education and community building. Here is a succinct version of the story.

Meeting authentic community needs seems easiest when there is a community partner who identifies a need the service-learners can address. In the case of this team, the chair of the CHC recreation committee was the partner who told the student team that the neighborhood needed more recreational spaces. At the CHC meeting that followed, residents proposed a recreation building but were told by representatives of City Hall in attendance that there were no funds for the project. An alternative was suggested: creating an open playground and playing fields. The students were directed to an empty lot that could be put to such use, but quickly discovered that more resources than expected would be needed to clear it, and that, in addition, the immediate neighbors were not in agreement with the proposed use for the space. Still searching, struggling, confused, and somewhat anxious about the passing of time, the group next attended a public meeting where participants would be discussing neighborhood plans for improvements that might include recreation: a competitive process was in place, through which the mayor's office would provide funds to those neighborhoods that had developed solid plans and had the organizational capacity to manage the funds.

The students, the only immediately visible outsiders at the meeting, fell unawares in the middle of a controversy. There was no plan in the making and no consensus; instead of a united community, they heard differences of opinions, angry accusations, and questions that went unanswered. As they recounted the situation later in class, the students realized that their CHC contact had not spoken for the neighborhood as a whole, nor had he given them important information they were now beginning to gather through class discussion and readings, information that allowed them to put the meeting in the larger context of the neighborhood funding initiative and the divisive effects of City Hall policies. At the meeting, however, they didn't yet know about this larger context that would help them make sense of the situation differently. Frustrated by what he saw as a chaotic meeting and a disorganized community, George, a member of the student group not known for his tact, stood up and delivered this message: "*you people should get it together. No wonder you can't get things done.*" The response was not what he and his friends expected. They described it as a lashing and, although they did agree that the comment was disrespectful and more than a bit brash, they were confused and angry at the intensity of the reaction. It didn't help matters when George added that he was there with a team of CU students who wanted to do a project to help the community: Was he that naïve—people asked—didn't he know the university was *the* problem?

Crossing Borders to Community Building

The encounter left the students stunned and upset but also eager for help in making sense of the situation. The incident and the cognitive and emotional dissonance that followed created an opening for a shift in consciousness which, through facilitation, led to different questions and eventually a different action. Growing in understanding through in-class group reflection, readings, and facilitated dialogue with their Upland teammates, the whole team eventually came to question their prior construction of the community's needs. The need for recreational space was real, but now they could put it in the context of inequitable policies that favored center city, realtors, and big players like the university and the business community over inner-city neighborhoods. Given this background, creating competition among the neighborhoods may be a good option for City Hall, as there wasn't enough funding for all the pent-up demands. But it was unfair. If competition was inevitable, maybe the team could provide some supports to the neighborhood group: how could they help, metaphorically speaking, level the playing field?

Considering their project in light of issues facing the neighborhood, their place in it, and the politics of power, the recreation group began to formulate an alternative.[12] At the meeting, they had picked up a 15-page official description of the neighborhood initiative and its requirements. They began to think that, instead of facilitating community engagement by providing the needed information, this document seemed to constitute a barrier to engagement. In what became a genuine dialogue that involved listening and making use of one another's capacities and resources, the joint high school–college team came to see the document, which neither the Upland students nor, by their account, neighborhood residents understood, as an exercise in (oppressive) power through language. The Upland students suggested they should rewrite the document in language they *all* could understand. The CHC leadership agreed. Here, finally, was a project that met an authentic community need and enacted their new understanding of the good: the team took the essential information in this document and created a pamphlet that was distributed in the neighborhood through our community partners.

One of the insights to emerge from this incident is that identifying authentic community needs in a service-learning partnership, at least in circumstances such as were met here, is more than an instrumental task that can be accomplished through typical community needs assessment methods: starting from a listing of possible need areas (housing, health, transportation, mental health, safety, etc.) such exercises produce new lists that identify community priorities. The pamphlet would not have been on such a list; it came out of dialogue and deliberation that uncovered a need for community education and advocacy as it emerged in interaction with the particular situation. The need revealed itself through the students stumbling on an approach to community-based research that was more in line with ethnographic inquiry and with the researcher reaching for insider understanding of the issue, which the high school and community partners provided. The approach was consistent with the four phronetic questions mentioned above, as it identified one of the ways power was exercised and one of the ways it could be countered so as to serve the community. This incident and its aftermath also showed what becomes possible when hidden dimensions of what is real are made visible through reflection and dialogue that explore personal and community issues in light of social structures and relations of power.

In turn, genuine dialogue would not have been possible without some qualities that were emerging or coming to light in participants through the process. To explain this, I need to turn to another aspect of the incident that was unpacked in its aftermath: George's "you people" comment and the community members' reactions to it. This issue was interwoven in the dialogue that led the team to envision their new service-learning project and is only separated out for ease of presentation. Skilled facilitation had included nurturing of qualities for collaboration and youth engagement. For the college students these qualities included humility, open-mindedness, empathy, deep listening, and a desire to understand; for their part, the high school students were coming to trust their partners and themselves, believe in their own capacities, and feel comfortable with voicing their understandings to the college students. The incident provided more food for thought, as the dialogue took up questions about how authenticity and racial identity figured in collaboration. What follows is a brief account of how Fatima facilitated the students' learning around this issue.

Fatima introduced short readings and discussion points that engaged the students in reassessing their assumptions about the neighborhood and helped them come to grips with the borders that kept them from seeing it from the inside and learning how local people understood its realities. One of the readings was a well-known piece on white privilege by Peggy McIntosh (1989); others were brief accounts of the history, politics, and economics of racial and ethnic groups in cities that helped locate the current state of city neighborhoods in the contexts of the politics of race and class. The whole class engaged in examining the incident through the lenses of these historical and systemic factors as well as their own personal and familial connections to these events. The phrase, 'you people,' provided an entrée into relations across racial and class divides and an opportunity to explore how the white students felt about and dealt with their own racial identity and the privilege that came with it.

Fatima was not from the neighborhood but, as an African American, she had insider knowledge. She explained why 'you people' could be interpreted as a racial slur: it lumped together the whole race in an offensive way and, especially in such a public context, named them as Others who were inferior to oneself. George and others insisted that the comment was not racist, but they accepted Fatima's interpretation and the class reflected on the deficit assumptions that informed how the white students had made sense of the meeting. Turning their attention to the service-learning projects, students were asked to consider economics and race as factors in their construction, and whether their projects were in line with service as charity or service as social justice.

The dialogue was difficult *and* stimulating, even in its moments of intense discomfort. It could have engendered hostility, resistance, and silences (which were not entirely absent from it) had it not been for prior work on relationship building both inside the college class and with Upland students, which had created enough trust for some truth telling, genuine exchanges of information, and fewer silences. The desire to understand seemed to win over the desire to ignore, as questions and realizations kept coming. Expressing how they felt being a minority in this setting, the white students began to reassess why Upland students were at times silent or absent: their own experience suggested that it happened when the Upland students did not feel safe enough to ask questions, express what they really thought, or got tired of not being able to be 'just themselves.' From there, the students made connections to relations of authority in education, asking one another what kind of teachers they would be, as many, inspired by the dialogue, committed to becoming teachers who would not silence their students.

This incident and subsequent readings and dialogue generated additional breakthroughs that speak to the transformation of habitus in the context of border crossing. Let me end this section with a long and revealing reflection from James, one of the other college students on the recreation team. I will let it speak for itself.

> At the beginning of the semester I felt totally out of place in this community . . . Basically, I felt as though I had died and gone straight to hell. Here

I am, an upper-middle-class white male in what I perceived as an impoverished black neighborhood. I felt there was no way I could possibly fit in here, no contributions I could make. Regardless of what I did, the Black students in this school will never accept me . . . As time went on, somehow I managed to fit in very nicely . . . As I reflect on my earlier feeling and the way I feel now, I look at what must have precipitated the change. One day in class, Fatima had us read the "White Privilege" article and I realize that this was why I was uptight . . . Being a White man in a white society produces a rather high level of arrogance. This seems to be the basis for the "White Privilege" syndrome. I felt I didn't belong here and I was scared to death. However, in the end, the Upland students accepted me very hospitably. I guess I was the one that had to accept them.

Summary and Conclusion

I will end by reviewing what this case offers with regard to changes that needed to be cultivated for the development of the border-crossing democratic civic professional and the processes that facilitated and supported those changes. The case was designed to give suggestive examples of changes in desired directions, meaning toward deeper, more pertinent, thoughtful, caring, and inclusive (wiser) understandings of what constituted the good in the situation and what actions to take to enact it, as well as changes in personal qualities (habitus, virtues) that supported these perceptions and enactments. Thinking with practice and especially wise practice meant that the focus was not on the professional or practitioner as such, but on the interaction between participants and the situation and the supports provided for wiser practice through spaces that facilitated the interruption of unwanted normalcies and supported emergent qualities, sensemaking that glimpsed what the good might be, and collective intelligence and action toward that good.

Thinking with practice also means thinking with the particular. What the good consisted of had to be constructed in the course of a partnership that was about doing service-learning projects with particular participants in a particular setting. This focus on particularity means that although tools, techniques, and knowledge can be adapted from one situation to another, to enact wise practice the wise practitioner is never finished learning. There is a guide and guidance, but it always involves judgment and rethinking what has or hasn't worked and what might work. What did the guided facilitation entail?

The guide to wiser professional practice was three pronged. It involved (a) a sense of the good, (b) interrupting various normalcies, and (c) providing supports for change in directions and practices that seemed to lead to the good. We had ideas about the good, normalcies to be interrupted, and likely supports prior to engaging in the partnership, but these understandings shifted and other aspects became visible through the practice itself. Undoubtedly many normalcies continued to be enacted that did not become visible to us and thus were not interrupted. Equally, some supports were more successful than others: such is the emergent and developmental nature of the process.

What the good was and how it was constructed was central, so let me start there. As this was a service-learning partnership, we began by constructing the good with reference to principles of service-learning practice and of collaboration across borders, armed with a degree of awareness of the main normalcies we needed to disturb in these areas. We knew we wanted there to be collaboration not only in the leadership team but also—and especially—in the joint teams of college and high school students. Although this aspect of the partnership should have pointed us in the direction of the principles of youth engagement and the related need to disturb the normalcies of youth-adult authority relations, this aspect of the good came clearly into view only when we became aware of its absence.

Once the general principles pertaining to the good were identified (through processes that were obviously not linear), they needed to be considered in light of the situation, understanding that each situation was unique. For instance, the service-learning project that came about through the third critical incident clearly shows that there is no single right way to enact the principle of meeting authentic community needs; this was simply a more appropriate or wiser construction of the good emerging through these particular circumstances. The circumstances included who was at the table (the qualities, knowledge, and orientations—habitus—of the students, instructor, and CHC leaders), what was happening around the situation (the neighborhood disarray, the policy context, and broader contexts of inequality) and the situation in the moment, especially the details around the critical incident. What was required in all instances was judgment in resolving on a line of action, weighing different possibilities in the context of the particular givens and a growing appreciation for how to be a partner with neighborhood groups in this situation.

Weighing possibilities pertains to the aspect of phronesis that involves making sense of the situation and moving toward a possible action that enacts how one understands the good. Again, this is guided by one's understanding of what is real and what is possible in the situation, which may be limited or enhanced by participants' qualities and habitus. For example, my desire to see assets rather than deficits in the high school students prevented me from grasping the complexities of teaching in the school; the single-minded focus of some of the college students on completing the task kept them from seeing and considering opportunities for enacting the good by engaging their high school partners. If these were constituted as obstacles in this instance, there were also *virtuous* qualities, such as the desire of many of the student-teachers to be developmental leaders who worked to support the engagement of their high school teammates, and the motivation of many of the high school students to take on more responsibility for the projects once their college teammates were gone.

In Chapter 4, I wrote about building *third spaces* that sustain the learning and change that are envisioned as the good. In this partnership, many spaces were created that presented opportunities for genuine cross-border communication, sharing of knowledge and understandings, and relationship building. To what extent did they become genuine third spaces for transformation? There were many occasions when the normal was interrupted and the discomforts and disorientations that accompanied such interruptions were explored; relationships were built that made it somewhat more comfortable to be vulnerable and disoriented—although this was perhaps the hardest part of the process. Some spaces were created through the interventions of instructors and community partners, others through the insights and actions of students, and still others through experiences that "just happened" and created stores of memories.

Facilitators' interventions that interrupted undesirable normalcies and furthered qualities and practices in support of the good included (a) changing what mattered in the course (e.g., the focus and types of assignments and the weights given to them), (b) directing students' attention to their own and others' emergent qualities and to alternative possible ways to think and act in situations, (c) introducing relevant and time-appropriate information and knowledge that contributed to more complex understandings of the situation, (d) supporting relevant capabilities (e.g., critical reflection, collaboration), and (e) creating spaces where power was shared and the above practices would be supported. It is important to remember that, at times at least, facilitators were not only course instructors but also participants—although our (the leadership team) normalcy of making decisions, being the 'knowers,' assuming sole responsibility for intervening, and like marks of authority was not interrupted as often as we should have. This meant, in particular, that genuine sharing among the students and collective intelligence based on that sharing did not happen as often as would have been wise.

One of the goals of the chapter was to explore how thinking with phronesis can help us enact wiser practice and support the cultivation of wiser practitioners. As I look back, my sense is that the framework enabled connections to be made that were not visible in the case prior to adopting this lens. In particular, it brought to light the interconnected nature of the practitioner's personal qualities (or virtues), how these influence understanding the practice situation and the possibilities for the good in it, and actual practice. It opened up areas for intervening and facilitating wiser practice. And it helped direct the focus of reflective practices (especially reflection on critical incidents) by aligning them with the three aspects of phronesis.

There is extensive literature on human development and developmental processes that stresses the importance of a balance of challenges and supports, critique and affirmation. In reconsidering this chapter in light of that literature, I wonder if there was perhaps too much challenge and not enough support. At least in the retelling, there seems to be more emphasis on a critique of problematic normalcies than on celebration of small victories and larger achievements. In the epigraphs to this chapter, Paulette Chevannes reminds us that if we want to be change agents we need to change ourselves. John Kretzmann and John McKnight also remind us that everyone has capabilities and gifts, that there is virtue in being able to express them, and that such expressions build community, both as bricks and mortar and as social bonds. As a facilitator of such processes, I have continued to search for wiser ways to practice.

The next two chapters are aligned with phronetic practice without foregrounding it to the extent that this one has. They will help us explore further and deepen understanding of the above questions and others, especially with regard to some of the issues that remain around interactions between young people and adults and between campus professionals and community partners, around challenges and supports, approaches to facilitation, and becoming comfortable with the discomfort border crossing necessarily entails.

Notes

1. The case narrative was drawn from unpublished documents written by the coauthors and other participants, including a conference paper by Fatima and Novella (Keith & Hafiz, 2002). Fatima and Jim also contributed ideas in conversation with Novella and reviewed and commented on the chapter in its final stages. The chapter is written from Novella's perspective and through her voice because cowriting was hampered by time and other constraints (unless otherwise noted, the first person refers to Novella).
2. Case documents include project reports, conference presentations, field notes and reflections, and final papers/projects the college students completed as part of their regular coursework (permission for use was granted). I have done my utmost to be faithful to original meanings and have retained actual wording in any cited passages. Some relatively minor modifications to the case have been made to suit pedagogical purposes. All direct quotes are from field notes and reflections, with the names changed or omitted to preserve anonymity.
3. CHC leaders were African American professionals; from the high school side, Fran and Hank (who joined the team in the third year) were white while Sharon was African American; the college faculty, including Pamela and the first teaching assistant were white. Fatima, who is African American, took over this role in the second year. Due to changes in the high school, Hank gradually replaced Fran as the main high school partner. I joined as instructor during the second year.
4. This is a simplified description of the approach, which involves a deep sense of the environment and students' emotional as well as academic orientations and needs and a caring, challenging and supportive learning environment. See Gay (2010).
5. A critical friend refers to a facilitative or developmental leader. It does not mean being critical of others in friendly ways, but working collaboratively on critically important, urgent issues. It requires creating sufficient trust, care, and safety in relationships and spaces that help participants face hard truths, ask uncomfortable questions, and engage in critical reflection. Drawn from critical pedagogy (Deans, 1999; Horton & Freire, 1990), the concept was introduced in school reform work by the Annenberg Institute for School Reform. It is also used in professional development (see http://www.criticalfriendsinternational.com/index.php/en/about-us/why-critical-friends).
6. Much of my learning in the realm of the emotions and the interaction of emotional habitus and situations is based on group work with Charles Rojzman and

Transformational Social Therapy (TST) (see Chapter 8) as well as friends, students, and colleagues involved in Temple's Graduate Certificate in Diversity Leadership and Transformational Intergroup Dialogues. The professional learning community of service-learning course instructors was also immensely valuable.
7. One of these incidents happened in the stairwell of Upland. On our way to class, Fatima and I saw a young man sitting on the steps, looking upset. Fatima stopped, asked what was the matter: he wanted to be in class but had been late and now was locked out. She offered to help. He replied that stopping to talk with him was already helpful and thanked her: he would wait for the period to end and go to his next class. As we continued up the stairs, Fatima said, "I love my people so much!" The emotion has stayed with me; I believe that witnessing and being part of such experiences changes us.
8. An excellent training manual for youth-adult partnerships was produced by a four-way collaboration (The Innovation Center et al., 2003). It has a storehouse of training exercises on topics such as 'real partnering,' 'shared leadership,' and 'team development.' Most exercises are short (20–30 minutes), interactive, and participatory, and include group reflection. See "Attributes of Leaders" handout, p. 123.
9. These differences recall the literature on gender and ethical orientation, where women's ways of knowing (and doing) tend to be more relational while approaches that identify with masculinity are more rational and analytical (see Belenky, Bond, & Weinstock, 1997).
10. We discovered that what he and other students described as "the paper work" were work sheets from Build a House of Service. We should have interrupted this fragmented construction of the curriculum, but did not—another normalcy.
11. There were tensions as the students explored the new structure and new roles and initially it became the college students' turn to be disengaged. Chapter 7 takes up this issue, naming the problem as the de-centering of the college students in a practice situation that was focused on the community, leaving them uncertain about who they were in relation to the project and what role to play.
12. This is an instance of the practice we developed of having short readings and resources (now usually Internet based) available when teachable moments happened. For a sample of relevant resources see the Tool Kits from the Asset-Based Community Development Institute (n.d.); Bigelow (2004), pp. 594–597 on a problem-solving process for unstructured problems; Connell (1993) chapter 1, Social Justice in Education; Kincheloe & Hayes (2007), especially chapters by Goldstein and Wyngaard on understanding 'city kids'; Small Group Skills (n.d.) for tips on facilitating and participating in small groups.

7

BUILDING TRUST, SHARING POWER, CROSSING BORDERS

The Art Sanctuary–Temple/Tyler Partnership

Billy Yalowitz, Karen Malandra, and Novella Zett Keith[1]

> I love these productions . . . not only did they give young people the opportunity to understand something about history, it gave all of us a chance to understand about the fact that we are involved in a place like North Central Philadelphia, we are involved as human beings that . . . have some kind of spark of decency in us and hopefully, some kind of decent vision of what the world might be.
> (Father Isaac Miller, pastor of the Church of the Advocate, cited in Yalowitz, 2005, p. 11)

> Art Sanctuary is not like a program to me, it's like a family . . . we help each other . . . if we got problems . . . we can come to Brother Jeffrey or Miss Lorene or Brother Billy.
> (Shaday, North Stars Youth Ensemble member, cited in Yalowitz, p. 12)

> When they did *Brown vs. Board of Education* . . . it brought tears to my eyes . . . it like did something to me. But the thing is, Shaday is learning more about her culture.
> (Ruth, North Star parent, cited in Yalowitz, p. 12)

The Art Sanctuary–Temple/Tyler partnership was a 5-year collaboration that culminated each year in a multimedia performance held in the sanctuary of the Church of the Advocate. It is a story about bringing to voice the struggles for equity and justice of an African American community by placing them at a center of a public performance. For the university partners, who were intentionally de-centered, it is a story about negotiating the interplay between outsider and insider, exciting and disturbing emotions, and enacting the meaning of living an integrated life.

The story interweaves three voices. The chapter starts in Novella's voice, experiencing the neighborhood and the performance and introducing the partnership and the partners while also interweaving some of Karen's narratives.

Billy's voice continues the narrative of how the partnership developed over its 5-year production cycle. Karen's voice tells the story of the university students and the border pedagogy process: as they were supported in engaging their own stories and path to transformation, they learned about community arts and about working in transformative ways with teens like Shaday and the Art Sanctuary partners. In between these two stories, Billy and Novella dialogue and critically deconstruct the concept of the ally, replacing it with resonance, which creates connections through empathy. The conclusion returns to the theme of what makes such partnerships and such learning possible. The stories are woven through with meaning making, through theories and interpretations that are not easily attributed to any of the authors but come from being in dialogue with one another. Novella was the main weaver, which means that interpretations at times will also reflect her own voice and the limits and unseen biases that come along with her understandings.

The Setting, *Reflections in Brown*, Church of the Advocate, May 2004

As Novella approaches the Church of the Advocate, just a few blocks from campus, she notices the vast physical improvements in the neighborhood. A once elegant corridor of large Victorian brownstones fronting marble stoops and more modest row homes has been coming back to life along the tree-lined street. Restored by a local community development corporation, the homes are now occupied by a blend of racially integrated working and middle-class families, college students, and public housing recipients. Gentrification is extending from this thoroughfare to the surrounding area, which just a few years ago was mostly a mix of abandoned, condemned, and rehabilitated homes and empty lots, the neighborhood of an economically dis-advantaged African American community.

Standing like a prophetic vision on the corner of 18th and Diamond Streets is a grey granite building that encompasses half a city block. The Church of the Advocate, a majestic French Gothic revival church dating to the late 19th century, seems again at home in its surroundings. Walk inside, however, and you are immediately struck by a different presence: 14 large murals fill the walls, depicting biblical themes as experiences of suffering and redemption in the struggles of African Americans. The murals have startled and offended many, grating against sensibilities, especially for those who were not raised, religiously speaking, on the themes of black liberation theology.[2] Commissioned in the 1970s by the legendary Father Paul Washington (Washington & Gracie, 1994), they proclaim that this is a social justice ministry, one that is about the uplift of black people and is at home with controversy. Back then, some 400,000 African Americans lived in this neighborhood, which was the epicenter of cultural and civil rights action in the 1960s and 1970s. Here local activists joined with others to fight for the desegregation of Girard College, a city-owned free boarding school for white orphan boys, part of a bequest to the city by Stephen Girard, an 18th-century shipping magnate. The area was also witness to three days of street fighting in 1964 which were considered the worst urban riot in the city, and countless other instances of African American political activism.

As a committed cultural and spiritual institution, the Advocate opened its doors to local warring gangs wanting to dialogue, civil rights leaders, and national groups: it was the site of the 1968 Black Power convention, the 1970 Black Panther convention, and the 1974 first "irregular" ordination of women priests in the Episcopal Church. Now, it opens its doors to thousands of folks monthly, who need services, participate in after-school programs, or use the site as a place for dialogue. Tonight, the open doors reveal the set for a performance. Stage and lights are ready, the audience is milling around, people greet one another, chat, go over to the art installation off to the left of the stage, depicting a one-room schoolhouse in the segregation era, including photographs, newspaper clippings, and other historical artifacts. It looks like this performance of *Reflections in Brown: Separate/Unequal/Still?* is going to play to another packed house.

The performance begins with a Griot invocation. Drawing on a West African ritual, the poet calls to the ancestors, pours libations in their honor, and creates a sacred circle of continuity connecting those who have gone beyond and those who will follow, literally setting the stage for the stories and the memories that create and connect this community. The members of the audience are mainly African Americans, with a smattering of whites—mostly, I assume, associated with the university or friends and family of the other white people who are floating around, working the equipment, students in a Temple/Tyler class, *Field Internship in Community Arts*, and their teachers, coauthors Billy Yalowitz and Karen Malandra.

The Griot and her entourage exit the stage and the North Stars, teenage members of an after-school program sponsored by the Art Sanctuary, the Advocate's art ministry, take their places on the stage. For the next two hours, stories of struggles around segregation and desegregation on the theme of the *Brown v. Board of Education* Supreme Court case unfold through dancing, poetry, music, and film. The teens, 17 African American students from Philadelphia middle and high schools, are the primary performers. They have been working on the production for months now, under the guidance of seven professional artists in the fields of poetry, music, dance, visual arts, with Billy as artistic director. Billy and Karen's 12 Temple students are a diverse group, in terms of college majors and age; most are middle class and female, two are African American, two are multiracial, and the rest are white. One of them, an African American graduate student, will appear on stage to perform a dance she has choreographed. Like the teens, the Temple students have contributed to the research, built props, and documented the process: the large screen projections that play behind the performers, the One-Room Schoolhouse art installation, and the public service–style announcements that play between scene changes are their work. Karen has facilitated visual arts workshops for the project and, in her capacity as teaching assistant for the college course, has performed roles too numerous to mention. Currently, she is working the lights.

The seven scenes that follow are amazing in their intensity and the quality of the performance. Oral history and archival research into how African Americans experienced this period have been transmuted into art, retelling stories of oppression and overcoming, from the segregated past to a still segregated present, recreating complex emotions and encompassing a vision and actions committed to continued struggle for social justice, still fought nowadays through the quest for educational equity. I am caught up in the performance, feeling the power of art to let me partake, as nothing else could, of these emotions and experiences: in this moment art creates a bridge to a human story that is our story. Here, in this sanctuary, I reconnect with one of my deepest desires, that each of us should be able to express, in a deep and meaningful sense, our own humanity and feel it as part of our common humanity. In this place and this moment, I am no longer the white woman from the university, the one who on first thinking "the neighborhood is coming back to life" thought about how it felt more comfortable and welcoming to her. Witnessing this retelling of the community's stories helps me see a different meaning to that phrase. What is 'coming back to life' is the strength of this community, which was merely hidden from my view: the Art Sanctuary is drawing from an activist tradition that has deep roots.

The Griot returns. Closing the performance and the circle of learning, she restores to the community its voice, truth, and power. As the applause dies down and the lights come back on, I look around, thinking about how the performance came about. What does it mean, for the artists and the audience, that people from the university, who are for the most part not members of this community of identity and memory, are participating in something so clearly focused on African American self-affirmation? On what basis and for what purposes did the university instructors and students gain access, and what did they and the community gain?

The description so far foreshadows two interrelated themes that can help us make meaning of this project. First, this is a case about community arts. While this point is quite obvious, less obvious is the fact that this process is associated with a theory of change that comports with criteria for socially just university-community partnerships: here we have the artist-as-citizen whose art can trespass boundaries and unsettle borders such as those between community and university, student and scholar, professional and vernacular. Community arts support the epistemological shift whereby university partners can begin to let go of their role as expert knowers; the challenge to the citizen artist is to lead this process not as a helper or missionary, or even as an ally, but as a partner.

The tradition dates back to anthropologist Victor Turner (Alexander, 1991; St. John, 2008) and his notion of *communitas*. Turner saw ritual and the meaning making that happen through performance as engines in culture. With the breakdown of 'traditional' societies, that engine gets dispersed into entertainment, and the community-arts process entails getting it going again. Mary Jane Jacob (1995) describes three categories of projects that are usually called community arts: bringing in outside resources to start a program that is created in isolation (emblematic), creating art on a subject drawn from the community but without its participation (supportive), and incorporating a community-building approach with an orientation to social change (participatory). Only the third approach is truly community arts and it involves dialogue with the community from the beginning. For Arlene Goldbard (2005), perhaps the leading community-arts scholar, this is "not a matter of technique . . . but of core purpose." When the individual artist's vision controls the work, it may be powerful and beautiful but it's not community arts "because it doesn't honor [its] underlying principle of equality of participation and its underlying aim of collective expression" (pp. 8–9). Community arts bring together oral history and community education, along with a community organizing piece. Oral history is not about university research as such, but about the stories that matter to the community. These stories had been privatized and the community-arts process, through a public performance, returns them to community knowledge (also see Borrup, 2005).

Beginnings: Partners Engaging in the Partnership

This is how Karen portrayed the partners and their interconnected needs and desires:

> Lorene said the children said "teach me, figure it out and teach me, take this life and distill it into something beautiful." Ms. Brown said "we need a program for our teenage grandchildren and the arts give a taste of life that gives hope." Carlotta said "I want to commission artists to make new work." Billy said "we need a community partner for our college students." The students said "we want to interact with the world." The teens said "we want to learn to dance, we want to create." The elders said "we want to tell our stories." The artists said "we can support you in making this happen." Each of us bolsters and complements the work that already exists in our individual spheres and collectively we are building a community arts program that meets all of our needs.
>
> (in Keith et al., 2003, p. 21)

Reflections in Brown was the fourth production in a cycle of annual performances created during the 5-year collaboration (2000–2005) between the Advocate community and Tyler/Temple. The partnership began when Billy and an arts organization, ArtWorks in Different Places (AWIDP), approached Lorene Cary, founder and director of the Art Sanctuary, to explore the possibility of an ongoing collaboration. Coming from a background as a left-wing Jew whose community was deeply engaged in the labor, civil rights, peace, and women's movements, Billy was drawn by the civil rights history of the Church of the Advocate and was interested in working with Lorene Cary. AWIDP commissioned artists to make new work through artists' residencies in Philadelphia neighborhoods. Billy and Carlota Schoolman, director of AWIDP, were interested in establishing a high-quality program in community arts at the university (this would become the Community Arts Practices Program—CAP—now in its 12th year), one that would cross boundaries of generations, class, and race, promote art as an agent of social change, and support the training of students and professional artists seeking to do this kind of artwork. The Tyler partners saw themselves as catalysts for launching a sustainable arts-based learning program in which the Advocate community would ultimately assume equal or majority responsibility.

Billy was well prepared for this partnership. An earlier play of his, *Black Bottom Sketches*, which he produced and directed in 1998, was based on the stories and voices of working-class African Americans living in the Black Bottom, a West Philadelphia neighborhood abutting the University of Pennsylvania campus.[3] The neighborhood was destroyed through the 'urban renewal' practices of the 1960s, conveniently making room for university expansion. Billy's work was already shaped by his long-term activist commitments but the experience of producing and directing the *Black Bottom* performance gave him a deeper understanding of the community-arts process, especially its insistence that there must be a joining of resources and knowledge (Goldbard, 2005; Thompson, Schaefer, & Brad, 2003; Yalowitz, 2011). As an artist, he knew how to get a theater performance up on its feet, and community members knew firsthand the history of their neighborhood and how institutional racism had made their life difficult. As a community artist, he could not go into the community naming the university's destruction of the neighborhood as the problem: the community knew its own stories and its agency and power could only be released through the stories it wanted to remember at this particular time. An outsider could only ask pertinent questions and facilitate this process: that was the genesis of *Black Bottom Sketches*.

When Billy approached Lorene Cary and proposed a partnership, she had not seen his play and thus probably didn't have a clear sense of his approach. A native Philadelphian and faculty member at the University of Pennsylvania, Lorene Cary is a prize-winning author whose novel about the Underground Railroad, *The Price of a Child*, was read by some 40,000 Philadelphians in 2003 when it was selected for the program *One Book, One Philadelphia*. The Art Sanctuary is dedicated to using the power of African-American art to transform individuals and the community. Cary explains that the idea came to her while reading from one of her books in a downtown Chicago bookstore: "I wanted to do what I was doing [there] in the inner city." As she put it, North Central Philadelphia would become the site for a cultural commons.[4]

Cary recommended Grands as Parents (GAPS) as a potential partner. Based at the Church of the Advocate, GAPS advocates for grandparents and relative caretakers who are raising their grandchildren and great-grandchildren. Eileen Brown, GAPS's president, was concerned about teenagers who were too old to attend the GAPS-run after-school program and were falling through the cracks. She initially thought the partnership could provide the teens access to artistic and educational resources as well as mentoring opportunities through long-term relationships with university students. GAPS partnered with AWIDP and Temple/Tyler to host a hip-hop artist-in-residence culminating in a public performance in Spring 2001, *'ill Salmon,* featuring the GAPS teen participants (who later became known as the *North Stars*) and supported by a class of Temple/Tyler students. This project also allowed Karen, as the teaching assistant, to begin her long-term involvement in the partnership.

The success of this experience paved the way for continued collaboration and launching of *The North Cycle*, which premiered three different performances between 2002 and 2004: *North Called Home, North and Beyond,* and the one featured at the beginning of this chapter, *Reflections in Brown: Separate/Unequal/Still? The North Cycle* would be followed by the last production of the partnership, *Souls of Young Folk*, as the partnership came to a natural close.[5] The original aims of the partnership have been more than fulfilled, as the Arts Sanctuary now owns and sustains this work. We go on to detail the process through which this goal was achieved. The section below looks at the connection between trust and power in the leadership team, while the section that follows will look at the transformation of habitus through border pedagogy, and how the university students experienced and were changed by the process.

Building Trust, Sharing Power: *The North Cycle*

There were issues of trust and relationship building in the partnership that stemmed in part from the social identities and locations of the leaders. The leadership of GAPS, Art Sanctuary, and the Advocate were professionals of middle- and working-class backgrounds, African Americans who were long-time members and activists of the North Central Philadelphia community. The leadership of AWIDP and Tyler/Temple were European American; Billy and Carlota Schoolman (director of AWIDP) were the grandchildren of New York Russian-Jewish immigrants, and Karen was the descendant of Ellis Island Italian working-class immigrants. They were all formed in different sociopolitical and historical contexts; they had all developed different leadership and management tendencies; and they held different positions in varied fields of power. This was the reality which they knew, owned, *and* had to question.

Building trust means that when conflicts happen—and they always will—the players are looking at the situation through many different lenses. For some race might name the barrier, for others it's communication or organizational styles, for others it's economics. At times, partners may not even agree on a barrier. The real barrier results from sweeping these issues under the rug, that is, from disengagement from the argument and the deafening silence that follows. When this happens, someone is pulling away from the group and the chance for educating the *other* and the group is lost. This type of critical reflection became a conscious process that was incorporated into the realities of all the participants involved in this project (Malandra, 2004).

Although this chapter does not address the many conflicts the collaborators had to go through, you, the reader, must be informed of their existence. There were struggles and delays constantly, that could and did at times become critical, caused by miscommunication or misinterpretation, the juggling of space and schedules, different approaches to engaging the various participants, and breached responsibilities: the list could go on. People are complicated and partnerships take constant nurturing. They require great persistence and commitment on your part as a border crosser. That is, a commitment to muster the ability to go back and forth, and through and around, again and again and again, the many borders of resistance and limitations either created externally or existing in your own mind (Malandra, 2004). We recount next how the process worked.

Years 1 and 2: Building Trust

'lll Salmon (2000–2001)

The first year Billy and Karen were involved with the Art Sanctuary was also Billy's first year at Temple University. AWIDP funding went to two artists who staged a hip-hop play with teens and local residents as performers. *'ill Salmon* provided an entry into the partnership, but it was a supportive community-arts process and not yet a participatory one.

The first two *North* productions were developed following the classic community-arts process. The place to begin is listening for the key issue—the one that, when it is told and art is created around it, will move things forward for the community and the partnership and will unlock initiatives in other areas. Following through on this ability to listen to community members and finding the key story is what begins to gain Billy the community's trust. The theme for the third North production, *Reflections in Brown*, came from outside the community but was aligned with its history of civil rights activism and community members wanted and felt ready to address issues that connected them to a larger community of memory (Booth, 2008; Ricoeur, 2004).

Year 2: Beginning of The North Cycle *and the Community-Arts Process:* North Called Home *(2001–2002)*

The partnership relationship could not be equalized as long as the Art Sanctuary was dependent on Temple/Tyler's Community Arts Practices Program (CAP) for the basic knowledge, funding, and resources to carry on the project. Equalizing the relationship was a developmental process and by the fifth year the Art Sanctuary was fully in charge of what was now an entirely sustainable venture. There was a gradual gaining of ownership by Art Sanctuary, as the annual performance became part of their organization and artists from the community started playing a central role. An important issue of trust and ownership started being addressed when Billy took over as artistic director in the second year and the Art Sanctuary assumed a larger role: the storytelling and story circles of the community-arts process began to create the vision of what would become the *North* projects.

Listening to dozens of life stories of community members was a first step in cocreating the productions and building accountability in relationships. Many of the GAPS participants had been community activists all their lives and, as mentioned earlier, the Church of the Advocate itself was quite prominent in its activism. The community-art project would focus on the church's and community's activist history. A key issue quickly emerged: connecting the young people of the community with the stories of the elders. The intergenerational piece is very important. Young people are separated out all the time, as are the elderly, and through the artistic process community elders pass on their story to the younger generation and recreate a whole community. People immediately sensed that they needed these storytelling performance rituals in the neighborhood life cycle. And the young people, as they began to hear stories like—"Your Grandma was a Black Panther"—sat up straight and listened differently to their elders.

One of the stories that built trust for the university partners and Billy's art process involved Miss Hattie, a community activist and grassroots organizer. After her interview at her nursing home, Trapeta Mayson, a poet who was part of the Art Sanctuary team, turned her story into a poem: "One day / holes big as pits lined up and down their street." When the city did not heed Miss Hattie's repeated requests for repairs, she "threw a big ole' block party / invited all the neighbors / . . . made politicians and on-lookers take notice." The story became a scene in the *North Called Home* (2002) production and was performed by GAPS elders, church pastor Isaac Miller, members of the church, and the youth ensemble. Miss Hattie died three weeks before opening night, but Trapeta performed the poem as a eulogy at her funeral, which was held at the church, and it became part of the keepsake book her family put together. Thus the community-art process played a ritual role in the community's grieving and celebration of Miss Hattie's life.

There were many indications that the performance process was becoming a part of the community, but the young people's questions provided an important spark. After the performance, the older ones would come up and ask, "what are we going to do next year?" and the younger ones would say they wanted to be part of the next performance. The community storytelling and performance project had entered the life cycle of the community and its expectations for an annual performative cycle and creation of meaning. For Billy, this is when Lorene Carey realized that this process could fulfill her deep desire to create a place with young people in North Philadelphia that would give them the experiences of deep nurturing she felt they needed. This realization led the Art Sanctuary to really start investing deeply in the project.

Sharing Power

Years 2 and 3: The North Cycle and North and Beyond (2002–2003)

Starting in the second year of *The North Cycle*, Billy worked closely with Lorene Cary, Trapeta Mayson, and Art Sanctuary staff on next steps in building the infrastructure of the partnership. This involved expanding the staff and roles of local artists, creating an after-school arts program for community youth that would offer classes in dance, poetry, and music throughout the school year, and developing more effective ways to attract and retain youth within the program. In addition, they began to look at Billy's role in the project. He was wearing the multiple hats of artistic director, Temple University faculty member, and coproducer. He wanted to address the contradictions of his participation in and leadership of the project as a white person and a university professor in a new way. So, they began the process of transferring more leadership of the project to Art Sanctuary, looking at both artistic content and project structure. In particular, they began to address the ways that social patterns of inequity were still active in the organizational power relations of *The North Cycle*.

One issue that had come up was Billy's relationship with Jeffrey Hart, the community youth organizer for the project. While Billy could tell that their difficulties—mostly about leadership styles and power sharing—had to do with issues of race, class, and power, he couldn't tell what to do differently. He was on the brink of looking for a new youth organizer when Lorene Cary intervened. She spent time listening to Jeffrey and Billy as they aired their differences, helping them to see that each of them had a deep commitment to the young people and to the work. Acknowledging cultural style differences in communication went a long way toward developing mutual understanding. But this was more than a question of communication styles. The structure of the university-community partnership at that point was such that Billy was in the position of being the decision maker about whether Jeffrey would continue on, and yet Jeffrey was the one who was rooted in the community. The work around their conflict was part of the process of shifting the power relations in the partnership. With Lorene's help, Jeffrey and Billy persevered, and they became close coworkers and friends, still with their differences. But here was a juncture where race and class differences and power inequity could have derailed the project significantly.

Cary spoke about these power dynamics when she participated in a group presentation about *North* in November 2004, at the *Imagining America* conference:

I wanted to underscore something that Billy said, when he shared the business about his relationship with Jeffrey and how pivotal that [growth] had been. I wanted to add something that he's probably too modest to put in . . . about the process of transforming relationships around race and class. You [Billy] talked about teaching that but I wanted to testify to your commitment to it. Which means that when we talked about it, you entertained the possibility, which very few folks do, understanding that in order for things to change, things had to change . . . right . . . (laughter). So consequently it means that the power relationship that existed before does not exist now. That means that it wasn't just that Jeff had a problem or Billy had a problem. It was that here was a relationship where two people who ought to be having equal input into this, have a relationship instead, where . . . one person has the power to decide whether somebody is on or off. As the program has evolved, you [Billy] no longer have that power. Can I tell you that that doesn't happen in this country very often! (clapping) Because usually power has to be gotten by hooking somebody off or shooting them (laughter) as opposed to somebody saying I want to make a change. And I'm thanking Billy very much for bringing the vision and then for having the generosity of spirit to let other people move the vision and for him to take different roles in it.

Year 3: "What to keep, what to let go?" North and Beyond *and the Advocate Murals*

In the work with the Art Sanctuary staff, the partners had decided to shift the process of selecting the content of the next year's production from GAPS and Billy to the community youth participants. They began by asking the youth ensemble, now calling themselves the North Stars, what they were interested in for a project theme. The North Stars were interested in their community's traditions and habits, both positive and negative, and in working with the questions Billy had introduced as part of his process: what to keep, what to let go. They decided to hold a community forum, inviting leaders from all over the city—artists, politicians, educators, parents, and grandparents—to ask this question. The young people wanted to keep and build upon the Church of the Advocate's tradition of activist art, and they became fascinated with the 14 murals that had been created in the church by artists Richard Watson and Walter Edmonds in the mid-1970s, commissioned by Father Washington. In choosing the murals as the theme of that years' work, the young people happened upon a controversy at the heart of one of the church's key issues: a struggling congregation and the perception of some of the lay leaders that the murals kept away potential new members. A second community forum was held on this issue, inviting congregants, project artists, the North Stars and their friends, and Temple students. Watson and Edmonds were invited for gallery talks in the church, and they explained that the symbolic violent images that attracted so much attention were not being understood in their full context. The murals were meant to be seen as a whole cycle, while walking around the perimeter of the sanctuary, much like the Stations of the Cross are meant to be experienced in motion. The artists were building on the narrative of Biblical Exodus to tell the story of Africans in America, including the freedom struggles from abolition through Black Power. The congregation, the North Stars, and the artists were able to agree on the goal that the production would unite the young people's interest in the murals and the congregants' interest in addressing the murals' meaning in a larger context.

The partners set to work to create the piece, *North and Beyond*. Project artists from the community now included poet Trapeta Mayson, choreographer Itola Byrd, and composer Monnette Sudler, who each studied the murals and created work with the North Stars in their respective media. Billy worked with the Temple students to create costumes and video designs. The resulting performance in effect moved the audience around the space to see the murals in their full cycle, from Creation to Enslavement to Passage and Uprising, through Grief and Healing and on to Re-birth. As director, Billy drew half-consciously on his Jewish tradition of the Passover Seder, in which this same cycle is reexperienced each year in a ritual storytelling meal. With live feed video, projections of Watson's and Edmonds's murals, and original music, choreography, and poetry, they created a kind of blockbuster community performance ritual.

Years 4 and 5: Reflections in Brown *and* The Souls of Young Folk *(2003–2005)*

The last two years of the partnership saw a continued shift in Billy's role from artistic decision maker to collaborator. In order to position the artists' ensemble to make the artistic decisions for the project, Lorene Cary was now placed at the center of the ensemble, which had grown to six artists. Billy's new role left him free to focus on involving the Temple students more personally in the *Brown* production. Paradoxically, with the Art Sanctuary artistic staff more in charge of the process, and with a theme that went beyond the stories of the local community, there was more space for inclusion of Temple voices. Transferring of the project's artistic leadership continued in the last year, as Trapeta Mayson became the lead artist for *The Souls of Young Folk*. Billy's role in that production was as faculty artistic consultant, while also engaging with the North Stars and teaching artists and supervising the Temple students' involvement and support of the North Stars with video and technology.

This shift represented the completion of a cycle of work in which the community has taken over ownership of the project. The North Stars project became an independent, ongoing program of the Art Sanctuary, with a roster of after-school arts workshops during the full school year, and an annual performance each spring of original community-based performance work. The performances have become very much a part of life for the Church of the Advocate and its community. The North Stars program has brought a youth voice and an additional community-arts process to the work of Art Sanctuary to reestablish and renew North Philadelphia's community-arts traditions that had been strong during the 1960s and 1970s.

Interlude: Becoming . . . Allies?

The story so far has been about the performance and Billy's and the community's involvement in it. The Temple students have been almost invisible. What was it like for them to support this production and what did they learn from it? In a conversation, Novella tells Billy that she's thinking one of the themes of this chapter should be about being an ally, although it needs to be unpacked; she thinks that the way Billy enacts it is really good. Billy nods, there's a pause, and then he says, "I don't use the term anymore." He adds that it has come to mean so many things, and in one enacting, it means "you need my help" and "I stand outside your story and try to help you. You're the oppressed person, I'm the oppressor, and I'm learning your narrative so I can be depended upon as . . . what? An advocate with the powers that be? A witness? It's just limited." And there's another, more personal question: "so I listen to your story and—just because I think your story is important and it's undervalued and marginalized . . . That's important, but where's my story in your story? How do we connect with one another?"

Billy and Novella talk a little about earlier uses of the ally, the problematic, romanticized, but also real history of cross-race alliances between working-class poor Jews living in adjacent neighborhoods to working-class poor African Americans in the 1930s and 1940s, and now, Novella's negative reaction to the occasional white men with placards, standing on corners in black neighborhoods, trying to organize them, telling them about their oppression. How do we envision the transformed relationships we would like to see enacted? Is it about recognizing our interdependence, Novella asks?

We continue to unpack these ways of seeing the work. Campus-community partnerships are often seen as an exchange—of knowledge and resources—that we have to try to equalize. An ally is someone from a privileged or advantaged group who works on behalf of those who are oppressed by their group (Munin & Speight, 2010); but to be an ally may also mean being stuck in a world of victims and oppressors and feeling guilty about being one of the oppressors. Billy suggests we see it as resonance. Resonance is freeing yourself from the bind of having to be either one or the other; it's about empathy and a deep sense of recognition, like an electric current joining negative and positive poles. A theater insider describes it well:

Empathy which includes listening and understanding other people's stories creates resonance. The root of the word *resonance* is revealing: the Latin

[Margin note: Tie group activity back to critical incident]

word *resonare*, to resound. Resonance, the Oxford dictionary states, refers to "the reinforcement or prolongation of sound by reflection," or more specifically, "by synchronous vibration." This occurs in the theater when the audience is on the same wavelength emotionally with the actor and production—when they feel "in sync." And true to the original meaning of resonance, this synchrony "resounds," prolonging an "AHA!" experience with the audience.

(Herendeen, 2010)

Novella tells Billy she remembers him talking about a question that one of Father Washington's sons, Michael, asked him at a performance: "Why are you telling *our* story?" Billy nods: for him it was a really meaningful moment. What began to come together for him was the sense that without resonance of your story and my story, the risk is that one winds up as the missionary. He asks: how do we connect through a sort of attunement of emotional energies, where something I feel and see in you and in your story mirrors and amplifies something in myself, in my story?[6] Novella tells Billy she doesn't think he was the missionary. The hook for him was in the performance, which enabled him to become a member of this community. So it gave him something. We're back at the exchange relation involved in reciprocity.

Billy answers that it gave him a lot. Part of his tenure was staked on this: ironically, he was getting credit for having created new knowledge that was about relationship building, which was problematized throughout his work. The question in his mind is, how do we structure projects from the beginning with a different epistemology. With his students now, he knows that when they're creating art about someone, in order for it to stay alive in a certain way they have to bring their own stories into it. They have to do the work about themselves: self-reflective work is embedded in the listening, and so there's an intersubjective piece, from the very beginning. It started to happen with *Reflections in Brown*, when the college students were asked to tell their stories of having been bussed and what integration was like for them.

[Margin note: What is story before & after you joined partnership?]

Border Pedagogy as a Transformative Process

The above conversation takes us to the space inhabited by the Temple students in the Field Internship course that prepared them to engage in community arts through the Art Sanctuary–Temple/Tyler partnership. This preparation included conducting local historical research, preparing props, serving in technical roles for the performance, and creating visuals and art installations. A major focus of the course, however, was personal and relational: in the context of a project that was centered on the community's stories, part of what the Temple students needed to do was to take on new identities as border crossers—to create new narratives of themselves, shifting their habitus—and thus new ways to work with this community. In this part of the chapter we focus on this transformative process, enacted through border pedagogy.

What sort of pedagogy can take the students into the space, as Billy says, of intersubjective resonance? He describes a guided process that involves both challenge and affirmation.[7] To cross borders successfully the college students needed spaces where they could step out of their comfort zone, accept that the ground for a transformed self must be prepared by disturbing and unsettling the old self (this is the 'challenge') and be supported and affirmed in doing so. The guide provides supports for challenge, reflective understanding, and affirmation, so that a process that at times feels like displacement and figurative homelessness is not avoided but is understood and felt as necessary because it carries the seeds of transformation and of new possibilities.

In this section we look at how border pedagogy was used to help the college students construct possible roles and identities for themselves, as they moved in resonance around the African American community's needs and work. The task goes beyond university faculty and students learning how to be in borderlands; it is also about creating public spaces where dialogues that further democratic life can happen. In her dissertation, Karen organizes these experiences as five semichronological moments of the community arts cycle: *prepping the self*, *role negotiation*, *integration* (that is, Temple and community partners coming together), *making the work*, and *aftermath*.[8] Space limitations do not allow us to delve into all of these moments equally. Each of them combines both challenge and affirmation, but *prepping the self* and *role negotiation* involve more challenges; *integration* and *making the work* entail more affirmation; and *aftermath* involves a balance of both. We explain what is involved in each moment but provide a more detailed account of three: prepping the self, integration, and aftermath. Karen was a participant observer in the class. Here she is writing in the present tense.

Prepping the Self

This process is about the initial class meetings and a storytelling circle during the fourth week of class, when the Temple students struggle with their own experiences with race and segregation, entering into dialogue with each other.

Initial Class Meetings

The initial weekly seminar meetings are structured to facilitate the students' move from their ordinary lives to new places of learning and being. The issues that the students will navigate throughout the process surface in these classes: segregation, otherness and race, negotiating relationships and collaborative art making, figuring out how to be an insider/outsider, and gaining a thoughtful understanding of community, identity, and educational inequities that is both personal and well-informed. To get at these issues, Billy assigns a mixture of readings and reflection exercises on community-arts projects, *Brown v. Board of Education*, racism, and white privilege. He uses class time to arrange reflective interactions among the students so as to build connections in the group and ensure that the students can view their own and their peers' experiences and biographies through different lenses. These investigations serve as preparation for integrating with the community participants and also become thematic content for the course and the performance.

Early on, the students voice trepidation about doing community work in a community that is not their own. Billy addresses fears about going into the neighborhood, explaining that most outsiders have been taught to fear it, but that the students' sense of it will expand as they talk and learn about race and the university's role in the neighborhood and how that informs their fears and hesitations. The trepidation about being outsiders in someone else's community is loudest when considering issues of race, power, and privilege. One of the white students captures a commonly shared feeling: "it makes me feel guilty, I do want to be a part of the community but I'm not [from the community]." Billy responds that the students are part of the Community Arts Practices Program, which is building a long-term relationship with the Advocate community. He describes his own experience and the fact that he still negotiates an insider/outsider position: "there are questions of power that are always an ongoing process." Billy and the students continue to wrestle with these questions throughout the course.

Class Essays

Compelling interactions during the fourth class meeting move the group to a space of togetherness that, among other things, results in a deepening commitment to one another and the community-arts process. In subsequent discussions, many students reference the sense of closeness and respect that was seeded that evening, with several noting that they really learned to listen. The students were given an assignment to create artworks and personal essays on their own educational histories in relation to the *Brown* decision, integration, and segregation. Encouraging responses in any arts medium, Billy had offered these guiding questions: "How much contact did you have with people from other racial/religious/class backgrounds? Is there a particular person from a different background with whom you developed a close relationship? What happened to the relationship? How did/does the Brown decision affect you?" The students will present their stories to their classmates.

While several students create artistic essays (paintings, collage, etc.), most write about their personal encounters with race, class, and other experiences with difference. Billy facilitates the class like a storytelling circle that is typical of the many he leads throughout the semester, in the classroom and at community sites. The circle includes spaces for listening and appreciation. He tells the students that "this is our warm up, with each other . . . [this] helps us to get used to sharing our stories around issues of race." One of Billy's rationales for asking students to speak their racial histories is to get them to begin to undo the 'touristic and missionary' tendencies that are commonly associated with privileged people working with *Others*, in particular white people working with people of color. He wants to foreground the privileged person's tendencies to exoticize the Other and to use an expert voice that says "we have the answers for you." Further, he wants the students to shift their views of the project from being solely about the *Brown* decision and the black community to seeing it also as being about their own stories and histories with the *Brown* decision and race. In this way, the assignment will help them begin to unlock some of the emotions and confusion surrounding their earliest memories of race. Billy believes that we must do this if we are to move toward resonance, or we will be quite limited in our ability to build relationships across these borders. The following are just a small part of the students' stories as they present them to their classmates.

Aubrey volunteers to go first. Visibly nervous, she props her painting on a chair, stands next to it and begins:

> I grew up in Philly and I grew up in a home where my father was racist. It's kind of really hard for me to talk about issues dealing with racism because it was such a problem when I was growing up . . . I couldn't understand why I couldn't get [my dad] to think in a different way . . . [When] I was maybe 14 and I started having close friends that were not white, that was like completely not allowed, forbidden.

Aubrey explains that one of the class readings, a booklet titled *Ending Racism* (Jackins, 2001) got her thinking again about this experience, adding: "I'm still enraged about that type of thing . . . and it makes me mad . . . I think it kind of hindered a lot of relationships in my life because I couldn't have those close relationships as a kid." Others share similar experiences that have also affected their present relationships. When Aubrey continues, she examines her experiences through the lens of her relationship with her father. She thinks he felt uncomfortable being around people who weren't like him; and yet, when he eventually relocated to Ohio, he shared an apartment with an African American man. Was this because of convenience—she wonders—or was it that "some of the things I've actually said in my life have made a difference, like, maybe [my being] a living example has made him change his mind."

Aubrey finishes and the class, not knowing what else to do, responds by clapping. They feel odd about this and one says, "it's something to do." However, as each subsequent student shares their story, they eventually work out that clapping isn't the response they're looking for; the talkbacks are. Several address Aubrey's story. Billy observes that she is challenging her own efficacy by questioning whether what she did made a difference. Sherron, an African American graduate student who later will draw from this dialogue to choreograph and perform a scene in the production, says that she appreciates Aubrey's honesty:

> [I used to] be skeptical of white people that were trying to help but as I get older I realize that you need to help because humanity is an integral part of you and you are an integral part of humanity as well . . . and I appreciate you making me aware of that, reminding me of that.

The class begins to talk about being a white ally. Aubrey is struggling with this newly named role, while Sherron grapples with continually accepting white folks as allies, themes they revisit through the semester. Yet by listening to each other's stories, the students are moving to a deeper level of dialogue, connecting 'undoing racism' with personal quests 'to be free.' For Aubrey and several other white students, Sherron's response is a key moment in experiencing the reality of a person of color.

Continuing to articulate their experiences with racism and education, several students' stories center on bussing and integration. The students make connections that underscore their evolving understanding of how the *Brown* decision continues to impact institutions and how these institutions impact their own experiences. Bertha describes that she went to a private school on the Main Line (a wealthy Philadelphia suburb), adding, "I was the poor one from Philadelphia," to which Billy responds, "So you had a bussing experience?" Bertha immediately says no and appears off-kilter and Billy replies: "When we associate bussing to our own experiences, we don't think it's happening, we jump back from it." A perceptible shift seems to happen as Bertha sees that, yes, she was bussed in the 1990s and had distanced herself from it.

Challenges to students' belief systems become the norm and frequently they are stirred by external prompts, such as Bertha experiences. These challenges open up pathways for others to examine their own experiences. For instance, the exchange between Billy and Bertha segues into realizations by Elisa and Tracey that they bussed themselves from insular communities to Temple University because they wanted integrative experiences. Like Bertha, Egan and Carmen also recall their own early bussing experiences. Like the majority of their classmates, they move from seeing bussing as something that happened "back then," to contextualize their own connection to the *Brown* decision by describing the effects of integration on their worlds.

Carmen, who was also bussed, says she had never thought about the *Brown* decision touching her personally, until now. Prompted by the assignment, she had a conversation with her mother who described her own bussing experiences in the racially tense city of Boston in the 1970s, when white parents "welcomed her bus with rocks and picket signs telling her to go back home." Learning of this, Carmen connects integration with her early public school experiences. She writes that she was one of two black girls in her grade and remembers feeling very different, "almost like a specimen." Yet she didn't feel unwanted: she was invited to birthday parties, sleepovers, and bat mitzvahs, but did not invite friends to her house, because she didn't think they were interested: "They were used to me coming into their community . . . The plan wasn't to remove them from *their* comfort zone, just me." She adds that she thinks her contribution to the school's diversity was useless "due to an ill-prepared system, leaving me in a community with awkward silence instead of discourse."

Pieces of Carmen's experiences resonate with everyone in the room as their stories interweave. Tracey became conscious of her whiteness "two weeks ago" because she's the only white girl who tutors during the day. Mariana shares a story of her own isolating experiences at hip-hop concerts, feeling like it wasn't her place to be there, an awkward white girl, but still going, because she loved it. Sherron responds that she, who is outwardly very different from Mariana, connects to that," because there's so many times where I feel awkward and when you [Mariana] share [your story], again, it's just like okay, I'm human, and I have those moments of feeling isolated too." Rochelle was the white girlfriend of the only black girl in her Catholic elementary school. Turning to Carmen, she says: "you should think about how you affected these white girls and maybe you affected them more than you think because I was one of them."

Starting from their own stories, they also focus on how the system neglected to prepare people for forced integration. Billy contrasts this lack of preparation with how the students, by examining their histories, are preparing themselves to integrate and work with the community. He stresses the inevitability of awkward moments and the importance of bringing this awareness into this project: "There will be these awkward moments. We're having awkward moments all the time, I'm having an awkward moment as I speak, you know as each one of you shares a story . . . So how can you kind of acknowledge it and what do we do with those things?" Billy's questioning will resurface periodically and almost become a mantra for the class, as students discover and discuss the comfort and awkwardness of a disoriented self and the ways the class community can help them find ways to exist with the discomfort.

Because of the structure and content of the assignment, disturbances to the students' selves are highly pronounced during this period of the cycle. As their comfort zones are penetrated, these intersubjective exchanges often result in their understanding of their personal histories. Memories of these disturbances are carried forward throughout the semester. Thus, three major things happen this evening: (a) students prepare themselves for the new relationships they are building with each other and the new relationships that they will build with the Advocate community; (b) students begin to research historical events and relate them to present circumstances, while also questioning power structures; and (c) students who have never been conscious of what it is like to be in the racial minority, now know it a little bit more intimately.

Role Negotiation

This part of the process involves considering the roles of the university partners and especially making spaces for the students in the project. As Billy mentioned above, the changes in the partnership leadership structure during the third year freed him to spend more time working with the students as *his* constituency. Prior to this point, given the importance of building trust, his main constituencies had been the community, artists, and organizations. The project's content during the third year also creates an opportunity for greater inclusion of the Temple students. Nonetheless, given that the Temple partners' role is clearly to facilitate and support community voice, role ambiguities remain.

The central question that guides Billy's approach to border pedagogy seems to be how to be on the sidelines. Billy tells the students that their role is one of support; he asks them symbolically to inhabit the margins, to be in the border spaces of interactions, to think about the scope of what's happening and to find their place in it: the college students are not central to the production and their voices are necessarily outside the community conversation. Living through this awkwardness, the discomfort of being in this location is necessary.

As Billy models his role as a community artist for the students, complexities come into view and manifold tensions are exposed. For instance, the community partners don't seem to consider the Temple students as their constituency and are themselves unclear about the students' role in the project. Jeffrey, the community youth organizer we met above, has even proclaimed that the community doesn't need the Temple students, whom he sees as learners and not as partners. The students, for their part, repeatedly avow to feeling like impostors, observers, and outsiders. Perhaps this tension itself makes the moments of integration magical. The college students all long for and celebrate these moments, which provide support through the tensions of being de-centered, of working with a community, on its project, while not being a part of it. Some of these feelings are explored in the last moment, *Aftermath*.

Integration

The first joint activity involving the college students and teens is a poetry workshop that takes place at the Art Sanctuary during the fifth week. This is one of several integrated forums in which the Temple students experience an insider view. Billy and Trapeta have developed a plan where the focus is on introductions. By this time, the college students are quite excited by the research they've discovered, their changing selves, and the expanding closeness they're feeling as a group. They've entered zones of discomfort with each other and crossed into zones of clarity that have produced mind-expanding and even exhilarating experiences. The integrated forum is a guided exchange that invites everyone to be in the center of the process. Although the teens are the central focus of the entire program, experiencing the occasional insider view is necessary for the Temple students' integration.

Metaphorically speaking, the college students bus themselves from campus to the Church of the Advocate where the teens have their workshops with Trapeta, who is their poetry instructor. Introducing herself, Trapeta says that we've all been personalizing legacies of *Brown* "and today we'll get to know each other a little better." While the Temple students centered on educational histories, bussing and integration, Trapeta's teens concentrated on the youth activism of the Little Rock Nine and Linda Brown, the 1967 student strike at the Philadelphia Board of Education, and the murder of Emmett Till. Taking different paths, both groups are focusing on racial identity and educational inequities. There are two activities. In the first, Trapeta mixes teens and college students into three groups and instructs them to create collective poems made up of the rhythmic noises that you would find in a classroom. Her students practiced this exercise the prior week and take the lead while the Temple students politely make space for the teen voices. Eventually, they are laughing, playing off of each other's ideas. The three groups get up to perform their versions of the noise poem: some stand up, some sit down, they clap, they cheer, they perform their noises . . . shh . . . shh . . . tap . . . tap . . . As one group speaks, the others start to change their ideas, becoming more engaged and inspired to perform better.

Following this exercise that rather quickly bonds the group, Trapeta asks them to pair off—one college student and one teen—and sit facing each other. She asks them to tell each other stories about a significant moment that changed their lives. Then they will each write a poem about the other's story. The previous camaraderie gives way to some hesitation and nervousness, but what transpires next is like magic and is described later by the college students as a "euphoric experience." Jacki writes in her journal: "Amazing workshop with Trapeta . . . and kids . . . [we] shared our life-changing stories in two minutes, then wrote poems about each other, unbelievable, so poignant, so close, so quick?" Trapeta asks people to speak their poems, and about half choose to do so. Cole (high school senior, African American, poet, 18) gets up to perform his poem in the first person from the perspective of Aubrey, his activity partner.

> I was 16 years old, carrying my child in a womb.
> And it still hurts knowing I won't be graduating in June.
> I stand back and admire my baby boy, even though I'm 26 years old I still receive joy
> every day I pick him up from school.
> As a teenager life was cruel with the baby daddy not around,
> Speaking of daddies mine looked down on me from the day I conceived,
> Not to mention my friends became few and distant.
> Ever since Michael came into the picture everything changed.
> I'm happy now I went back to school.

The room erupts with appreciative hollering and clapping. Aubrey jumps up and hugs Cole. She and others are visibly moved by feelings of connection with the young people and appreciation of Cole's developing craft. She quickly composes herself and her voice steadies as she finds power in Cole's story. She points to herself every time she speaks "I write because I have to."

> I write because I have to, it gives me life.
> I write because I have to, it use to be my secret.
> I write because I have to, it lets my feelings be mine
> I write because I have to because if I won't who else will?
> It is my voice, my knowledge; it is what changed me . . .
> From the depth of my soul, I feel words.
> It is my voice, my knowledge
> It is what changed me so I write because I have to.

Cole smiles broadly. He is proud to hear what is spoken of him: he stands, and they hug each other. Aubrey the teenage mother expresses the soul of Cole, the passionate teenager, and Cole pays respect to the teenage mother finishing school. In her final written reflection of the semester, Aubrey recalls the impact of the experience: "I felt when Cole and I had the poetry thing that night like we had an instant bond . . . like going through that together was one of the significant points of the project." Many of the exchanges are equally powerful and connective, as the poetic dialogue spawns visible joy and respect. Admiring the teens' artistic sensibilities and abilities, the Temple students quickly become supporters of the evolving poets. Appreciative of their attention, the teens are interested in more interaction with the college students, which will come later in the form of a joint performative activity in the subway, dubbed 'subway activism.'

Later, in separate conversations with Billy and Trapeta, Karen finds out that they both were really pleased with the joint workshop. Although this is the third year they are working together, they've never integrated their two classes with as much preparation. Trapeta explains what was different—and better—this time in the Temple students' involvement:

> This puts [the college students] more on an equal footing. It kind of puts you out of the "we're here to help you" and it made it more like "we're learning" and we want to absorb this and we want to learn. You can teach us and we can teach you. And I think . . . the kids came away feeling "you know we're teaching something" and they read their poems and the reactions they got, the response and the support. I think they were really into it.

She explains that the first year the message from the Temple students was "we're here to help" and there was a sense of them being in charge. The second year, she didn't feel like they had a real sense of ownership and were only periodically "on board." This year was different: "I think with this sharing back and forth, I think that opened the door."

Billy also reflects on the workshops, explaining that initially, when he and Trapeta had talked about joint workshops, he had been eager for the Temple students to have a lot more interaction with the teens. But Trapeta didn't agree. Billy continues:

> That time was really valuable to her and them. And that's a piece of community arts happening right there. . . . If we stand back and we see and honor that and we got to play a role in [the teens] getting to deliver their poems and being changed forever . . . when we stepped out of the way and didn't get the interactions that we wanted to have, that's actually being an ally.

Making the Work

The process here involves producing all the materials that are part of the performance. Visual art-making workshops that take place on Saturdays during the 'production month' before the performance become community gatherings, providing more spaces for integration. Everyone comes together to create masquerade and costumes for the performance: community artists bring their families, college students bring their children and roommates, the teens bring their siblings, friends and parents, and Art Sanctuary staff come by to participate. In the workshops, art making is blended with joking and playing. Using their skill sets to paint props, create publicity, sew, and make masks, after weeks of role ambiguity the Temple students experience being able to contribute in ways that make them integral to the process. They later report being more comfortable in their relationships with the artists, the teens and other young people from the community when they were able to converse through the art-making process.

The Temple students also create video and cross into the production roles of stage managers and lighting operators. They had previously recorded the oral history interviews with civil rights activists and gathered archival photos and films. Their visual and narrative research is now edited into short films that are projected solo or intermixed with the live dance and poetry scenes. Three students collaborate on the art installation that is set up in the Sanctuary for the performances. This period is marked by a lot of fervor and work. There isn't much time to linger on the discomforts and disconnects that difference might bring. Rather, everyone is focused on getting the show up and running. Each student interjects a moment into the larger conversation and in small but significant ways, helps to shape the meaning of the overall experience for themselves and for the audience.

The Aftermath

The final part of the process takes the form of an informal group reflection at Billy's house, over a dinner he cooks for the students. The students' dialogue goes from the afterglow of the performance, to questions about what they wish they had experienced, how to maintain the relationships that were started, and issues of power, race, and cultural difference. Many students think seriously about whether, when the structure of the class goes away, they will be able to sustain the relationships they seeded. And they discuss how to keep these types of experiences in their lives.

They revisit repeatedly the major theme of the course, which revolved around issues of integration, and their contribution to the performance, which did not emphasize integration as a theme. Their experiences as members of this process have existed mostly in the margins. They alternate between trying to find a fit and pulling back and being supportive of helping to facilitate community voice. Billy notices this and says:

> I have a lot of regrets about what I didn't get to do with all of you because I'm more and more realizing that you are my constituency, you're the group that I am committed to [work with] and that's no less valuable in any way. Anything that you made and anything you wrote is incredibly valuable . . . it's just that we were shining the spotlight on young people and Black artists in the Black community.

He shares that this process has left him questioning, "What's community arts at a university that's in an African American community?"

Finally, at the end of the evening, Billy returns to the issues of integration and relationships offering that for him, one of the most important aspects of doing community art is about making the choice to build cross-cultural relationships. He says:

> I think as a white person for myself, this is about refusing to lead a segregated life. A couple of you have said that. And I think you get to refuse that, you get to decide to build those relationships even when you feel awkward, and even when you are questioning in the way that people were doing very thoughtfully, am I taking up too much room here, how much resource am I using.

Sherron responds that "Black people do that all the time. . . . When we're around white people—she explains—we make ourselves uncomfortable asking if [we] are taking up too much room." As she emphasizes, these are the historical and cultural legacies of racism: "It's just less of a choice for us [to be uncomfortable] because the world is presented to us as white." Her comment stresses that white people are privileged in not having to be uncomfortable, so that entering into discomfort is a choice they make when they decide to work toward changing social inequities.

By the evening's end, a number of students voice that they are at a crossroads where they have to make the decision to keep up these types of interactions, to lead integrated lives. Jacki's comments in her final reflection paper sum up their concerns:

> 18th and Diamond seems so much closer now. The space between seems activated, more comfortable . . . But at the same time I realize that it is only with effort that these boundaries stay permeable. I had brunch with my family in Northern Liberties [middle-class, gentrified, Philadelphia neighborhood] on the Sunday after the project. I was hyper-aware of the homogeneity of my everyday world . . . the way our society is structured it takes constant vigilance to know and understand "others".

Summary and Conclusion

Like the last chapter, this chapter ends with questions that take us back to the main theme of the book: What does the case contribute to our understanding of the democratic civic professional who is engaged on the path to border crossing? How are transformative moments on this path created, moments that cultivate the desired new identities and practices? A brief summary of the main themes in the chapter, with help from the border-crossing partnership framework, will help us address these questions.

The overarching theme is community arts as a social change process, with three important features: (a) the oral history of a community that had been marginalized was taken from privatized spaces into public, performance spaces and passed on from one generation to the next and from one community to other communities; (b) these were the stories the community wanted to tell, stories that released its energies and celebrated the human spirit that came through those who participated in its struggles for justice; (c) the partnership centered the community and its stories and de-centered the university partners, who contributed to creating performance art from the stories but, as outsiders to this community, remained intentionally on its margins.

Two main aspects of phronesis can help us understand the democratic civic professional engaged in border crossing (here, perhaps more elegantly, the citizen artist): embodied virtues, including an orientation to ongoing inquiry, and practice that enacted living well or *the good*.

- As the main community artist from the university, Billy embodied a commitment to walk this path and use self- and other-awareness and inquiry to understand how to be and stay in this borderland. Some of the virtues he embodied, which were acknowledged by community partners and students, included humility, deep listening, courage, emotional self-understanding and empathy, and willingness to show emotions and be vulnerable. He also understood clearly (and was supported in it by community arts theory and practice) how to position his knowledge and capabilities in the partnership and what needed to emerge from the community. He was committed to staying with the discomforts of ambiguous roles and uncertainty about how to be on the margins, having to invent how to do it and admitting to not knowing.

- For Billy, living well, or enacting the *good*, meant an ongoing search for living an integrated life and cultivating this desire and possibilities in others—here, his students, but at other times, also the audiences of his performance work. With regard to this particular partnership, this meant moving from being at the center, as the originator of the vision, to inhabiting the margins, as the community partners followed their own vision and took ownership of the project. Practices that were part of de-centering included building trust with the community by telling its stories, sharing power with community artists, engaging the North Star teens in identifying the theme for upcoming productions, and working more closely as time went on with the college students, enacting border pedagogy and guiding them through the process of being de-centered community artists.

Much of the work was done relationally and pedagogically. In the community, Billy became Brother Billy to the North Star teens; Lorene Cary addressed him as one who had "the generosity of spirit to let other people move the vision"; and he became a close coworker and "friends, still with our differences" with Jeffrey. With the group that he increasingly saw as his own constituency, the Temple students, he was a model and a mentor, creating an environment in which the students became able to interrogate their experiences with racial and educational inequality and develop cross-race relationships.

The border pedagogy process disturbed and transformed the students' habitus in ways that supported border crossing in three main ways.

- Billy's qualities and character came through in the ways he enacted his role as teacher and as community artist; he was transparent about the process and his own self-examination and discomfort, which gave the students insights about their own process and about the tensions in community arts. As artistic director and the professor of the course, he made spaces for emotional and creative exchanges with his students. As process participant, he stood with the students as they all attempted to understand and navigate the dynamics of *Reflections in Brown*—its interracial relationships and thematic content. He addressed the students as having complex and multiple identities and built spaces for listening and for reflection. Modeling his process and becoming comfortable with their own process and vulnerabilities, the students made their own spaces for sharing partial understandings and figuring out how to be in this change process.

- Two sorts of spaces for transformation were created: the semiprivate group reflections in seminar classes and the more public interactions in the arts workshops and public spaces. These spaces were organized around different ways of working together. They included reflective dialogue, art making, art process, and experiencing. Thus, they could engage different realms—artistic, creative writing, intellectual, relational, and emotional—transcending the limitations and reaping the advantages of each. For example, the perspective the college students gained while sharing their class essays had tremendous value in supporting their growing understanding of racial inequality and the advantages and disadvantages that went with different social positions. The perspectives gained in the poetry and visual arts workshops were important for different reasons: here, the college students transcended their feeling of being outsiders, as the process of creating together became an organic way to develop relationships. This shuffling of sites and positions helped them learn to live in and with the ambiguity of the process.

- The destabilizing tensions of the process disturbed and reoriented the students' habitus. This was achieved through the balancing of experiences that were destabilizing and challenging with others that were exhilarating and affirming. Feelings of excitement and joy were heightened during the integration and making-the-work stages. They also coincided with a decrease in the college students' feelings that they "did not quite fit" in the process. Although it was not possible to go into all the details of the process in this chapter, this pedagogical work did, overall, enable students to develop capacities to resist previous constructions of race, move toward more equitable understandings, and make different choices. New communities were formed through exhilarating encounters that eased the tensions of the hard work of disturbing the habitus.

We would like to end with some thoughts about how the partnership furthered democratic and civic work. It should be fairly easy to see how this work is profoundly *political*, given its emphasis on redressing power asymmetries and unequal resource distribution in the community and on enacting critical pedagogy in the classroom. But the value of the work goes beyond the immediate. Democracy is not only about political processes but also about cultural and social ones (Chapter 3). The work of the citizen artist is to surface suppressed narratives so they can be reinserted into larger, national narratives about who we are, narratives that build on our different stories. These are stories that the dominant narrative constantly suppresses, and reinserting them into this larger narrative is about communicative democracy (Young, 2000): as research on Truth and Memory (n.d.) work in many countries has demonstrated, such communication can be profoundly healing and enable real participatory democratic work to begin.

The citizen artist contributes to communicative democracy in two ways. For the community whose narrative has been marginalized, the collective memory contributes alternative stories that affirm the community's strengths, resilience, and power, explain its pain and its internal struggles and violence, and stand in opposition to the dominant story of psychological and cultural deficits, defeats, and weaknesses. Making these repressed stories public also interrupts and disrupts the dominant narrative and potentially engenders a collective "we" who remember all of our stories. We need to repair the injustices of the past (Booth, 2008) not because we were personally responsible but because we are implicated in narratives that still want to forget. Reparations and social justice don't have to come by way of a calculative redress of what 40 acres and a mule would mean nowadays. They can be achieved through symbolic means that signify a willingness to hear and listen and recognize the other through inclusion: a listening that is followed by affirmation that in fact this is who we have been and at times still are, but we will struggle against our desire to ignore and we will do better.

Notes

1. This chapter is dedicated to Karen, Novella's and Billy's friend, collaborator, and former student, who passed away on April 9, 2009. It draws from her dissertation research on the Temple-Arts Sanctuary program (see Malandra, 2007), a chapter that Karen had drafted for an earlier version of this book (Malandra, 2004), and additional research and writing by Billy and Novella. The first part, including the description of the setting and *Reflections in Brown*, was written by Novella. Billy and Novella wrote the rest of the section and Billy is the main author of the second part. The last part, on border pedagogy, was edited by Novella using Karen's work. Novella wrote the conclusion, still in conversation with Karen's and Billy's work. Part of the proceeds of this book will go to the education fund for Karen's young daughter, Isabella. I thank Jacques and Kathy for giving their full support for this use of Karen's work.
2. Billy routinely takes his community art classes to the Advocate and notes that students struggle with this, especially those who adhere to traditional (white) Christian religion. See murals and descriptions here: http://www.churchoftheadvocate.org/african-american-experience-murals.html.
3. Billy was well known in regional theater circles. In 1999 the *Philadelphia Inquirer*, a major local newspaper, named him 'best choreographer' and another one, *City Paper*, had termed him 'the best unclassifiable theater artist.' His bio is available at http://tyler.temple.edu/faculty/billy-yalowitz.
4. Quotes are from the Art Sanctuary website. See www.artsanctuary.org. Since 2010, the Art Sanctuary has a second location and its offices, including a gallery, are now located in center city Philadelphia.
5. Following this production Billy would move on and the work of the Art Sanctuary with the North Stars also developed in new directions. Performances took up topics from New Orleans and Hurricane Katrina and the Liberian civil war, before returning to more local and personal themes. The spring 2009 performance, *Dad's Day*, aired the community's struggles with fatherless families. For Billy, this topic took a lot of bravery: it is a "deeply painful issue in the African American community, but the desire and courage to bring it into the public arena had to emerge from the community, in

its own time." For him this is the essence of community arts, looking for "the story that needs to be told." (Billy, conversation with Novella, May 2009).
6. Maybe this is a reason that in youth–adult partnerships the role of the adult ally, once embodied, seems easier to enact. There is resonance between the adult who was once a young person.
7. Other writers describe the process as a 'learning partnership' that entails a combination of challenges and supports (Baxter Magolda, 2012). Transformative learning theory and practice involves disorienting experiences, reflection, dialogue and authentic practice (Mezirow, Taylor, & Associates, 2009). A major tradition that emphasizes the connection between personal transformation (or conscientization) and social change is based on Paulo Freire's (1991) critical pedagogy. Also see Chapter 6.
8. Karen describes this cycle in detail. See especially summarizing Table 2 (Malandra, 2007, p. 182), which describes each of the moments and introduces the pedagogical practices and conditions in them as well as the changes in habitus that occur in each moment.

8

CULTIVATING CIVIC CAPACITY FOR DEMOCRATIC COLLABORATION

The Maville–TST Project for School Success

> Just about every experiment with participatory democracy to date has failed because people thought it would be enough to include all voices and opinions, thereby releasing a collective knowledge or intelligence that would match the knowledge of experts. In reality, collective intelligence can only emerge if and when people are freed of their fears and regain trust in themselves. This goal is not easily reached, however, because lack of trust comes from the very depth of our being.
>
> (Rojzman, 2009, p. 94)

The partnership cases featured in the last two chapters helped us understand some of the ways that democratic civic professionals can grow and cocreate spaces for collaboration and cross the borders created by social divides. Specifically, the chapters explored two broad themes: (a) how to develop and enact capacities that help one stay in the discomfort of borderlands and so uncover and address oppressive normalcies and unequal power relations, and (b) what sorts of structures can support such capacities. Here, cultivating capacities involved both the dispositions of the habitus and practices that changed the rules of the game by instituting new roles, rules, formal requirements, pedagogies, and so on. Cultivating capacities meant that the sum total of experiences created something that stayed with participants and provided a reservoir of practices and resources to inform current and future efforts.

The cultivation of civic capacity, which is the focus of this chapter, takes us a step further. Civic capacity is what stakeholders display when they are able to join in a concerted effort to address a pressing community problem they all share. The following interconnected aspects need to be present (Stone, 2001, 2005):

- An orientation to action toward specific goals
- Multiple stakeholders (usually both government and nongovernment)

- Mobilization around a major issue the stakeholders face ("the conscious creation of actors seeking to establish a context in which extraordinary problem-solving can occur" (2001, "Discussion")
- Furthering the well-being of the whole community and not just a segment of it
- An organic process: it is about the particular rather than the general and about developing relationships: "who is included and on what terms" (2005, p. 231).

Conceptually, what is central is power as the capacity to act; when multiple stakeholders are involved, cultivating this capacity puts the stress on interdependence or, in our terms, on creating democratic spaces and partnerships that include sufficient resources to sustain the effort (Hochschild, 2008).

This chapter illustrates the development of civic capacity in a *banlieue*—the French social equivalent of a US inner city—located in the Paris region. A group process, Transformational Social Therapy (TST), brought together participants from across deep divides and enabled them to collaborate on school reform.[1] TST was created by French social psychologist Charles Rojzman in the course of more than 20 years of practice and has gained wide recognition in France and internationally for its ability to humanize social institutions while also healing individuals (Tarpinian, 2010). The approach is especially interesting because it has succeeded in settings that were torn by violence and intractable conflicts, getting deeply divided people to work together on particularly *wicked* problems facing them and their communities.

Collaborative efforts across such borders are essential but are also notoriously hard to achieve. For instance, the well-studied participatory model of school reform in Chicago was fairly successful in middle-class neighborhoods but hardly so in neighborhoods with wide socioeconomic disparities between educators and parents. Researchers agree that nothing short of repairing the social fabric of these communities is required (Bryk, Bender Sebring, Allensworth, Luppescu, & Easton, 2010; Stone, 2005). The chapter illustrates how TST theory and practice were utilized in Maville, a site that exemplifies these barriers, to repair relationships and achieve stakeholder collaboration on a community-wide school change plan. The stakeholders included middle-school students, their teachers, education system administrators, and community members.

The chapter looks at the beginning of the project, which is where the approach that brought together distrusting would-be partners is most visible. Specifically, it focuses on four 2-day meetings, two with students and two with adults. A mixed group of student and adult participants came together for one day during the fourth meeting. The chapter begins with some background that exposes a context of structural inequalities and deep mistrust. The theory and practice of TST are reviewed next, followed by some details about the project and the results of the intervention. The subsequent section provides sufficient details to illustrate the TST process and add to our understanding of its theory and practice.

192 Learning About Professional Practice

As with the previous two chapters, a summary and conclusion take us back to the democratic civic professional and the contributions the case makes to understanding this professional's work.

The Setting

Once the home of an industrial working-class, Maville is now an economically depressed area whose residents are described by the municipal website as "young and multicultural": their ethnic origins are in North and West Africa, the Caribbean, Eastern Europe, Asia, Turkey, Spain, and Portugal. One in three is under 25 and many are of Muslim origins. France is estimated to have the highest concentration of Muslims in Western Europe—around 6.5 million, or some 10% of the population. The government is not legally allowed to maintain statistics by ethnicity, race, or religion, but the connection between these factors and economic and educational deprivation seems unmistakable. For instance, overall unemployment between 2001 and 2007 stood around 10% but was some 40% for North Africans. Young people (18- to 24-year-olds) of Muslim origins, who constitute 8.5% of the age cohort in the general population, are 40% of the age cohort in the prison population. At the time of the intervention, youth unemployment in the administrative region of Seine-Saint-Denis, where Maville is located, was 50%, the highest in all of Europe. The poverty rate in this area was one-third higher than the average for the greater Paris region (Chrisafis, 2006).

Academic attainment is also inequitably distributed. In her study of Muslim girls in Seine-Saint Denis, Trica Keaton (2005) found high rates of failure and dropping out, gross underresourcing, and intensive tracking leading to nonexistent jobs. The teachers did not fare much better than the students: massive teacher and student protests took place in the late 1990s, citing "concerns over inferior facilities, inadequate funding, crushing course loads, high teacher turnover, low salaries, and the elimination of critical teaching positions in a system in which classroom sizes have doubled and tripled over the years" (p. 407). In the initial phases of the Maville–TST project, community tensions were especially high, schools were generally in disarray, and there were widely reported riots in *banlieue* neighborhoods (Chrisafis, 2006).

These circumstances make the ring towns around Paris and other major cities areas of social isolation, political marginalization, and seething resentment where disturbances are not uncommon (Canet, Pech, & Stewart, 2008; Lawrence & Vaisse, 2006; Le Goaziou & Rojzman, 2006). Analyzing the riots of October–November 2005, Coleman (2006) concludes:

> The rebellious youth of the 1980s, who had some hopes in reforms . . . have been replaced by totally desperate kids and young adults who know they have no future, and in fact nothing to lose. To be beaten up, to be arrested

by the cops and to go to jail, is seen not as a failure but as an heroic act, as a necessary test.

("Deep Origins of Youth Revolt")

Various government entities hoped that educational improvements would pacify young people and increase public safety. A national education reform policy that had created networks of 'feeder' schools (from early childhood to middle schools) and called for joint planning by these school networks, parents, and local community-based organizations was revived in 2004–2005 and thus provided some resources for the Maville–TST project (Hargreaves, 2009; Héraud, 2007). The principal of the middle school that headed the network, Collège Picasso, had previously participated in TST professional training offered by the Charles Rojzman Institute. He invited the Institute to facilitate a planning process that would bring together students, teachers, and administrators from network schools, students' families, and representatives of civic and municipal organizations, under the joint leadership of a high-level representative of the Ministry of Education and the principal himself. Collaboration would not be easy: the teachers were for the most part inexperienced and 'white' French, teacher turnover was high, and a garrison mentality pervaded many of the schools (Pugin, 2007); in turn, many neighborhood residents, both French- and foreign-born, felt estranged from all French institutions. Collège Picasso was known as one of the most challenging schools in the country (Héraud, 2007).

TST and Collaboration: From Toxic Emotions to Democratic Dialogue

The main goal of TST, which begins with exchanges within a group and leads to transformative action, is to foster democratic practices and healthy multicultural and multiethnic democracies. Its premise is that institutions and communities can be healed and transformed by helping the people within them address the violence (as defined below) that prevents them from working together; without this work, violence is likely to lend support to fear-based authoritarian groups and regimes. Collaboration is facilitated by creating a *group*, also described below, that constitutes a supportive environment in which participants can let go of some of their masks (R. Craig, 1994; Goffman, 1959) and engage in authentic dialogue.[2] How does TST cultivate collaboration among hostile and mistrusting participants? I describe first its general theory of action and then the main components of the practice.

The TST theory of action was developed in conversation between TST practice and insights from several fields, including especially psychoanalysis, group therapy, action research, and consensus organizing.[3] An important foundation is located in psychodynamic theories of violence, which look at how basic needs for human development and human connections are met (see Staub, 2003). Pathways to meeting one's needs are found at the level of intra- and interpersonal relations (starting with the infant in the family) and social institutions and organizations. If the environment does not provide healthy pathways, the attendant anxiety fosters unhealthy and even pathological ways to meet one's needs. On this view, violence is thus not the problem but a solution to the problem of meeting basic human needs in environments that are unhealthy. A nonobvious example of a pathological social environment is one that promotes extreme social selfishness which fosters a disregard for the well-being of others. In a form of violence directed toward oneself, people can also construct themselves as powerless victims, manipulated by all-powerful authority figures and systems. Given its interest in healthy democracies, TST is especially concerned to heal pathological authority relations and foster a healthy self-determination, or autonomy, as the basis for collaboration.

TST group process centers on reweaving social relationships by healing emotional wounds and creating healthier spaces for meeting one's needs. 'Negative' views, emotions and behaviors are accepted, as it is important for participants to feel and understand who they are in their everyday lives. Experiencing emotions (one's own and others') rather than only engaging in intellectual processing creates an embodied experience that holds the potential for transforming the emotional habitus. In the context of group supports, individuals begin to heal and the healing positively impacts the group and others beyond it. As blocks that prevented connection and communication are removed, participants become motivated to work together for change in workplaces, organizations, and communities. They can now communicate openly and engage in conflict without violence, sharing information they would not previously have revealed or even thought was valuable. Actions that are informed by the resulting collective intelligence are generally more suitable and creative than expert-driven ones, even when the latter include some form of community consultation.

Table 8.1 provides a schematic overview of this framework. The first column illustrates the links between human needs, the fears that arise from unmet needs, and the violence that results as an adaptation. We use masks (second column) for self-protection and to hide our fears and vulnerabilities; the list includes some of many possible masks and signals that just about all the behaviors in the initial stages of group formation are masks. The third column illustrates moves by the facilitator to build an environment that supports healthier expressions and relationships.

Like all schemas, the table simplifies a complex reality. First, the items listed under violence are not inherently harmful. Guilt and shame, for instance, may be associated with introspection, empathy, and moral development. Second, the categories are fluid: guilt, which is about one's behavior, is here linked to an unmet need for power because the feeling that one did something (or everything) wrong can be felt as an absence of power; similarly, shame as a sense of worthlessness may lead back to lack of recognition. Any form of violence can be

TABLE 8.1 Heuristic for TST Facilitator's Practice

Needs	Fears	Violence (toward self/others)	Masks of Self-protection	Facilitator's Practice
Human connection (love, belonging)	Being rejected, abandoned, unloved	Abandonment (self-hate, rejection)	Not needing anyone Perfectionist Not responsible	Knowledgeable about the process but not an expert on the problem
Recognition	Being despised, disrespected, worthless	Humiliation (shaming, negative judgment, misrecognition)	Lacking self-confidence or overconfident Compliant	Create connections Support expressions of doubt, fear, and negative emotions Listen
Power (to act, agency)	Being judged, having no agency	Blaming (scapegoating, 'guilt tripping'; feeling like a victim)	Controlling Bully Defensive Perennial victim	Recognize talents, knowledge, contributions Model acceptance, non-judgment; treat fairly
Safety (security)	Being attacked, abused	Mistreatment (emotional, physical attack/abuse) Rigidly controlling Fanaticism	Pathological submission to authority or rebel	Promote shifts: from dependency to self-determination; victim to responsible agent; binary dualisms to complexity

Source: Adapted from Rojzman, 2009, pp. 55–57.

linked to different human needs, however; recalling the discussion of habitus, field, and capital should remind us that there are myriad possibilities and each of us develops in particular ways that suit our experiences and circumstances.

This leads to the third point. The table is not a script that the facilitator follows. Consistent with the phronetic framework, practice is about perceptions and insights about what may be going on in the concrete situation—and here the reference is to each participant's unique habitus. Additionally, the facilitator's actions are not skill- and rule-based but are rooted in embodied understandings and virtues (in TST terms, the facilitator's *posture*). The TST facilitator is not the expert who analyzes from a distance but a wiser practitioner who asks thoughtful questions in the spirit of exploration and helpfulness. Think of the table, then, as a heuristic, an experience-based framework for making educated guesses about what may be going on in the particular situation and resolving on action based on these intuitive judgments. Finally, a reminder that intra- and interpersonal realms constitute the intersection between the personal and the social: organizations, especially hierarchical ones, can be violent and foster violence.

Violence

As suggested above, violence is not only grave physical and emotional harm to self and others, but also includes more subtle expressions, for instance, the micro-aggressions and micro-insults discussed in Chapter 2 under the rubric of everyday racism. For example, the fear of not being loved may become the violence of manipulation and demands for 'love': no longer self-determinate, people are there merely to serve one's needs. Violence is thus quite pervasive and may even seem *normal*.

An important part of TST practice is the transformation of violence into conflict. What distinguishes the two is not the strength of the emotions: anger, for instance, is not necessarily violent. The key qualifier is how the self and other are constructed in the moment. Being fully human means accepting imperfection in ourselves and others: we are neither saints nor devils. We are thus violent toward ourselves and others when we fear, hate, and reject the shadow side. We tend to assuage fears about our unmet needs by perpetrating the forms of violence we have experienced, especially but not uniquely in our formative early years—which perpetuates cycles of fear and violence. The toxic emotions that are so generated may be directed toward oneself, one's family and colleagues, as well as feared Others through group categorization.

The defense and pretense, to ourselves and the outside world, constitutes a mask (or even an armor) that is necessary when the dangers are real, but perhaps less so when they are imaginary. Yet, through the lens of our fears we can't tell them apart. The TST facilitator intervenes by creating a group environment in which participants can express their fears and vulnerabilities, understand the difference, and experience healthier ways to meet their needs.

Creating a (TST) Group

As mentioned above, TST works through small groups comprised of people who are suffering from the violence of a particular setting or institution. In deciding who should be in one or several simultaneous groups, a major criterion is that everyone who is part of the problem should be included, with as much heterogeneity as possible. Thus project sponsors need to reach beyond the usual volunteers, involving even those whom they may see as the problem and whose initial reason for participating may be to accuse others of wrongdoing: so-called naysayers, cynics, and troublemakers are needed because their perceptions and views carry understandings of the situation and information that are essential for the change project. Another criterion for group formation involves separating participants who normally engage with one another through hierarchical authority relations. In the Maville–TST project, this was the rationale for working separately with students and adults.

A TST *group* is more than an aggregate of people who are brought together for a given purpose. It is intentionally created and comes about when enough trust is present so that people can overcome the fears that prevent them from showing their emotions and vulnerabilities and speaking their minds with the other participants. This means that in the beginning there is no group as such. All participants wear masks and enact their normal categorizations: they will gravitate toward those with whom they feel comfortable and avoid those whom they perceive as threatening. Interrupting this normal in-group/out-group formation, creating relationships across the entire group, and thus fostering trust is an important part of the facilitator's work. Growing trust—in oneself, the group, the facilitator, and the process—helps participants take the important step of moving from feeling like victims of powerful others to seeing themselves and those others as complex human beings who are responsible agents and who thus can act differently. This also engages the motivation of participants to work together toward change.

The TST Facilitator

Like other practices that are informed by depth psychology, TST facilitation requires prior in-depth work on oneself, so as to face and understand one's own psychic wounds, shadow side, and violence, and not be manipulated by them. Rojzman refers to the facilitator metaphorically as a wounded healer: a human being, imperfect, not superior to others, vulnerable, and prone to the same emotions, fears, biases, and violence. This does not mean there is a (false) equality. The facilitator has a deeper understanding and compassion for self and others, the capacity to perceive and interrupt one's violence, an orientation to healing, and a method or approach. She or he is an expert in leading the group toward an agreed goal that involves working together while group members have the knowledge necessary to resolve the problem.

In a phronetic sense, the facilitator is a wise practitioner enacting practices that arise from an authentic self and from the orientations of the habitus. Among the important qualities of the facilitator are capacities for authentic human connection and for therapeutic listening: a way of being present, not passively or simply accepting but engaging with the person's deep core, gently pushing them to go deeper in their understanding of what is going on. Four practices stand out. The facilitator:

- Makes no distinctions among participants. This posture, which arises from empathy and compassion, helps participants be less judgmental of others and show the same consideration and respect for everyone. It also contributes to an egalitarian environment that feels safe.
- Makes room for and mitigates fears. When participants speak of their fears, it allows the facilitator to hear the violence behind them; in a receptive environment, this speaking will help reduce the power of fears to feed violence and allow conflicts to surface. The facilitator does not stir up conflicts but allows those that are under the surface to emerge and be aired.

- Supports the development of relationships and cooperation among all participants. An important process, mentioned above, is the move from binary dualisms to complexity, especially in the context of shifting from powerless victim to responsible agent. In the process, participants share information that is usually available only to in-group members but is vital to the group's full understanding of the issues at hand. This fosters the creation of collective intelligence.
- Supports a democratic relation between leader and group members, leading them from dependence on or rebellion against the authority figure to interdependence and self-determination or autonomy.

The next section describes the beginning of the Maville–TST project, illustrating the movement from mistrust to trust and to collaboration. An additional issue in the case involves the quality of intergenerational relationships and youth–adult partnerships. I continue to explain the TST process in the context of the presentation.

The Maville–TST Project

The TST project started officially with a meeting (March 14, 2005) that included principals and teachers from the school network, a member of the local Community Governing Council, and the two network lead administrators.[4] The meeting served to affirm the purpose and goals of the project (to set in place actions that would promote students' academic achievement), explain the TST process, and allow participants to express their ideas and what they hoped to achieve. The leadership team then proceeded to recruit members for two groups that would be taken through the TST process: a group of 8 to 10 eighth and ninth graders from Collège Picasso and one of 10 to 15 adults—professionals (educators, social workers) from various levels in the school network, parents, and community members from local organizations. The student group met separately and started earlier than the adult group, since it was expected that students and adults would not speak freely together before participating in the TST process. Facilitators would decide when and how to introduce the students and their ideas into the adult group.

Student participants met for 4 days in two sessions held in April and May 2005. Members of this group also participated in two meetings with the principal and vice principal of Collège Picasso, held in April and June 2005 and one meeting with the adult group in October 2005, at the adults' invitation. The adult group met for a total of four 2-day sessions (only two of which are presented in the case details) that began in May 2005 and ended in October 2006. Each day lasted around 5 hours. The adult sessions were held at approximately 6-month intervals. Between sessions, adult participants engaged in various school improvement activities.

The intervention succeeded in creating the groundwork for collaboration and by the second adult-group session in October 2005, the adults and students were able to have an open dialogue that informed subsequent action plans.[5] The meetings also helped initiate collaboration between educators, parents, and community-based social workers and organizers (Héraud, 2007). The project was extended, with intensive follow-up in 2007–2008 through Ministry of Education funding. Considering that its aim was to stimulate organizational, community, and system change, TST proved to be an effective relatively short intervention that left in place people who had experienced that it was possible to collaborate and were motivated to be change agents.

The Maville–TST Process

Inviting Participation

On the day the project was announced to students, a flyer was posted in the school. It was drafted by Théa, one of the TST cofacilitators, who spent several days there as an observer. It shows how diverse participants, including disengaged students, were invited to participate.

> **School Isn't Perfect?**
>
> In this school there are students who are struggling, hurting, not doing well, afraid of failing; students who feel alone, attacked, and like they're victims of injustice. If you're having problems, if you're angry, disillusioned, enraged, frustrated or even if you're happy (why not?) join us for four days of dialogue and collaborative research. Any 8th and 9th grader can become a "young researcher" . . . The group's mission will be to find solutions to students' problems, your problems . . . Do you have something to say? What ideas or criticisms do you have? Come, you can change the school!

The flyer speaks to underlying TST principles and the way TST departs from the norm. Identifying participants, even those who may be disaffected, as "young researchers," signals that everyone has useful information and that even negative judgments are valuable. Whereas programs are often aimed at a particular problem and construct youth as the problem, here the problem is not defined: the goal is to change the school, not to change the students to suit the school. The flyer also names some of the emotions students may be experiencing, whether positive or negative, without passing judgment. The last words, "you can change the school," announce that the students have power: they can become change agents rather than remain powerless victims whose only choices are, in TST terms, the violence of obedience, rebellion, or abandonment. The flyer speaks to this initial mindset; it is not yet time to point to the other side: in order to change the school the students will also have to change themselves.

Students themselves find this approach and its language unusual and continue the discourse of student-as-problem: when a new student joins the group on the second day (April 26, 2005), a member of the original group tells him that the project's goal is "to do something about disruptive students." The facilitator corrects him and reminds him of the larger, civic purpose: "we want to do something for all the schools, to help all students succeed, and not only deal with those who are disruptive." Nine students respond, seven boys and two girls between the ages of 14 and 17, all of North African and African origins and all considered school troublemakers. The unorthodox recruitment method had yielded the desired results.

From Mistrust to Dialogue

Four scenes provide rich details on key aspects of the practice and will serve to illustrate the TST process. The first scene comes from the initial meeting of the student group (April 25, 2005). Here, the focus is on enabling collaboration by reducing mistrust and creating enough trust in the group, the facilitator, and the process. This account is more detailed than the first meeting with adults because it exemplifies the TST method, which was similar for both groups. The next scene takes us to the second weekend (May 3–4, 2005), when, in an atmosphere that supports much more trusting and open communication, the students create and perform several role plays about their experiences in and around school. The adult group watches a video of these role plays on the second day of their first session (May 23, 2005). The third scene is about this virtual encounter, in the course of which the adults come to see the students' information as trustworthy and thus as an essential component of the collective intelligence for school reform. The fourth scene is a joint meeting of students and adults during the adults' second session (October 18, 2005); this meeting becomes the occasion for a dialogue between students and adults as mutually trustworthy partners.

Give This Project a Grade

At the agreed starting time on the first morning (April 25, 2005), only the facilitators (Charles and his assistant, Théa) and a school staff member are present. A few calls and reminders are sent out and eventually nine students arrive. Charles starts by explaining the goals and organization of the project and how the students' work will dovetail with the work of the adults. He reiterates the importance of their knowledge about promoting school success in this neighborhood: the students should be open about any criticisms they have and think about how they want to communicate their criticisms and ideas to the adults. Charles' introduction is not greeted with enthusiasm: students sit slumped in their chairs, look at their phones, seem guarded and indifferent. Charles invites them to introduce themselves and speak briefly on how they feel about the project: "Do you believe that this work will produce good results and help students succeed in school? Give it a grade, from 0 to 20."

TST practice is already visible in this introduction. Asking the students to grade the project accomplishes three things. It inverts typical relations between students and the adults who normally rule their lives; it signals that negative expressions (doubts and criticisms) are acceptable; and it gives the facilitator information about participants' fears. There is also a notable absence: activities to develop ground rules and trust-building exercises. While processes such as intergroup dialogue usually begin by creating rules for behavior (Dessel & Rogge, 2008), the therapeutic foundations that inform TST offer a different (and not artificial) path to achieving the relative safety and trust required for a group to collaborate. There are only three rules that are already implied and that Charles will communicate at a different time: obligatory attendance, confidentiality, and freedom to participate as one wishes to. Attending means being present: if any of the participants want to sleep, be silent, listen to music, play with a cell phone, or otherwise refuse to join in, they are free to do so. The seeds of new authority relations are being planted here as the students are invited to act rather than react to the authority figure.

The facilitator would see the students' seeming initial indifference and hostility as masks that will begin to be lowered when the conditions for collaboration are created. A typical teacher may take offense at behaviors that infringe the rules, while for the social therapist they are masks that would be solidified by the teacher's or facilitator's defensive or offensive reaction (other masks) and would lead them to enact together a play of violence rather than cooperation. Again, the goal is not to obtain compliance but to create conditions that will make it possible for participants gradually to let down some of their masks.

Returning to the activity, grades range from 7 to 12 out of 20, as the students share their hopes for the project and the obstacles they anticipate. On the positive side, they seem to consider this a good idea that they wish could work. Then they almost immediately proceed to the obstacles, all of which point to the teachers: they always want to be right and have the last word, there is no give-and-take, they won't listen and some won't want to do it. Time is also mentioned as an obstacle; the initiative may work for a while but not for long, and one week won't change much. Breaking the solid wall of student victims and teacher oppressors, one student remarks that "it's not only the teachers—some of the students don't want to change, either." After this, Charles proposes they talk about who bears responsibility for the students' failure. He asks them to complete a sentence on their own, after which they will talk about it together: "if we don't succeed it's because the students _____ or because the teachers _____. Explain why."

Before moving on let me comment on these questions in light of TST practice and theory: could the facilitator have started simply by asking the students to describe the problem as they see it? The issue here is about focusing the question on the main actors and inviting the students to consider their agency. At this point, relationships have not yet been established that allow masks to come off and the facilitator understands that the ensuing conversation will be mainly about their needs and fears, which include their need for him to hear and respond to their grievances. Nonetheless, the door is open for the probing questions that will come.

If perspective taking and impartiality were the goal, the students' responses would show that it's too early for that—or that something else is going on. They ignore the *blank* that would have assigned responsibilities to students and continue to air their grievances toward the teachers. The students explain how teachers create the problem by giving examples of unfairness, prejudices, categorizations, and preferences that they construe as fundamentally unjust. When students need academic support, none is provided: teachers show no care for them personally and no concern about the family problems they experience. We begin to sense the emotions and needs behind the utterances. If he were acting as a teacher or a typical adult, Charles might mention the students' failure to follow his directions; he might ask pointed (and leading) questions that invite them to admit they are not simply innocent victims. But at this point they would likely hear this as a judgment and a ruse by an adult to trick them into admitting they are the guilty ones. Instead, he will lead by being present, asking questions, suggesting activities and exercises that help them see more—entering their world as an adult who is enacting a different kind of authority figure.

As mentioned above, Charles's listening for the students' fears and wounds is not an analytical exercise. He asks probing reflective questions and invites them to entertain the notion that reality is more complex than the binary one portrayed through their masks: are all teachers like that (answer: no, not all); how are students responsible (answer: students create problems, as well, they're not all obedient; we're not all saints, either!). Once again, the purpose for inviting them to move beyond categories is to help them begin to envision a path to change: complicating the picture and humanizing the teachers means they are real people who are in some ways like them, with feelings, fears, prejudices, and also gifts, and to whom they can relate. He also reminds them that the objective is to convey their understanding of the problem to the adults and they should think about how to do it. Here, the facilitator is exercising his professional responsibility to guide the process toward the goal that project sponsors previously agreed on, but the reminder may also motivate students to move from powerless victims to responsible agents.

As the environment becomes relatively safe, including an adult authority figure who cares, takes them seriously, listens, and invites reflection, the quality of the students' participation changes: they start using their agency to consider how to change the school environment rather than to blame, resist, and rebel—and to invite one another to walk this path. One of the students suggests they make posters "to make teachers and students reflect." Another one proposes they make a film that shows the students' perspective on what happens when they are thrown out of class and then suspended. A brainstorming exercise ensues, in which they generate words about teachers and students. Charles does not interrupt what seem clearly expressions of their violence. Théa writes in her notes: "a list of around one hundred words is quickly generated, many of which are quite violent toward the teachers. [The students] laugh and throw out the words without thinking." The brainstorming newsprint also has negative words about students.

Small groups work together to create phrases based on the brainstorm, and in a whole group discussion that follows they decide on a number of slogans for teachers and for students, for the school posters. The first include: "I treat you with respect, you treat me with respect," "Moussa, Kadhidja, Kader = Maxime, Bertrand, Géraldine,"[6] "Tell me when I'm doing well, too," "I exist, why don't you see me?" "We all want the same things," "Why don't you give me support? We need support so we can improve," "Don't get physical," and "If you're wrong, accept it." For their peers, the slogans are, "Put yourself in the teachers' place; their job's not easy," "School is not the hood," "Bastard, prick, fuck-up, these aren't words for school," "Pride, for both students and teachers, that's what gets us stuck in power games," "Problems between students and teachers are often created by misunderstandings. Do you agree?"

How would the facilitator perceive and make sense of these interactions—again, as hunches rather than prescriptions? A lot seems to be happening: first, Charles seems to have gained the students' trust: the very fears they had expressed about the teachers are not present in this room, with these adults; the students are being taken seriously as contributors to the project and are not experiencing the usual adult violence; their knowledge is not ignored or belittled. The fact that they engage in the exercises although earlier no one had given the project high marks means that their doubts and fears are being assuaged. Working in small groups, they are getting more comfortable with one another as well, taking some risks by revealing some truths about their in-group. Masks are being removed, in a process that will continue the following day while they make up the posters and begin to plan for the film. On the second day, they and the facilitators have a meeting with the principal to discuss their planned actions and gain his approval.

Clowns, Rabble . . . and More

The following weekend the group is joined by two additional adults from the Rojzman Institute and everyone works on the film the young people are planning. The purpose for bringing the additional adults, as Charles explains, is not to help the students but to add more information about experiences in school, from their own perspective. The large group is often split into smaller ones, and the adults will sit in with the small groups and contribute to their conversation. The first day (May 3) is mostly geared to help the students get more clarity and a deeper understanding of the problems they raised in the first session; they also continue to explore sources of difficulties and develop ideas about what can help students be more successful. Following Charles's direction, they break into small groups and create two story lines, one of a student who is academically successful and one of a student who is failing. To get ideas for the stories, he tells them they should talk personally about their own lives and families, both in the neighborhood and at school.

The students start by talking about two binary student categories that lead to success or failure: clowns (*bouffons*) and rabble (*cailleras*). The clowns, who are successful, stay at home and study, always obey adults, and are boring. The rabble are school troublemakers who are the opposite of obedient: they rebel, don't care what the teachers say, don't bother to do the school work, and just have fun. They often also have family problems. As to why this is so, there doesn't seem to be an answer: some do well, others don't. While developing the role plays, however, the students begin to correct their initial statements: "it's not always like that," "there are lots of different circumstances," and "there are different kinds of clowns; it's not necessarily bad to be a clown." Reflection grounded in personal experiences disrupts the binaries, other categories come to light, and the mask of in-group unity begins to fray. In this new atmosphere, the students plan and try out different scenarios.

The process continues on the next day (May 4), when 11 role plays are filmed: three in a classroom, six of meetings between teachers and parents, one showing parents and their child at home, and one featuring a meeting of teachers and students. The scripts and the conversations around their development show an increasingly nuanced understanding not only of each setting but of their interaction. Comparing the scene of parents and children at home to those of parents with teachers shows a pervasive powerlessness that manifests in different ways. The adults show more understanding of the children at home than at school: they ask their child why she behaves that way and worry about what will happen to her: "do you want to become a servant?" With the teacher, the parents seem ashamed and at a loss for what to do other than simply agree with their pronouncements. There is no dialogue, no real communication, everyone is stuck, nothing leads to resolution.

What makes a good or a bad teacher? A comparison of the different role plays is an exercise in complexity. In an early scene, being a good teacher means being present to and understanding the students' academic needs and how they connect with their personal lives. The teacher walks around to the students' desks as they work, asking how things are going and if there are any problems. When he sees that a student hasn't understood the lesson, without shaming him he asks another student to come sit next to him and help him. When a student says he doesn't have the book, he lends him his. The teacher always smiles and speaks nicely to the students. Classroom order seems to be maintained here mostly by the teacher being the students' ally and asking them to be his. When students don't listen and comply with his requests, he asks them for "some respect." He approaches a student who continues being disruptive and says, "stop, otherwise the principal will say that I'm incompetent."

The teacher's approach leads to a classroom that is not chaotic but does not engage the students in their academic work. The students explain that the teacher is too permissive and not exercising enough authority. However, in another role play, a very strict teacher (a "bad" one) also has trouble keeping control of the class. When the student who is role playing the teacher is asked if he (as teacher) is responsible for the chaos, a negative answer introduces yet another factor: "the students have just come back inside from their break, sometimes they're just like that." There is a problem about relationships, however, as one adds that the teacher "is strict, but he's alone"; and also, "on the one hand, I understand him, on the other hand, he's not necessarily right."

What is emerging is that students want guidance by responsive and responsible adults and that no one, themselves or the adults in their lives, knows how to connect in enabling ways. Here, interactions with the facilitator and other adults from the Institute provide a demonstration that the youth-adult roles they desire are possible: guided with respect and supports, they have learned to trust and work well with adults. The violence in this setting has decreased to a remarkable extent and it is suggestive to see it as the result of the students meeting their needs in healthier ways. TST seems to have succeeded in changing the social environment according to plan, engendering the capacity for collaboration that will be an important part of building civic capacity for school reform.

They See Us So Well

The 2-day session with the adult group, on May 22, starts in ways that mirror the students' session. Group members are invited to introduce themselves and say who they think bears the main responsibility for the lack of school success. At the end of the round of introductions and comments, members are asked to talk in pairs with someone with whom they disagreed or whose views shocked them, which is designed to foster connections across potential in-groups. The next day (May 23), Charles tells the group about his work with students and the film that is ready for viewing. Many of the reactions are strongly negative: participants expect that the students' portrayals of them will be stereotyped, caricatures even; the anticipated (excessive) criticisms are only the views of problem students; shock, dismay, and even disgust are expressed about some students' violent comments about teachers.

Charles agrees about the subjective and partial nature of the students' views. He also admits that he is unsure about how to reach the goal of having the two groups work together. His sense of the previous day's conversation is that, interesting though it was, it did not move the group toward understanding what to do about the problem. He returns to the theme of powerlessness and where to place responsibility for what needs to change: "We are steeped in a sense of powerlessness. We can't change others. So we need to talk about how we can change, what can change in ourselves, here and now." They will have to figure out not only how to collaborate inside this group but also with the students, being attentive to include their different motivations in the plan for school success.

An activity is proposed: each person in the group should reflect on what he or she does that contributes to the problem. As the students before them, the adults are asked to enter into a dialogue in which they speak personally rather than distancing themselves by speaking only about their roles, groups, and categories. Charles explains that talking about their difficulties may help them grapple with the realities of the situation, find solutions that are adapted to these realities and thus overcome their sense of powerlessness. The activity continues on the theme of inviting participants to connect with their own power and agency: they will find the answers. The starting point is to move from the intellectualizing and distancing process of the previous day, which is another mask, and take the risk of speaking personally, honestly, and emotionally.

Perhaps sensing that this is the real issue, participants start talking about the risks involved in the activity; several express reservations and claim their right to not make themselves vulnerable. In the end, through a facilitated exchange similar to the students', they agree to engage as was proposed. This exercise in vulnerability seems to set the groundwork for another vulnerability-inducing activity with which they now agree: watching the students' film.

The film seems to transform the adult's perception of the students and the information they can contribute toward collective intelligence. One teacher comments, "I didn't realize they see us so well" and others concur, reflecting on the students' keen powers of observation. The film's depictions of interactions involving parents and students also match the adults' impressions and knowledge. There is also more empathy, although not complete trust. One participant's comment captures this new feeling: "sometimes I think, poor kids; then, other times, I wouldn't want to meet a group of them in the dark." After the viewing, the adults engage in a reflective conversation that connects the students' perceptions of school to their own experiences as students.

The TST process here is sufficiently similar to what the students experienced and does not need further explanation. What is of interest is the way students are transformed in the adults' eyes. First, they become trustworthy sources of information for collective intelligence; second, they are humanized through their emotions and thus become worthy of empathy. Let me briefly comment on each. Co-constructing knowledge, especially across borders, requires more than pooling information from different sources. The information has to be trustworthy and it has to be turned into knowledge. In this, developing collective intelligence bears similarities to the action research process—in fact, the students were invited to participate as "young researchers." Research becomes trustworthy when it addresses ways to reduce biases and the findings are credible. In the circumstances of this case, with participants who can be described as defended subjects,[7] it is difficult to imagine achieving trustworthiness without the TST process. The first two scenes showed the multiple ways the process strove not only to reduce bias but to break through the students' defenses, or masks, and help them understand the situation in depth. The adults' assessment confirms their credibility and relative lack of bias.

The film also succeeds in humanizing the students for the adults, just as the first two scenes show the adults being humanized for the students. Binary constructions have been interrupted and enough has been achieved in the process of building trust and reducing fears to enable the two groups to take the next step in working together. What appears to move the adults in these directions is seeing the students as capable of feeling and understanding human emotions. The fact that they understand the teachers means they are capable of empathy. The film also shows that they are concerned about their families and need their involvement in their education. Research on categorization shows that attributing human emotions to a group helps us connect to them and this seems to be happening here (Leyens et al., 2003): in a sense, the students can be trusted, they can be reached, through their emotions and needs. As the knowledge from the film begins to be integrated into the adults' knowledge, one senses that the wealth of diverse experiences is beginning to suggest some possible paths out of powerlessness and into action.

Meet Again in Three Months? No, in Two Weeks!

On the first day of the adults' second session (October 17) the group is floundering: in marked contrast with the pleasant experience of the voluntary summer school, the start of the school year has been ridden with crisis and participants feel like they're drowning in "an ocean of difficulties." As he has done before, Charles suggests that "the only way to move forward is for everyone to be able to work together." The group decides it wants to come together with the students: can a meeting be arranged for the next day? Some phone calls later, six students are on board.

To prepare for the meeting, the group develops a short list of areas they want to explore together with the students: better communication, peer pressure, violence in school. They also engage in an activity Charles proposes: "Pretend that you are the same as you were [in middle school] . . . but you are going to this school, in this neighborhood. What's going on? How do you react?" The exercise produces especially interesting insights about how the school system works. The initial impression is one of two completely separate and different worlds: as students, the adults had acted respectfully toward the teachers, even if they disliked them. Then they discover a common foundation: "the system was founded on fear of the teachers [and that fear] . . . kept us quiet." Strangely, it worked: "the more violence there was from teachers, the more quiet the students got." Here, however, it seems that the students are more afraid of their families, especially their older brothers, than of the teachers. The exploration of these commonalities and differences energizes participants and gives them a new sense of purpose for the upcoming meeting with students. The next day, the students arrive on time and for the next 3 hours no one calls for a break and everyone engages in a lively dialogue. At the end, Charles suggests that the group meet again in 3 months, and the students exclaim: "no, no, [let's meet] in two weeks!"

At the beginning of the joint meeting, the director of one of the network primary schools takes the lead in explaining why the adults wanted to meet and what they hoped to achieve. They have been grappling with the question of how to improve the school and are determined to find ways to help all the students succeed, but they have not been making progress and would like to hear the students' ideas about the problem: "What kind of changes do you think would help?" As was decided on the previous day, the director proposes that they explore together what it means to have "a good day at school." The students agree and the adults start the conversation.

This introduction is noteworthy for the way the students are addressed. The adult—an educator, and thus an adult-who-is-supposed-to-know—admits that he and his peers don't have the answers and need the students' knowledge. Evidence from the research on youth-adult partnerships has established that adults find it difficult to act as partners because they are oriented to seeing young people as immature children in need of direction, which they may compensate for by being permissive (Camino, 2005). We encountered this tendency in the college students in Chapter 6 and more broadly in the ways professionals often address community members. In this case, as the role plays showed, it also happened between teachers and parents. Similar ways of relating are typical of hierarchical and authoritarian relations. Here, the students are being treated as trusted young adults and as partners, which is how Charles has addressed authority relations in both groups.

Two themes describe a good day at school for the adults: good relationships and meaningful, satisfying work. The two are related, since work well done means that the students are learning and are satisfied; the teachers are making a difference and feel useful, and "everyone leaves happy." Meaningful work goes beyond happiness: it is about genuinely educative experiences that open up new worlds for the students and create "magical moments in the classroom." The main theme for the students is a safe and educative school environment: there are no fights, they have few problems understanding what they are being taught, the teachers are encouraging and give them help when they need it. Reading these expressions through the lens of needs, we perceive a need for positive power, recognition, human connection, and safety—understanding also that participants' needs and fears have expressions that are unique to each one. We can also begin to glimpse the pain that is their companion as, day in and day out, these needs are not met and the opposite of a good day at school is the norm.

Overall, the meeting is starting well. There is banter and a quite refreshing camaraderie. In response to the students' question (did they enjoy going to school?), adults share what their own schooling was like. The responses amaze the students who exclaim: "same for us, nothing has changed!" As children, the adults only liked school because they got to see their friends; they were afraid of the teachers and tried hard not to get in trouble, but the adults "were always right." When they get into more substantive aspects of the school, the conversation continues as if in the spirit of 'critical friends.' Issues touch on class size, schedules, students' complaints about teachers' behaviors that were already visible through the role plays: throwing them out of class, not bothering to explain, labeling them and calling them names, not giving them the chance to redeem themselves.

As the meeting progresses, we see some risk-taking, as young people and adults speak more openly about how they feel, showing their vulnerabilities. One of the teachers confesses that he is constantly afraid of losing control of the classroom and that this makes him less tolerant of even minor infractions by students. A student is upset because of an unjust punishment: it shows the teacher doesn't care about him. Adults and students engage one another, ask hard questions, disagree. When the adults want to talk about the peer pressure they see some students exert on others, the young people explain that for them that's not the real issue: some students are weak, and the problem is rooted in the differences between school and neighborhood. The conversation takes an amazing turn when one of the adults suggests that maybe the students should accept more responsibility for the problems. He asks: "what if the students just aren't working hard enough, or aren't motivated?" This question starts an exploration about the meaning and purpose of school: what should the focus be? What is a relevant curriculum? How does the school see the future for which it is supposedly preparing the students?

Dialogue is about the free flowing exploration and creation of meaning in a group. Unlike debate, which involves adversaries who each muster supports for their own position while looking for weaknesses in the other's, dialogue is about exploring, connecting, and together reaching toward new understandings. Brazilian educator Paulo Freire, known for his dialogical approach to liberatory education, adds that dialogue is an epistemological relationship that is humanizing and life affirming: I cannot know myself except in dialogue with you. It is thus "an indispensable component of the process of both learning and knowing" (1991, p. 17). In dialogue, we listen and respond authentically, as our participation is distinguished not by holding on to our positions but by epistemological curiosity—meaning that we truly understand that we are all learners. Showing our vulnerabilities is an important way of connecting and building trust. Daniel Yankelovich (1999) recalls Martin Buber's *I and Thou*, for whom "life itself is a form of meeting and dialogue is the 'ridge' on which we meet" (p. 15).

This sort of existential meeting seems to be taking place here, and as young people and adults engage in the dialogue they are creating a common (third) space for collective intelligence. Unlike the understandings of the problem each group expressed at the beginning of the project, this dialogue is rich with insights and yields information that can inform action. The exchange also has a felt-sense of abundant energy and motivation for change: they are partners, a team, no longer alone facing an insurmountable and unending problem. How did participants become partners who saw one another as having trustworthy information for changing schools? Let me go back to the first scene and trace the path that was travelled.

Summary and Conclusion

The case narrative has focused on four scenes that highlight the movement from initial mistrust toward dialogue and collective intelligence. These, in turn, constituted a foundation for civic capacity in the form of a shared plan for collaborative action on school reform. The first and third scenes showed that at the beginning of the intervention both students and adults made sense of the situation and exercised their agency largely through violence. All the potential stakeholders saw themselves not as responsible actors but as victims, who were thus powerless to change an impossible situation and the system of which it was a part: they could only blame others and react. When insights from all the scenes are combined we see that encouraging participants to express the emotions behind these defensive masks was a key to building trust and moving to collaboration and the free sharing of information. Importantly, the case shows that the participation and engagement of unwilling and mistrusting would-be partners (both students and adults) was gained initially not by appeals to the common good and the institution's stated need for collaborative planning, but by welcoming the expression of grievances. Here was the initial motivation for participating and engaging—a motivation that would probably have been squelched by typical (*normal*) processes that insist that "violence" be left outside the room.

The TST process was particularly attuned to enabling these expressions and doing so in ways that created self-awareness, connections, relationships, and trust. Reflecting on the creation of collective intelligence as an outcome of the process, it is instructive to compare the action proposals the adults made at the beginning and the "keys to school success" they drafted at the end of the second weekend. As shown in Table 8.2, the comparison is quite suggestive of the changes that took place.

I have seen lists similar to the one in column A before; they mostly come out of deficit and expert-based assumptions that families need to be helped to understand the school and educational system (while educators don't need to be similarly helped to understand families and neighborhoods) and that the problems, caused by the neighborhood and not the school, can be alleviated by taking students out of the neighborhood. To me it's a rather sad list that speaks to an

TABLE 8.2 Adult Action Proposals, First and Last Day

Action Proposals: First Day	Keys to School Success: Last Day
Invite parents to school, in order to (a) reduce inconsistencies in messages students get from home and from school; (b) communicate with parents about how school works.	*The School*: Reconsider the school schedule Match school work and rhythm of family life Consider that students perform at different levels Introduce peer collaboration and supports Support and stabilize teams, both in school and in the network
Bring parents and other stakeholders to the table to understand reciprocal expectations and create "something in common"	Make spaces for conversations Find ways to legitimate the necessary violence of the educational system
Take students on cultural and other outings outside the neighborhood	*Consider issues in the affective domain*: Motivation and effort Being valued
Motivate students by valuing their successes	Trust Respect and consideration

Source: Field notes; adapted from Keith, 2011.

overwhelming sense of powerlessness, a list that is also *normal* as it is informed by what Rojzman would say are common prejudices (such as we all have) and not by a real understanding of the situation on the ground.

The list in column B seems to come from a deeper understanding of the situation. My sense is that it shows considerable insight, but its contents may not seem all that unusual—until we recall the starting point. The qualitative difference between the two lists could hardly be due to the additional quantity of time—3 more days—that the adult group spent together. The more concrete ideas in column B suggest an understanding of the problem that is both broader and more grounded in the reality of the situation. In turn, this understanding draws from a new epistemological relation between educators, students, and community members: we are no longer in a world of experts-who-are-supposed-to-know (but here feel quite helpless) but one in which adults and students make valued contributions to the collective knowledge.

The last item under "the school," concerning "ways to make acceptable the legitimate violence of the educational system" is especially suggestive of new understandings about the place of the school within the educational system. Deep reflection, dialogue, and collective intelligence grounded in the adults' and students' experiences have revealed violent aspects of school-as-institution. It seems that the students' and adults' new understandings of themselves, the other, and their authority relations have translated into understandings of and relations to the institution, which has now also become a site for action rather than reaction: the school is becoming a site where the effects of a violent system are mediated by conscious and responsible professionals. Recalling Palmer's insights about professionals in pathological institutions (Chapter 4), the new partners seem to have come to the realization that, here and now, living a divided life is not a valid, *livable* option. They are becoming moral beings who are about changing the institutions in their lives by cultivating communities of discernment and support.

Thinking with the border-crossing partnership framework, this chapter has emphasized how the TST process and facilitator encounter the practice situation, starting with planning for and inviting participation, to creating a group, and supporting its collective intelligence. The details of the case point to TST itself as wise practice that supports the cultivation of wise practitioners. Let me briefly take each phronetic aspect in turn: embodying the virtues, making sense of the situation, and constructing and enacting the good in and through that situation.

I pointed out earlier that the TST facilitator's training is directed in great part toward cultivating an embodied sense of self that is about seeing one's shadows and enacting the wisdom of a wounded healer—qualities that make the being of the facilitator an essential aspect of the process. After a relatively short intervention, we see these qualities beginning to emerge in the practitioners involved in the process. For instance, like the facilitator, the adults are able to show themselves to the students as they are, with their uncertainties and doubts: they don't pretend to know, but show a genuine humility in asking the students to share what they know with the erstwhile experts. Humility is also refreshing because, in this situation, letting down some of one's masks builds the group's strength: as it turns out, the students saw through the masks anyway.

The case also documents changes in the ways participants made sense of the situation. Recall that in the Change from Within Programme the administrator provided cues for seeing differently through the suggestion of "looking for the positives" and that these new ways of seeing were supported by the Circle of Friends. Here, the facilitator, enacting TST theory and practice, looked for and suggested cues that enabled participants to see through the violence embodied in their emotional habitus and the ways that violence was (partly) responsible for creating the situations they suffered. For example, the TST facilitator's gentle but constant probing of sensemaking that pitted all powerful perpetrators against powerless victims helped participants consider their part in constructing the situation and thus provided a path from powerlessness to responsibility.

Finally, constructing and enacting the good in the particular situation was exemplified by the joint exercise about a good day at school—an exercise in genuine collective intelligence that was the culmination of all the prior preparation. The wise practitioner here is clearly not the single (virtuous) professional but an incipient virtuous community that is learning how to communicate more openly and honestly about the complex reality of the situation, who they really are in the face of it, and what they can do together. Bridging some of the borders that divided it, this is also a community that is making connections between institutional and personal violence and healing. In helping participants transform victimization into responsibility and create new ways of relating to authority figures, one another, and institutions, the process has demonstrated the possibilities of professional intervention to create educative sites for living and working democratically though the borders that normalcy creates.

Notes

1. This case was also featured in Keith (2011), which includes an extensive discussion of bodies of research and theory that relate to TST theory and practice. The names of the town and schools are changed to preserve anonymity.
2. Unless otherwise noted, references to TST theory and practice are drawn from Rojzman (2008, 2009), Rojzman and Pillods (1999), and Rojzman and Rojzman (2006). All except Rojzman and Pillods are in French. Novella Zett Keith is responsible for any translations. In French, TST is simply *thérapie sociale*. "Transformational" was added to its English name in part to distinguish it from an American form of social therapy that focuses on the health of the group and was developed by Fred Newman at the New York East Side Institute (see http://www.socialtherapygroup.com/approach.html). For the TST website see http://www.institut-charlesrojzman.com/.
3. For general background on consensus organizing, see Eichler (2006); group therapy, Yalom and Leszcz (2005); psychoanalysis, Winnicott (1987).
4. Data sources used in this chapter are verbatim notes and thematic summaries of the planning meeting and all meetings with students and adults. When the date is stated in the narrative, it should be understood that the source is field notes for that particular day. Théa Rojzman collected and transcribed verbatim data for most of the group sessions and wrote thematic analytical summaries that included observable nonverbal behaviors. Charles Rojzman provided clarifications and further analytical commentary relating the project to TST theory and practice. Novella Zett Keith translated from the French and analyzed the data.
5. Data analysis looks mainly at the youth–adult connection and does not unpack differences in the adult group. The selection of this focus, which was deliberate, doubtless misses an equally compelling story that awaits retelling.
6. The first set are recognizably ethnic names (Arabic, African), while the second set are 'white' French.
7. The *defended* subject, a psychoanalytic concept, was introduced into psychosocial research methods by Hollway and Jefferson (2000). Anxiety created by threats to the self and subconscious defenses against anxiety impede transparent communication. The researchers employ narrative approaches to overcome this problem. By addressing and contextualizing the emotional undercurrents beneath the conscious level, the TST process described in this case appears to constitute a valid method for producing trustworthy knowledge in psychosocial research.

PART 4
Going Forward

9

LOOKING BACKWARD TO GO FORWARD

As is fitting for a final chapter, the goal of this one is to look backward in order to go forward. The chapter offers a partial review of the book's main ideas, a distillation of the important conclusions, and some questions that you, the reader, might take forward into your practice. I hope that in addition to my list you will also develop a short list of insights and questions that come from your own interests and needs, which will help you grow into an ever-wiser border-crossing practitioner and democratic civic professional. If you are reading this book in a group setting, I invite you to do this with a circle of friends and as an exercise in collective intelligence. I begin with a brief review of the purposes of the book, the broad questions it set out to explore, and the path this exploration has taken.

Looking Backward

This book has considered two intertwined questions: what does it mean to be a democratic civic professional who engages in partnerships across campus-community divides and what supports are needed to become one. In the language of the higher education engagement movement, the questions have to do with supporting professionals who can move beyond community engagement as outreach to engagement as partnership. As I hope has been clear all along, my stand in this regard is resolutely on the side of universities serving as agents of democracy and social justice in our global age. I see campus-community partnerships as spaces where we can learn to work together in the spirit of mutual respect and power sharing, helping to bridge social divides that have been growing along with social, economic, political, and ideological polarization. I thus took to heart the message of the higher education engagement movement that democratic engagement is stalled and set about to understand the obstacles on the path and the way forward.

Many have focused on what needs to change systemically and organizationally—looking for instance at ways to make engagement part of the core mission of higher education institutions, aligning the structure of faculty rewards to new visions and missions, and undertaking the needed organizational development.[1] These issues are absolutely essential and are complementary to the task I set for myself. For instance, resources are needed to support networks and spaces that bridge campus and community and, indeed, provide the necessary professional growth opportunities. For my part, I chose to focus on the border-crossing aspects of campus-community collaborations, which involve often hidden dimensions of power and authority that community members may perceive as lack of respect and recognition. I thus emphasized the relational side of partnerships more than the organizational side and looked for obstacles mainly in the *normal* ways of being and enacting a professional, in normal or traditional practices, and in understandings of knowledge for practice. The first task in creating the democratic civic professional, then, involved looking for and interrupting normalcies that ran counter to its enactment.

This approach required both understanding what the new professionals should be like and what normalcies stood in their way. With regard to the first, I examined the research about what community partners desire in their higher education counterparts as well as constructs of the professional as expert, social trustee, and civic or civic-minded and democratic practitioner. Looking for normalcies that stand in the way took me in directions that are often seen as "outside" and "inside": I sought these normalcies in historical trends, institutionalized practices, and embodied dispositions. I hope I have conveyed sufficiently that the dichotomy is a false one. History and institutions are embodied in ourselves and, in turn, our dispositions and, broadly, our habitus, are tied to our collective experiences and structural social locations (for instance, as raced, classed, and gendered persons); they are not simply 'personal.'

I found in the historical periods of modernity and, more recently, neoliberalism pervasive and deeply held orientations to knowledge that emphasize certainty and systematicity and a preference for technocratic approaches to dealing with problems. These approaches favor efficiency, the expert professional as sole problem solver, technical/instrumental questions over value questions, and support engagement as outreach. Along with outreach through the expert professional, they also favor the separation of knowledge creation and its application: the researcher develops the knowledge base, the practitioner applies it, and the best research yields findings that are general rather than specific to a given situation. In their neoliberal form, these orientations create a passion for calculability as reflected in metrics and for knowledge as a marketable commodity. All of these are among the normalcies to be interrupted on the way to democratic civic professionalism. The critical and humanistic traditions in modernity do offer supports, generating democratic practices and like-minded professionals, but at the moment they seem overshadowed by neoliberal policies and orientations.

The second normalcy handed down by the modern period pertains to diversity; it is not about the expert's knowledge but about the binary constructs of Self and Other, which divide the world into those who are dominant, define reality, know, and are agents—Self—and those who are dominated or oppressed, defined, not knowers, not doers—Others—and are mainly known to Self in terms of their (supposed) deficits. Transforming this relation is especially important in border-crossing collaborations and I explored it through the lens of social justice as self-determination and recognition: the literature shows that these orientations are highly valued by community partners and their absence generates profound mistrust. These are important additions to the literature on collaboration, which does advance practices that may disrupt the normalcy of the expert but is limited when the collaboration involves crossing borders and not only boundaries.

Reviewing this literature brought us closer to understanding the construct of the democratic civic professional as border crosser and the kinds of supports needed to cultivate this 'new' professional. What we know about professionals and the professions suggests that we need to consider, beyond knowledge and skills, the professional and personal habitus to be cultivated and the kinds of collective supports (such as cross-border learning communities) needed for enacting the desired practice. Problematizing the notion of practice revealed the complexity and particularity of the practice situation: practice resides at the intersection between the practitioner, the situation, others who participate in the situation, and the contexts and systems in which all of these are embedded. Clearly, no practice situation is ever like any other and it is to this uniqueness and particularity that the practitioner's knowledge, understandings, and skills need to be attuned. Instead of the application of research-based best practices we have qualities of perception, insight, and judgment and learning through experience, cases, and thinking tools.

Enter phronesis (wise practice or practical wisdom) and the wise practitioner. This discussion helped clarify how knowledge for (wise) practice was different from two other types of knowledge: knowledge of things that are timeless and context independent (e.g., scientific, theoretical) and technical, skill-based knowledge. When considering the democratic civic professional and related practice through the lens of phronesis, knowledge for practice meant making sense of the practice situation, which involves perception, insight, and deliberation more than the analytical-technical methods traditionally associated with research; sensemaking is also guided and supported by values, the personal and professional qualities of the practitioner, and communities of learners—or circles of friends. Professional identity thus includes the virtues—the intellectual and character qualities—the practitioner embodies. Instead of technocratic, efficient, and value free actions we have practice that is guided by situated ethics and questions about the *good*: how will the practitioner's actions in this particular situation contribute to lives worthy of human dignity?

Phronesis is about virtuous or wise practice, but how do we get there? The discussion took up normalcy again, embodied here in the habitus and its interaction with particular fields of practice. In the previous iteration, normalcy referred back to modernity and its 'taken-for-granteds' (or hegemonic assumptions). That discussion had emphasized the process of normalization as described by Foucault, which is created through the power of language, or discourse. Its naturalness makes the normal mostly invisible to us—which is one reason for sifting through the long periods of history to catch normalized discourses in the making. This framework was especially useful for asking initial questions about obstacles to the good in campus-community partnerships, such as a technocratic mindset, the legitimacy of the discourse of the professional expert, and the discourse of rationality (and power disguised as rationality) and efficiency to justify decisions and actions taken.

Adding Bourdieu's habitus, field, and capital to the repertoire of thinking tools was consistent with Foucault's focus on the power of the normal but took us closer to actual practice and practitioners. In both our everyday and professional practice, we embody and recreate normalcies through the dispositions, attitudes, and orientations of the habitus, which partakes of history and collective experiences as well as experiences in more personal realms. Thus the importance of critical incidents whose disturbances, with guidance, help us glimpse those normal ways of being, thinking, feeling, and acting that are usually below the level of conscious awareness. The habitus is not necessarily virtuous in phronetic terms: it is about the qualities and orientations we develop as we interact in fields of practice and struggle with others over resources (capital) that are valued in those fields.

Using these thinking tools in the context of the phronetic framework shed further light on the guidance practitioners need as they reach toward wiser practice. The point was to consider the practitioner-in-context, the practitioner-situation interaction, and the ways the situation and, overall, the field of practice could be modified so as to cultivate qualities and sensemaking that would support desired constructions and enactments of the good.

While the earlier discussion of collaboration had pointed to differences between boundary crossing and border crossing, the ongoing development of the border-crossing theme fleshed out what was needed as a pre-task to enable partnership basics such as trust and open communication to be put in place:[2] the call was to disturb normalcies, especially with regard to the expert professional and Self-Other dichotomies and create border or third spaces that supported mutuality, shared power, respect, empathy, and recognition. Out of these spaces would emerge genuine collaboration informed by collective intelligence.

As elaborated in the book, collective intelligence entailed much more than polling and pulling together the knowledge, understandings, and action preferences of stakeholders, even if this was done collaboratively, through dialogue and deliberation. Here, collective intelligence became a new kind of wisdom. In the classic Aristotelian phronetic framework, wisdom is embodied in the person of the philosopher-king, the wise practitioner who is guided by his or her virtues and insight to construct and enact the good as is appropriate to a particular situation. The philosopher-king does not construct the good as an individual but as the perfect(ed) vessel through which flow ways of being excellent and ways of living well that carry the values of an entire community. But what is wisdom and its vessel when there is no community, a pseudocommunity, or the (possible) community is fractured? The task then is to facilitate and support the capacity of stakeholders and participants in a situation to become collectively wise; this is done by constructing processes and situations that help them mine their experiences, glimpse one another's knowledge and understandings, be in conflict, build relationships, and engage in more trusting, open, participatory, and respectful dialogues about what is worth doing, what is real, and what is possible.

Three processes were thus identified as being at the heart of collaboration across borders: disturbing the normal, Self-Other transformation, and creating collective intelligence. The next section provides selective examples from the cases in Part 3 that suggest how to engage these processes in ways that cultivate the capacities of the would-be democratic civic professional. I briefly review how aspects of the cases relate to each process and to the phronetic framework.

Three Processes for Collaborations across Borders

Relating the three border-crossing processes to the three phronetic aspects of the border-crossing partnership framework fleshes out the main tasks to be undertaken by the democratic civic professional. Table 9.1 captures this interaction. We can think of the processes in the left column of the table as a spiral that is also a continuum: as we move through interrupting and disturbing the normal, to Self-Other transformation and to collective intelligence we discover new normalcies to be interrupted, more nuanced aspects of Self-Other relations to be transformed, and deeper levels of collective intelligence. The three aspects of phronesis are listed in the top row. The items in each of the intersecting boxes were drawn from the cases in Chapters 6, 7, and 8 and thus are not in the order of general rules. Remember that situations are unique: the items could be used as a starting point for inquiry, but you should not assume that they will necessarily come up in each practice case.

If we think of interrupting the normal in terms of embodying the virtues, the items in the box (expert problem solver, etc.) are those orientations (or qualities) that come through modernity and the habitus, constitute obstacles, and generally need to be interrupted in order for virtues to emerge. When we engage in sensemaking through the lenses these orientations create, instead of seeing the practitioner and community partner as part of the practice situation and of social systems, we see them as separate individuals (the modern unencumbered self). The connection between the virtues and sensemaking should be clear: as orientations that constitute obstacles are disturbed, we begin to look at the situation

TABLE 9.1 Main Focuses of Professional's Practice in Border-crossing Partnership Framework

Aspects of Phronesis & Border-crossing Processes/Practice	Embodying the Virtues	Making Sense of the Situation	Constructing and Enacting the Good
Normalcies to be interrupted/disturbed	*Modernity and modern mindset:* expert knower/problem-solver; in-control technocrat; task-oriented (instrumental) leader *Habitus-field-capital:* dispositions and rules of the game that perpetuate advantage victim–oppressor binary	*Modernity and modern mindset:* individual as separate from situation/community problems/deficits as personal *Habitus-field-capital:* Structures and dispositions that support oppressive categorizations and self-serving understandings of the situation	*Modernity and modern mindset:* outreach, charity approaches to community needs; needs constructed from outsider/expert perspective *Habitus-field-capital:* disadvantaged ('at-risk') communities/populations as deficient and as the problem
Self-Other transformation	Developmental leader Heal relationships to enable dropping masks and showing vulnerability Accept (partial) responsibility—both are responsible actors	Awkwardness, uncertainty, and habitus disturbance as potentially positive Community and its members as human beings with capacities, emotions, and needs like one's own	Create structures that support: youth–adult ally; de-centering Self; resonance; respectful, equitable relationships authentic dialogue; all forms of social justice
Collective intelligence	Diverse group supports disturbance of habitus and cultivation of virtues Dialogue, reflection, and empathy enable all to share their information Entertain hope; motivated	Create supports for participants to share trustworthy information New knowledge contributes to novel, complex understandings of the situation	Co-construct possible actions that address authentic needs in the practice situation Create policies, practices, and relationships that support 'living well' for all stakeholders

differently. Thus interrupting and disturbing the normal is not just a matter of growing personally into a wiser practitioner but of seeing more of what is real in the situation. Similarly, if these orientations and sensemaking are not interrupted, proceeding to the next box we will construct the good largely in terms of outreach and charity to a community that is "in-need" and "at-risk." This means that, while we may be doing some good, in phronetic terms (recalling social justice values espoused by the community) we are not constructing the good at all.

Moving to the second row, Self-Other transformation can begin to take place once some obstructing normalcies have been interrupted. Here we begin to see some phronetic virtues—those of the developmental leader, for instance—and ways of making sense of the practice situation through these lenses, accepting and mining our disturbance as a positive event, looking for capabilities in the community, developing relationships grounded in the humanity of the other. The good here is constructed as processes that support Self-Other transformation. In the third row, the pre-task has been sufficiently accomplished and virtues and sensemaking that support collective intelligence are present. It is thus possible to construct and enact a good that, like the consensus approach we encountered in Chapter 2, benefits from information from all stakeholders and develops new understandings of the problem and new possibilities for action. Let me now briefly discuss the border-crossing processes, bringing in relevant examples. I take each one in turn but the discussion straddles the categories because, like the three aspects of phronesis, they also are interconnected.

Interrupting and Disturbing the Normal

In the context of the border-crossing partnership framework developed in the book, deciding which normalcies are helpful and thus can be retained and which constitute obstacles that must be interrupted is guided by one's sense of the good to be advanced in the particular situation. The good is always situation specific: how and what we see depends on emerging understandings of the reality of the situation and the possibilities it contains. In turn, as all the aspects of phronesis are interconnected, what we see and grasp in the situation is influenced by our habitus or, in phronetic terms, our virtues.

The cases explored this process with regard to normalcies that touched on the personal, relational, and organizational or associational levels of practice. For our purposes here, I focus on two types of normalcies: those that arise from modernity as discourse and mindset (also embodied in the habitus) and those that are specifically from one's habitus in interaction with various fields and capitals—understanding that they encompass all the above levels. In the Upland case (Chapter 6) I became aware of and began to shed the normal modern mindset of the expert and problem solver; I also became aware that in this particular situation I tended to be self-absorbed rather than direct and thus saw the situation through the lens of my desire to ignore. My self-awareness grew in the context of relationships, experiences, practice, and supportive circles of friends; all of these helped me become more open to the reality of the situation at the school and develop relationships that were more in line with being critical friends with my partners. We were thus able to seize the opportunity to make significant changes in the program (such as doing longer-term projects in the school) which furthered the good of student engagement and genuine partnerships in the student teams. With each turn, possibilities emerged that were not in view earlier.

Another normalcy seen in that chapter was that many of the college students (as represented by Alex) made sense of the high school students' behaviors through the lens of personal problems and character deficits rather than seeing the behavior as part of an interaction with the practice situation, including a response to the college students' own behavior. Not seeing these interacting factors, they concentrated on the tasks to be done at the expense of relationships to be developed. The students who embodied the qualities of the developmental leader (Jessica) were more in tune with the capabilities of the high school students, believing they could change, and changed their practice in ways that made the change possible. They thus engaged in Self-Other transformation. Like the student team in the third incident ("You people should get it together") they were able to pull together all the team members' information and develop a more thoughtful project that furthered the good of youth engagement and enacted the principle of working with the community and not doing service to it.

In all the cases, disturbing the normal was also achieved through partnership practices; practices that accorded with one's construction of the good also served to disturb the normal and support desired virtues. In Chapter 7 (the Advocate case), Billy's shedding of power took the form of including the North Stars teens in the process of deciding the theme of the next performance. De-centering the college students also interrupted a normalcy in service learning practice that constructs mutuality as equal participation or as the college students serving as young adult-youth allies (as happened in the Upland case). When the two sets of students met, as in the poetry workshop, there was Self-Other transformation through resonance, as they connected with one another, in a sense, by becoming the other, as they expressed through poetry each other's very human, emotional experiences. In Chapter 8 (the Maville case), normalcy was disturbed by inviting participants who were among the most marginalized and rebellious in the institution and finding expression for their "negative" emotions: violence was addressed through healing relationships rather than through the more normal repression and punishment.[3]

Self-Other Transformation

The previous section already indicated that a major purpose of disturbing the normal is Self-Other transformation, that is, to change the relationship of privilege and oppression where a dominant side is the definer and agent and the Other is defined and acted on. There is no possibility of collaboration as long as this remains the case, and thus embarking on this transformative process is essential to democratic engagement. As a quick reminder, Otherness is about much more than identity: the normalcy that the Other is deficient and incapable becomes justification for denying participation and recognition, and thus for maintaining a pervasive social, political, and economic injustice. In terms of recognition, Otherness makes it difficult to maintain one's self-worth in those areas where the oppression is strongest, such as the education system, and thus, as Chapter 8 showed, is implicated in educational failure.

Otherness was also visible when, as in the example I gave earlier, the college students did not have a developmental and young-adult ally relationship with the high school students. This did not necessarily mean that they saw them as Others; perhaps they judged them as they would judge a peer: "you didn't come through and so I'm not going to go out of my way to give you another chance." But they tended not to see the influence of their own dominance in the Self-Other relationship, how their whiteness and their privilege were seen by students on the other side. They did not see—as I did not, at first—the enormous weight of the intersecting oppressions of race and class and living in such a marginalized community, the sense of powerlessness and lack of hope that education can make a difference in one's life.

Staying with otherness before embarking on transformation, we can see its devastating effects on the high school students at Upland (Chapter 6). In commenting on a version of the chapter, coauthor Jim Peterson pointed out the incredibly oppressive effects of lack of hope in the educational system. The school and community were sites where:

> the majority of the residents had lost hope in the value of education to create positive change. . . . self-esteem was absent (a sense that the power to change was possible) from the majority of students and their families. The main cause of depression is a sense you have no power to control your destiny. A spark of interest, a small awakening, a sign of hope was a cause of celebration.

The vast majority of students faced a reality that they could hardly escape. Whereas the teachers could try to escape the reality of the school when they went home, there was no escape for the students, for whom home provided no relief. Being constructed as an Other by dominant parties did not make them puppets, as they defined themselves by different measures from the dominant standard. Music, dance, rap, and "fooling around" become their escape. Nonetheless, the oppressive nature of the relationship could not be shed because it was structural as well as personal, bringing together the combined effect of extreme poverty and social inequality, disparaged racial identities, and a school and neighborhood near the bottom of the social scale.

In this context, what did Self-Other transformation mean? On one level it meant taking the developmental leadership approach to changing the relation so that the high school students were able to begin to define the situation, to see themselves, vis-à-vis the college students, as powerful, knowledgeable, and having something to contribute. Let me quote Jim fully in retelling a very moving and powerful story that can be seen as part of Self-Other transformation and the Other exercising agency not by rebellion but through restored hope:

> for some of the students, [working on projects in the school, in partnership with the college students] instilled in them the power to change; by making a small change in their community, they were able to transform their destiny. I will never forget a former student . . . stopping and jumping out of his car screaming, "I got my college degree in Criminal Justice and it was your class that made me believe it was possible." College students perceived him as the kid [who was] not focused.

Thus, changing course structures and practices in ways that lead to greater collaboration and participation was itself part of the Self-Other transformation process.

Regarding Chapter 7, I already alluded in the previous section to the self-marginalization and de-centering of the college students who were literally removed from the possibility of being the definers. This could have happened even if they did not consciously engage the community in that way: the teens might have gone quiet, as they did in the Upland case. The point is that Self-Other is a structural as well as personal relation and this is what the process of transformation needs to address. The Advocate case did so by separating the two groups and taking them through a process that Billy constructed as involving both challenge and affirmation. The teens were taken through a process that may have been similar, learning a painful history but one whose struggle for justice gave them agency and a sense of self-worth. The community-art process also affirmed the community's power to choose which of its stories it wanted to tell.

Thus Self-Other transformation here was organized around separation and de-centering of the dominant group, which accepted (not without struggle) that the community of Others needed to find its power in this way, through separation. Understanding the different experiential meanings of integration would not be achieved by integrating the two groups for a common learning experience. Subsequently, they would have the capacities that would enable them to be equal partners. Self-Other transformation also happened through the process, in the college classroom, of disturbing the habitus and making space for conversations that shared experiences and worlds where the students could affirm their connections and common humanity. The guilt and vulnerability of the white students were expressed as well, and so lost some of their oppressive power.

The cases in Chapters 7 and 8 showed that the Self-Other relation is oppressive to both sides and that the transformation affects both. The college students' difficulties in accepting the separation and questioning their role in a community that was not their own manifested, at least for the students who participated in this course, a strong desire to connect, a growing understanding that segregation diminished their lives as well. Self-Other transformation was a very strong theme in Chapter 8, which adopted a particular process, TST, to accomplish it. What was especially powerful was the practice of assuming responsibility, the idea that we give up our power when we construct the situation as one of victims and oppressors and that we begin to reclaim our power when we accept we are all responsible agents. We certainly saw the teachers suffering a tremendous sense of powerlessness. All parties denied the other's humanity and, in a meaningful sense, both were Others to one another. Of course, the teachers' denied humanity and suffering were of a different order than those of the students: like the Upland teachers, they could go home both physically and figuratively, to privileged identities. In the language of TST, Self-Other involves violence and the transformation of this relation was healing. Working with the students to change the school was not only an exercise in action research leading to school reform: it meant a personal transformation, the weight of the world becoming a bit lighter on their shoulders.

Collective Intelligence

The final process is in some ways almost the starting point of a regular collaboration. Think of a planning exercise, where knowledge and information are pulled together by the stakeholders and there is deliberation about possibilities and what action to take. However, we would be missing something essential if we missed the motivation and emotions that accompany collective intelligence, which, especially in the Maville case, was accompanied by an eruption of energy.

I hope the cases have amply demonstrated that in border-crossing collaboration much more work needs to be done before coming to collective intelligence. The Maville case in Chapter 8 illustrates in much more detail than any of the others the process to collective intelligence as well as the outcome. But this process and its outcomes can also be glimpsed in the other cases. For instance, in Chapter 6 the third critical incident involving college students and neighborhood residents made the college students vulnerable and created a strong need and motivation to redeem themselves. Their tremendous faux pas revealed, to themselves and others and in ways that could not be glossed over, that they were inept outsiders, ignorant of the ways and problems of this community—which the high school students, as insiders, understood quite well. This very vulnerability was instrumental in changing the relation of college and high school students. It provided an opportunity for Self-Other transformation from which collective intelligence could emerge.

The incident was a powerful experience that demonstrated to all parties the value of neighborhood knowledge, but this would not have been enough for them to move to collective intelligence. Three steps were essential to the process: facilitation that helped the students create useful knowledge out of the experience, facilitation of the interaction between college and high school students, and the presence of a project they needed to accomplish together. Without these elements, the more likely outcome would have been each side retreating to its own group, the one to lick their wounds and explain away the incident, the others to laugh, for once, about the outsiders' incompetence. Both sides, in other words, would have dished out different kinds of violence in ways that were invisible to the other but effective nonetheless in supporting ongoing Self-Other relations.

Coming from professional orientations that stress the technical and instrumental, we should not underestimate the role played by the need to accomplish something together, which was not only instrumental. It was as if the critical incident awoke another need, to see each other's humanity. There was more than instrumental motivation for sharing information. This is an important aspect of collective intelligence as developed here: it is not just an instrumental/technical matter of sharing information but of being motivated to share it because we have something to gain by doing so, and that something is psychic as well. It releases energies that are normally held in a depressing cycle of despair through powerlessness, hopelessness, and feeling like victims. The mutuality of motivation was much stronger in the Maville case, where there was so much more at stake: transforming the school not only as an exercise in school reform, but to transform the students' and teachers' daily lives. It was this hope that supported the motivation to take the risk of being vulnerable. What we saw in Chapter 8 was a movement between despair and hope that pushed the group toward the willingness to take the risk to engage with one another.

The Advocate case shows still another face of collective intelligence. Here the students and community members gave voice to their stories—the ones *they* wanted to tell—through the oral history and arts process and through border pedagogy. As Billy progressively shed his role as artistic director, the community became the agent who pulled together the information that went into the performance. The artistic distillation gave this knowledge of who they were back to the whole community—and especially to its young people—so they could see themselves in new, more hopeful ways. Thus the artistic production brought together what each stakeholder knew in ways that, like in the Maville case, generated new energies. The point is that collective intelligence was grounded in a deep need and interest in the project to be done together; emotions were involved and everyone stood to gain something important and meaningful. They took risks. And out of it came a sense of celebration and a release of hope.

Going Forward: Some Things to Remember and Questions to Keep Asking

These are some questions that came to my mind as I was thinking of how to conclude this chapter and the book. As I said in the beginning, my hope is that you will also develop your own lists and, perhaps, share them with me.

As you enter a partnership:

1. Who are *you* and who are *they*? Not only as individuals but as people with histories, emotions, and experiences that are part of who you and they are (remember the habitus-field-capital interaction).
2. What qualities do you have that are valuable and useful in this particular situation? What qualities create obstacles and make the work challenging for you?

Working in partnership:

3. What is this particular situation like? Who are you and who are they in it? What is visible and what is invisible but still part of the situation? How do all these influence the situation and interactions?
4. When you make sense of the situation, what does it remind you of from your past? What influences what you see and how you see it? Talk to others who might see it differently.
5. What emotions are you experiencing? What are the sources of your emotions and especially your emotional *reactions*? How do they relate to things you have experienced in your own life and your identity group has experienced historically? In what discourses do the stories you tell yourself about these emotions and reactions fit?
6. Put yourself in the other's place and ask the same questions.
7. Try being a little vulnerable: share some of your fears with others, in moderation, even if you're afraid to do it. Take some risks and drop your masks a little. Do it with people you wouldn't normally seek out for this kind of sharing, even those you don't immediately like.
8. How might ways of being and acting that are normal to you be power games and engender reactions and resistance in the other?
9. If you're dominant, try marginalizing yourself a little!
10. As a facilitator and guide, support all of these; help create relationships and circles of (critical) friends.

Conclusion

What needs to change? I still believe that the academic has a considerable contribution to make but I am no longer sure about what that contribution is. The process of thinking about the subject matter of this book and about practical wisdom has changed me. And yet, changed perceptions are a source of creativity.

With this book, I have wanted to promote a vision of the common good and the good society. It is a society with more equity and justice, a deep sort of democracy, one in which we are able to work together—to struggle together—and build a common future out of a fractured, oppression-ridden, and very imperfect past and present. I see the purpose of university-community partnerships as, somehow, furthering this vision. This does not mean we will achieve consensus and that differences will disappear. Differences can be enriching and some truths can be found (partial though they always are) in the spaces between different stories, different positionalities, and very different experiences. Thus my vision is not one in which differences are erased and dissolved, but one in which we can surface more of these repressed emotions, memories, and stories and use them collectively to begin to heal ourselves, our institutions, and societies. The starting place is to make whatever difference we can make wherever we are. What is your vision? Think about it. Join with others. Reach together toward a hope that is not afraid to see reality as it is rather than as illusion and thus becomes the ground for forging new human possibilities.

Notes

1. As I completed this chapter, I received an e-mail announcement for the second annual Engagement Academy for University Leaders. The Engagement Academy is a national effort that dates back to 2008 and aims to create institutional capacity for community engagement in higher education. For background information and resources see http://www.cpe.vt.edu/engagementacademy/.
2. The term 'pre-task' comes from Charles Rojzman's work. It refers to all that is involved in creating a *group*, before which there can be no meaningful or *real* collaboration.
3. James Comer's (2004) School Development Program also emphasizes developing relationships by addressing violence, emotional stress, mental health, and healing. This is a long-standing successful program, quite unique in taking this approach to educational change. Comer is a psychiatrist based at Yale University.

REFERENCES

Adichie, C. N. (2009, October). *Talks: Chimamanda Ngozi Adichie: The danger of a single story*. Retrieved May 24, 2010, from TED Ideas Worth Spreading: http://www.ted.com/talks/chimamanda_adichie_the_danger_of_a_single_story.html

Alexander, B. C. (1991). *Victor Turner revisited: Ritual as social change*. Atlanta, GA: Scholars Press.

Alexander, M. (2010). *The new Jim Crow: Mass incarceration in the age of colorblindness*. New York: New Press.

Alterman, E. (2012, April 26). *Think again: How classical liberalism morphed into New Deal liberalism*. Retrieved October 4, 2012, from Center for American Progress: http://www.americanprogress.org/issues/media/news/2012/04/26/11379/think-again-how-classical-liberalism-morphed-into-new-deal-liberalism/

Anderson, J., & Honneth, A. (2005). Autonomy, vulnerability, recognition, and justice. In J. Christman & J. Anderson (Eds.), *Autonomy and the challenges to liberalism* (pp. 127–149). New York: Cambridge University Press.

Anzaldúa, G. (1985). *Borderlands/La frontera: The new mestiza*. San Francisco: Aunt Lute Books.

Archer, L. (2008). The new neoliberal subjects? Young/er academics' constructions of professional identity. *Journal of Educational Policy, 23*(3), 265–285.

Argyris, C. (1991, May–June). Teaching smart people how to learn. *Harvard Business Review*, 99–109.

Arnold, M. E., Dolenc, B., & Wells, E. E. (2008). Youth community engagement: A recipe for success. *Journal of Community Engagement and Scholarship, 1*(1), 56–65.

Asset-Based Community Development Institute. (n.d.). *ABCD toolkit*. Evanston, IL: Northwestern University School of Education and Social Policy, Asset Based Community Development Institute. Retrieved November 11, 2013, from http://www.abcdinstitute.org/toolkit/

Association of American Colleges & Universities [AAC&U]. (n.d.). *Civic engagement value rubric*. Retrieved March 11, 2012, from http://www.aacu.org/value/rubrics/pdf/civicengagement.pdf

Austin, J. E. (2000, Fall). Principles for partnership. *Leader to Leader, 2000*(18), 44–50.

Banks, J. (2008). Diversity, group identity, and citizenship education in a global age. *Educational Researcher, 37*(3), 129–139.

Barber, B. R. (2004). *Strong democracy: Participatory politics for a new age*. Berkeley: University of California Press. (Original work published 1984).

Barker, D. W., Allen, A. D., Robinson, A., Sulimani, F., VanderVeen, Z., & Walker, D. M. (2011, March). Research on civic capacity: An analysis of Kettering literature and related scholarship. Kettering Foundation Working Paper 2011–1. Retrieved November 20, 2013, from http://kettering.org/wp-content/uploads/Barker-Civic-Capacity-Final-KFWP-2011–011.pdf

Bartunek, J. M. (2007). Practitioner collaboration need not require joint or relevant research: Toward a relational scholarship of integration. *Academy of Management Journal, 50*(6), 1323–1333.

Battistoni, R. M. (2013). Civic learning through service learning: Conceptual frameworks and research. In P. H. Clayton, R. G. Bringle, & J. A. Hatcher (Eds.), *Research on service learning: Conceptual frameworks and assessment* (vol. 2A, pp. 111–132). Sterling, VA: Stylus.

Baty, P. (2012, June 26). *Rankings don't tell the whole story—Handle them with care*. Retrieved June 26, 2012, from University World News Global Edition: http://www.universityworldnews.com/article.php?story=20120626171938451

Baxter Magolda, M. B. (2012). Building learning partnerships. *Change Magazine, 44*(1), 32–38.

Beere, C. A., Votruba, J. C., & Wells, G. W. (2011). *Becoming an engaged campus: A practical guide for institutionalizing public engagement*. San Francisco: Jossey-Bass.

Belenky, M. F., Bond, L. A., & Weinstock, J. S. (1997). *A tradition that has no name: Nurturing the development of people, families, and communities*. New York: Basic.

Bensimon, E. M. (2007). The underestimated significance of practitioner knowledge in the scholarship of student success. *Review of Higher Education, 30*(4), 441–469.

Benson, L., & Harkavy, I. (2002). The role of community-higher education-school partnerships in educational and social development and democratization. *Universities and Community Schools, 7*(1–2), 5–28.

Benson, L., Harkavy, I., & Puckett, J. (2007). *Dewey's dream: Universities and democracies in an age of education reform*. Philadelphia: Temple University Press.

Berger, B. (2009). Political theory, political science and the end of civic engagement. *Perspectives on Politics, 7*(2), 335–350.

Biesta, G. (2007). Why 'what works' won't work: Evidence-based practice and the democratic deficit in educational research. *Educational Theory, 57*(1), 1–22.

Bigelow, J. D. (2004). Using problem-based learning to develop skills in solving unstructured problems. *Journal of Management Education, 28*(5), 591–609.

Blass, E. (2010, December). The failure of professional self-regulation: The example of the UK veterinary profession. *Journal of Business Systems, Governance and Ethics, 5*(4), 1–12.

Boas, T. C., & Gans-Morse, J. (2009). Neoliberalism: From new liberal philosophy to anti-liberal slogan. *Studies in Comparative International Development, 44*(2), 137–161.

Bologna for Pedestrians. (2009). Council of Europe Portal. Retrieved June 26, 2012, from http://www.coe.int/t/dg4/highereducation/EHEA2010/BolognaPedestrians_en.asp#P132_13851

Bonnen, J. T. (1997). The land-grant idea and the evolving outreach university. In R. M. Lerner, & L. A. Simon (Eds.), *University-community collaborations for the twenty-first century: Outreach to scholarship for youth and families* (pp. 25–70). New York: Garland.

Booth, W. J. (2008). The work of memory: Time, identity, and justice. *Social Research, 75*(1), 237–262.

Borrup, T. (2005, September). *What's revolutionary about valuing assets as a strategy in cultural work?* Retrieved March 16, 2012, from Community Arts Network Reading Room: http://wayback.archive-it.org/2077/20100906203706/http://www.communityarts.net/readingroom/archivefiles/2005/09/radical_whats_r.php

Boud, D., Cressey, P., & Docherty, P. (Eds.). (2006). *Productive reflection at work: Learning for changing organizations.* London: Routledge.

Bourdieu, P. (1977). *Outline of a theory of practice* (R. Nice, Trans.). Cambridge: Cambridge University Press.

Bourdieu, P. (1989). Social space and symbolic power. *Sociological Theory, 7*(1), 14–25.

Bourdieu, P., & Wacquant, L. J. (1992). *An invitation to reflexive sociology.* Chicago: University of Chicago Press.

Boyer, E. L. (1990). *Scholarship reconsidered.* New York: Carnegie Foundation for the Advancement of Teaching.

Boyer, E. L. (1996). The scholarship of engagement. *Journal of Public Service and Outreach, 1*(1), 11–20.

Boyte, H. C. (2003). A different kind of politics: John Dewey and the meaning of citizenship in the 21st century. *The Good Society, 12*(3), 1–15.

Boyte, H. C. (2004). *Everyday politics: Reconnecting citizens and public life.* Philadelphia: University of Pennsylvania Press.

Boyte, H. C., & Fretz, E. (2010). Civic professionalism. *Journal of Higher Education Outreach and Engagement, 14*(2), 67–90.

Boyte, H. L., & Hollander, E. (1999). *Wingspread declaration on renewing the civic mission of the American research university.* Retrieved November 20, 2013, from Miami University Office of Civic and Community Engagement, Research on Civic Health and Engagement: http://www.miami.edu/index.php/civic_community_engagement/resources/research

Bringle, R. G., & Hatcher, J. A. (2002). Campus-community partnerships: The terms of engagement. *Journal of Social Issues, 58*(3), 503–516.

Bringle, R. G., Studer, M., Wilson, J., Clayton, P. H., & Steinberg, K. S. (2011, June). Designing programs with a purpose: To promote civic engagement for life. *Journal of Academic Ethics, 9,* 149–164.

Brint, S. (1994). *In an age of experts: The changing roles of professionals in political and public life.* Princeton, NJ: Princeton University Press.

Brint, S. (2001, March). *Gemeinschaft* revisited: A critique and reconstruction of the community concept. *Sociological Theory, 19*(1), 1–23.

Brookfield, S. D. (2011). *Teaching for critical thinking: Tools and techniques to help students question their assumptions.* San Francisco: Jossey-Bass.

Bryk, A. S., Bender Sebring, P., Allensworth, E., Luppescu, S., & Easton, J. Q. (2010). *Organizing schools for improvement: Lessons from Chicago.* Chicago: University of Chicago Press.

Butin, D. W. (2006). The limits of service-learning in higher education. *Review of Higher Education, 29*(4), 473–498.

Camino, L. (2005). Pitfalls and promising practices of youth-adult partnerships: An evaluator's reflections. *Journal of Community Psychology, 33*(1), 75–85.

Campus Compact. (n.d.). *TRUCEN.* Retrieved May 27, 2012, from Campus Compact: http://www.compact.org/initiatives/civic-engagement-at-research-universities/

Campus Compact. (n.d.). *Who we are.* Retrieved February 2, 2010, from Campus Compact: http://www.compact.org/about/history-mission-vision/

Canet, R., Pech, L., & Stewart, M. (2008, November 18). *France's burning issue: Understanding the urban riots of November 2005*. Retrieved December 5, 2009, from Social Science Research Network: http://ssrn.com/abstract=1303514

Carnegie Foundation. (n.d.). *Community engagement classification*. Retrieved April 16, 2011, from Carnegie Foundation for the Advancement of Teaching: http://classifications.carnegiefoundation.org/descriptions/community_engagement.php

Carr, W. (2006). Philosophy, methodology and action research. *Journal of Philosophy of Education, 40*(4), 421–435.

Castells, M. (2010). *The rise of the network society* (2nd ed.). Malden, MA: Blackwell.

Catalano, R. F., Berglund, M. L., Ryan, J. A., Lonczak, H. S., & Hawkins, J. D. (2004, January). Positive youth development in the United States: Research findings on evaluations of positive youth development programs. *ANNALS of the American Academy of Political and Social Science, 591*(1), 98–124.

Center for Democracy and Citizenship. (2012). *Reinventing citizenship: The practice of public work*. Retrieved July 20, 2012, from University of Minnesota Extension: http://www.extension.umn.edu/distribution/citizenship/dh6586.html

Chevannes, P. (2011, June 10). *The change from within programme*. Lecture, Temple University International Service Learning Summer Abroad Program. University of the West Indies, Mona, Jamaica.

Chrisafis, A. (2006, April). *We will not be thrown away! France's student uprising*. Retrieved January 4, 2007, from *The Nation:* http://www.thenation.com/doc/20060424/chrisafis

Clayton, P. H., & Ash, S. L. (2004, Fall). Shifts in perspective: Capitalizing on the counter-normative nature of service-learning. *Michigan Journal of Community Service Learning*, 59–70.

Cochran-Smith, M., & Lytle, S. L. (2009). Teacher inquiry as stance. In S. E. Noffke & B. Somekh (Eds.), *The Sage handbook of educational action research* (pp. 39–49). Thousand Oaks, CA: Sage.

Coleman, Y. (2006, January/February). *The French riots: Dancing with the wolves*. Retrieved January 4, 2007, from Solidarity: http://www.solidarity-us.org/node/33

Comer, J. P. (2004). *Leave no child behind: Preparing today's youth for tomorrow's world*. New Haven: Yale University Press.

Community-Campus Partnerships for Health [CCPH]. (2007). *Achieving the promise of authentic community-higher education partnerships: Community partners speak out!* Retrieved May 2, 2011, from University of Washington: http://depts.washington.edu/ccph/pdf_files/CPSReport_final1.15.08.pdf

Connell, R. W. (1993). *Education and social justice*. Philadelphia: Temple University Press.

Corporation for National and Community Service [CNCS]. (n.d.). *Our mission and guiding principles*. Retrieved October 16, 2011, from Corporation for National and Community Service: http://www.nationalservice.gov/about/role_impact/mission.asp

Craig, C. J. (2013, January). Coming to know in the 'eye of the storm': A beginning teacher introduction to different versions of teacher community. *Teaching and Teacher Education, 29*, 25–38.

Craig, R. (1994). The face we put on: Carl Jung for teachers. *Clearinghouse, 67*(4), 189–191.

Cress, C. M., Collier, P. J., Reitenauer, V. L., & Associates. (2005). *Learning through serving: A student guidebook for service-learning across the disciplines*. Sterling, VA: Stylus.

Crossley, N. (2013). Pierre Bourdieu's habitus. In T. Sparrow & A. Hutchinson (Eds.), *A history of habit: From Aristotle to Bourdieu* (pp. 291–307). Lanham, MD: Lexington Books.

Darling-Hammond, L., Chung Wei, R., Andree, A., Richardson, N., & Orphanos, S. (2009). *Professional learning in the learning profession: A status report on teacher* development in the United States and abroad. Dallas, TX: National Staff Development Council and School Redesign Network.

Deans, T. (1999). Paulo Freire's critical pedagogy in relation to John Dewey's pragmatism. *Michigan Journal of Community Service Learning, 6,* 15–29.

Denning, S. (2011). Reinventing management: The practices that enable continuous innovation. *Strategy & Leadership, 39*(3), 16–24.

Dessel, A., & Rogge, M. E. (2008). Evaluation of intergroup dialogue: A review of the empirical literature. *Conflict Resolution Quarterly, 26*(2), 199–238.

Dreese, D., Dutton, T. A., Neumeier, B., & Wilkey, C. (2008). A people's history: Teaching an urban neighborhood as a place of social empowerment. *transFORMATIONS, 19*(1), 138–158.

Dryfoos, J. G., Quinn, J., & Barkin, C. (Eds.). (2005). *Community schools in action: Lessons from a decade of practice.* New York: Oxford University Press.

DuFour, R. (2004, May). What is a professional learning community? *Educational Leadership,* 7–11. Retrieved October 23, 2013, from ALLTHINGSPLC: http://www.allthingsplc.info/pdf/articles/DuFourWhatIsAProfessionalLearningCommunity.pdf

Dunne, J., & Pendlebury, S. (2003). Practical reason. In N. Blake, P. Smeyers, R. Smith, & P. Standish (Eds.), *Blackwell guide to the philosophy of education* (pp. 194–212). Malden, MA: Blackwell.

Durlak, J. A., Weissberg, R. P., Dymnicki, A. B., Taylor, R. D., & Schellinger, K. B. (2011, January/February). The impact of enhancing students' social and emotional learning: A meta-analysis of school-based universal interventions. *Child Development, 82*(1), 405–432.

Egart, K., & Healy, M. P. (2004). An urban leadership internship program. In M. B. Baxter Magolda, & P. M. King (Eds.), *Learning partnerships: Theory and models of practice to educate for self-authorship* (pp. 125–150). Sterling, VA: Stylus.

Eichler, M. (2006). *Consensus organizing, building communities of mutual self interest.* Thousand Oaks, CA: Sage.

Ekman, J., & Amnå, E. (2009). Political participation and civic engagement: Toward a new typology. *Youth and Society Working Paper 2009: 2.* Sweden: School of Social Sciences, Södertörn University.

Ellett, F. S. (2012). Practical rationality and a recovery of Aristotle's 'phronesis' for the professions. In E. A. Kinsella & A. Pitman (Eds.), *Phronesis as professional knowledge: Practical wisdom in the professions* (pp. 13–33). Rotterdam: Sense.

Emerson, K., Nabatchi, T., & Balogh, S. (2012). An integrative framework for collaborative governance. *Journal of Public Administration Research and Theory, 22*(1), 1–29.

Epstein, J. L., Coates, L. S., Sanders, M., & Simon, B. (1997). *School, family, community partnerships: Your handbook for action.* Thousand Oaks, CA: Corwin.

Essed, P. (2002). Everyday racism. In D. T. Goldberg & J. Solomos (Eds.), *A companion to racial and ethnic studies* (pp. 228–245). Oxford, UK: Blackwell.

Felman, S. (1982). Psychoanalysis and education: Teaching terminable and interminable. *Yale French Studies, 1982*(63), 21–44.

Flyvbjerg, B. (2001). *Making social science matter: Why social inquiry fails and how it can succeed again.* Cambridge: Cambridge University Press.

Foucault, M. (1984). *The Foucault reader* (P. Rabinow, Ed.). New York: Pantheon.

Freire, P. (1991). *Pedagogy of the oppressed (anniversary edition).* New York: Continuum.

Fung, A. (2006). Varieties of participation in complex governance. *Public Administration Review, 66,* 66–75.

Gadamer, H.-G. (1989). *Truth and method* (2nd ed.). New York: Continuum.

Gajda, R. (2004). Utilizing collaboration theory to evaluate strategic alliances. *American Journal of Evaluation, 25*(1), 65–77.

Gay, G. (2010). *Culturally responsive teaching: Theory, research, and practice* (2nd ed.). New York: Teachers College Press.

Gherardi, S. (2009). Introduction: The critical power of the 'practice lens'. *Management Studies, 40*(2), 115–128.

Gibson, C. M. (2006). New times demand new scholarship: Research universities and civic engagement, a leadership agenda. Tufts University & Campus Compact. Retrieved January 16, 2013, from http://www.compact.org/initiatives/trucen/new-times-demand-new-scholarship/

Giles, D. E., & Eyler, J. (1994). The theoretical roots of service-learning in John Dewey: Toward a theory of service learning. *Michigan Journal of Community Service Learning, 1*(1), 77–85.

Gini in the bottle. (2013, November 26). *The Economist*. Retrieved April 10, 2014, from http://www.economist.com/blogs/democracyinamerica/2013/11/inequality-america

Giri, A. K. (2006). Cosmopolitanism and beyond: Towards a multiverse of transformations. *Development and Change, 37*(6), 1277–1292.

Glass, C. R., Doberneck, D. M., & Schweitzer, J. H. (2011). Unpacking faculty engagement: The types of activities faculty members report as publicly engaged scholarship during promotion and tenure. *Journal of Higher Education Outreach and Engagement, 15*(1), 7–30.

Goffman, E. (1959). *The presentation of self in everyday life*. New York: Anchor Books.

Goldbard, A. (2005). *Art/vision/voice: Cultural conversations in community*. Retrieved January 30, 2010, from Maryland Institute College of Art, CAP Casebook: http://www.mica.edu/Documents/community/artvisionvoice_casebook.pdf

Goldsmith, S., & Eggers, W. D. (2004). *Governing by network: The new shape of the public sector*. Washington, DC: Brookings Institution.

Habermas, J. (1971). *Knowledge and human interests* (J. Shapiro, Trans.). Boston: Beacon.

Hager, P., Lee, A., & Reich, A. (2012). Problematising practice: Reconceptualising learning and imagining change. In P. Hager, A. Lee, & A. Reich (Eds.), *Practice, learning and change: Practice-theory perspectives* (pp. 1–14). Dordrecht: Springer Science + Business Media.

Hamilton, N. W. (2002). *Academic ethics: Problems and materials on professional conduct and shared governance*. Westport, CT: American Council on Education/Praeger.

Hammes, T. X. (2010, 1st Quarter). Private contractors in conflict zones: The good, the bad, and the strategic impact. *Joint Force Quarterly, 2011*(60), 26–37. Retrieved March 11, 2014, from http://oai.dtic.mil/oai/oai?verb=getRecord&metadataPrefix=html&identifier=ADA536906

Hansman, C. A. (2001, Spring). Context-based adult learning. *New Directions for Adult and Continuing Education, 89*, 43–51.

Hargreaves, A. G. (2009, September 24). *'Race' and the republic*. Retrieved January 12, 2010, from Indiana University Center for European Studies: http://vimeo.com/7599513

Harkavy, I., & Puckett, J. (1994, September). Lessons from Hull House for the contemporary urban university. *Social Service Review*, 299–321. Retrieved September 29, 2005, from http://comm-org.wisc.edu/papers96/hull.html

Hart, A., & Wolff, D. (2006). Developing local 'communities of practice' through local community-university partnerships. *Planning, Practice & Research, 21*(1), 121–138.

Hatcher, J. A. (2008). *The public role of professionals: Developing and evaluating the civic-minded professional scale*. PhD dissertation, Indiana University. Retrieved March 22, 2012, from https://scholarworks.iupui.edu/handle/1805/1703

Hatcher, J. A. (2011, Spring). Assessing civic knowledge and engagement. *New Directions for Institutional Research, 2011*(149), 81–92.

Haub, C. (2009, Fall). Our national demographic future: U.S. population could reach 438 million by 2050, and immigration is key. *Pop!ulation Press, 15*(3), 10–12.

Hazelkorn, E. (2011, July 31). Global: Do rankings promote trickle down knowledge? *University World News, 182.* Retrieved August 8, 2011, from University World News: http://www.universityworldnews.com/article.php?story=20110729142059135

Hemsley-Brown, J., & Oplatka, I. (2006). Universities in a competitive global market: A systematic review of the literature on higher education marketing. *International Journal of Public Sector Management, 19*(4), 316–338.

Héraud, J.-L. (July 2007). *De la reforme au changement: Une étude de cas—La mise en oeuvre de la reforme Ambition Réussite dans le réseau d'enseignement prioritaire Garcia Lorca.* Master's thesis, Université de Marne la Vallée, France.

Herendeen, E. (2010, June 2). *Creating resonance.* Retrieved August 10, 2013, from Contemporary American Theater Festival at Shepherd University: http://catf.org/creating-resonance/

Hesse, H. (1973). Inside and outside. In *Stories of five decades* (pp. 258–270). New York: Farrar, Straus & Giroux. (Original work published 1920).

Hochschild, A. R. (2003). *The managed heart: Commercialization of human feeling.* Berkeley: University of California Press. (Original work published 1983).

Hochschild, J. L. (2008). Clarence N. Stone and the study of urban politics. In M. Orr & V. C. Johnson (Eds.), *Power in the city: Clarence Stone and the politics of inequality.* Retrieved December 22, 2013, from http://scholar.harvard.edu/jlhochschild/publications/clarence-n-stone-and-study-urban-politics

Hollway, W., & Jefferson, T. (2000). *Doing qualitative research differently: Free association, narrative and the interview method.* Thousand Oaks, CA: Sage.

Honnet, E. P., & Poulsen, S. J. (1994). *Principles of good practice for combining service and learning.* Racine, WI: Wingspread.

Horton, M., & Freire, P. (1990). *We make the road by walking: Conversations on education and social change.* (B. Bell, J. Gaventa, & J. Peters, Eds.). Philadelphia: Temple University Press.

Horvat, E. M., & Davis, J. E. (2011). Schools as sites for transformation: Exploring the contribution of habitus. *Youth & Society, 43*(1), 142–170.

Howard, J. P. (1998). Academic service learning: A counternormative pedagogy. *New Directions for Teaching and Learning, 73,* 21–29.

Howard, R. W., Berkowitz, M. W., & Schaeffer, E. F. (2004). Politics of character education. *Educational Policy, 18*(1), 188–215.

Hoy, A., & Johnson, M. (Eds.). (2013). *Deepening community engagement in higher education.* New York: Palgrave Macmillan.

Hoyt, L. (2010). A city-campus engagement theory from, and for, practice. *Michigan Journal of Community Service Learning, 17*(1), 75–88.

Huber, J., & Harkavy, I. (Eds.). (2007). *Higher Education and Democratic Culture: Citizenship, Human Rights and Civic Responsibility.* Strasbourg: Council of Europe Publishing.

Hursthouse, R. (1999). *On virtue ethics.* Oxford: Oxford University Press.

Hurtado, S., Ruiz, A., & Whang, H. (2012). *Assessing students' social responsibility and civic learning.* Presented at the Annual Forum of the Association for Institutional Research, New Orleans. Retrieved December 22, 2013, from http://www.heri.ucla.edu/pub/AssessCivicLearning.pdf

Inkeles, A. (1975). Becoming modern: Individual change in six developing countries. *Ethos, 3*(2), 323–342.

Jackins, T. (2001). Working together to end racism; Healing the damage caused by racism [Pamphlet]. Seattle: Rational Island. Retrieved July 10, 2009, from http://www.rc.org/uer/UERPublications.html

Jacob, M. J. (1995). An unfashionable audience. In S. Lacy (Ed.), *Mapping the terrain: New genre public art* (pp. 50–59). Seattle: Seattle Bay Press.

Jacoby, B. (2009). Civic engagement in today's higher education: An overview. In B. Jacoby & Associates (Eds.), *Civic engagement in higher education: Concepts and practices* (pp. 5–30). San Francisco: Jossey-Bass.

Jha, J., & Kelleher, F. (2006). *Boys' underachievement in education: An exploration in selected Commonwealth countries*. London: Commonwealth Secretariat and Commonwealth Learning. Retrieved April 6, 2013, from http://dspace.col.org/bitstream/123456789/85/1/BoysUnderachievement.pdf

Juris, J. (2007). A new way of doing politics: Global justice movements and the cultural logic of networking. *Recherches Sociologiques et Antropologiques, 38*(1), 127–142.

Keaton, T. (2005). Arrogant assimilationism: National identity politics and African-origin Muslim girls in the other France. *Anthropology and Education Quarterly, 36*(4), 405–423.

Keith, N. Z. (1999). Whose community schools? New discourses, old patterns. *Theory Into Practice, 38*(4), 224–234.

Keith, N. Z. (2005). Community service learning in the face of globalization: Rethinking theory and practice. *Michigan Journal of Community Service Learning, 11*(2), 5–24.

Keith, N. Z. (2010). Getting beyond anaemic love: From the pedagogy of cordial relations to a pedagogy for difference. *Journal of Curriculum Studies*, 1–34 (first published on December 7, 2009).

Keith, N. Z. (2011). From mistrust to collaboration: Using Transformational Social Therapy to support participation in school–community educational reform in a French *banlieue*. In C. Hands & L. Hubbard (Eds.), *Including families and communities in urban education* (pp. 235–266). Charlotte, NC: Information Age.

Keith, N. Z., Cavanaugh, C., Islam, S., Hafiz, F., Mather, K., & Soler, J. (2003, March 1). *Partnerships as new ground: Between private enterprise and democratic possibilities*. Practitioner Keynote, Ethnography in Education Research Forum, University of Pennsylvania, Philadelphia.

Keith, N. Z., & Hafiz, F. (2002). *Working with the community*. International Service Learning Research Conference, Nashville, TN.

Keith, N. Z., & Keith, N. W. (2010, June). Philosophy of modernity and development in Jamaica. *CLCWeb: Comparative Literature and Culture, 12*(2), Article 6.

Kellogg Commission on the Future of State and Land Grant Universities. (1999, February). *Returning to our roots: The engaged institution*. Washington, DC: National Association of State Universities and Land Grant Colleges. Retrieved October 16, 2014, from http://community-wealth.org/content/returning-our-roots-engaged-institution

Kemmis, S. (2010). What is professional practice? Recognizing and respecting diversity in understandings of practice. In C. Kanes (Ed.), *Elaborating professionalism: Studies in practice and theory* (pp. 139–165). Dordrecht: Springer.

Kettering Foundation. (n.d.). *Our focus*. Retrieved June 29, 2012, from Kettering Foundation: http://kettering.org/who-we-are/our-focus/

Kettl, D. F. (2000). *The global public management revolution; A report on the transformation of governance*. Washington, DC: Brookings Institution.

Kincheloe, J. L., & Hayes, K. (Eds.). (2007). *Teaching city kids: Understanding and appreciating them*. New York: Peter Lang.

Kinsella, E. A., & Pitman, A. (Eds.). (2012). *Phronesis as professional knowledge: Practical wisdom in the professions*. Rotterdam: Sense.

Korza, P., Schaffer Bacon, B., & del Vecchio, M. (2008). *Arts & civic engagement tool kit: Planning tools and resources for animating democracy in your community*. Washington, DC: Animating Democracy.

Kretzmann, J. P., & McKnight, J. L. (1997). *A guide to capacities inventories: Mobilizing the community skills of local residents*. Chicago: ACTA. Retrieved August 19, 2001, from http://www.abcdinstitute.org/docs/CapacityInventories.pdf

Küpers, W. M. (2013). The art of practical wisdom: Phenomenology of an embodied, wise 'inter-practice' in organisation and leadership. In W. Küpers & D. Pauleen (Eds.), *A handbook of practical wisdom; Leadership, organization and integral business practice* (pp. 19–46). London: Gower.

Ladson-Billings, G. (2004). Culture versus citizenship: The challenge of racialized citizenship in the United States. In J. Banks (Ed.), *Diversity and citizenship education: Global perspectives* (pp. 99–126). San Francisco: Jossey-Bass.

Lather, P. (2004). Scientific research in education: A critical perspective. *British Educational Research Journal, 30*(6), 759–772.

Lawrence, J., & Vaisse, J. (2006). *Integrating Islam: Political and religious challenges in contemporary France*. Washington D.C.: Brookings Institution Press.

Leander, A. (2009, November 30). *Habitus and field*. Working paper, Copenhagen Business School, Department of Intercultural Communication and Management. Retrieved April 2, 2011, from http://openarchive.cbs.dk/handle/10398/7966

Lee, A., Dunston, R., & Fowler, C. (2012). Seeing is believing: An embodied pedagogy of 'doing partnership' in child and family health. In P. Hager, A. Lee, & A. Reich (Eds.), *Practice, learning and change: Practice-theory perspectives* (pp. 267–276). Dordrecht: Springer Science + Business Media.

Le Goaziou, V., & Rojzman, C. (2006). *Les banlieues [The poor ring cities]*. Paris: Le Cavalier Bleu.

Levy, P. (1995, October). *Pour l'intelligence collective [For collective intelligence]*. Retrieved July 19, 2005, from *Le Monde Diplomatique*: http://www.monde-diplomatique.fr/1995/10/LEVY/1857#nb1

Lewicki, R. J., & Wiethoff, C. (2000). Trust, trust development, and trust repair. In M. Deutsch & P. T. Coleman (Eds.), *The handbook of conflict resolution: Theory and practice* (pp. 86–107). San Francisco: Jossey-Bass.

Lewicki, R. J., & Tomlinson, E. C. (2003, December). Trust and trust building. Retrieved April 28, 2009, from Beyond Intractability: http://www.beyondintractability.org/node/2608

Leyens, J.-P., Cortes, B., Demoulin, S., Dovidio, J. F., Fiske, S. T., Gaunt, R., . . . Vaes, J. (2003). Emotional prejudice, essentialism, and nationalism. *European Journal of Social Psychology, 33*, 703–717.

Lockwood, T. C. (2013). Habituation, habit and character in Aristotle's *Nichomachean Ethics*. In T. Sparrow & A. Hutchinson (Eds.), *A history of habit: From Aristotle to Bourdieu* (pp. 19–36). Lanham, MD: Lexington.

Long, S. (2002). *The new student politics: The Wingspread statement on student civic engagement*. Providence, RI: Campus Compact.

Lukes, S. (2005). *Power: A radical view* (2nd ed.). London: Palgrave Macmillan. (Original work published 1974).

Macedo, S., Alex-Assensoh, Y., Berry, J. M., Brintnall, M., Campbell, D. E., Fraga, L. R., . . . Walsh, K. C. (2005). *Democracy at risk: How political choices undermine citizen participation and what we can do about it*. Washington, D.C.: Brookings Institution Press.

Malandra, K. (2007). Interrupting habitus and community-based arts: Pedagogical efficacy in a university/community collaboration (Order No. 3268170, Temple University).

ProQuest Dissertations and Theses, 287. Retrieved April 4, 2010, from http://search.proquest.com/docview/304827516?accountid=14270. (304827516)

Malandra, K. B. (2004). One community's collage: Art making for social change. Unpublished draft chapter, Temple University.

Marklein, M. B. (2008, December 4). Studies examine impact of part-time college faculty. Retrieved January 16, 2010, from *USA Today:* http://usatoday30.usatoday.com/news/education/2008-12-03-part-time-professors_N.htm

Markoff, J. (1996). *Waves of democracy: Social movements and political change.* Thousand Oaks, CA: Pine Forge.

Martin, S. D., Snow, J. L., & Franklin Torrez, C. A. (2011). Navigating the terrain of third space: Tensions with/in relationships in school-university partnerships. *Journal of Teacher Education, 62*(3), 299–311.

Mathews, D. (2004, April 7). *Six democratic practices.* Kettering Foundation Working Paper Draft. Retrieved May 27, 2012, from Public Policy Center: http://www.publicpolicycenter.hawaii.edu/documents/PPC2Keynote_001.pdf

McGee, M. C. (1998). Phronesis in the Gadamer versus Habermas debates. In J. M. Sloop & J. P. McDaniel (Eds.), *Judgment calls: Rhetoric, politics, and indeterminacy* (pp. 13–41). Boulder, CO: Westview.

McGregor, J. (2009, March 11). Smart management for tough times. *Business Week.*

McIntosh, P. (1989). *White privilege: Unpacking the invisible backpack.* Retrieved January 10, 2014, from University of Michigan Institute for Social Research: http://www.isr.umich.edu/home/diversity/resources/white-privilege.pdf

McKnight, J. L. (1995). *The careless society: Community and its counterfeits.* New York: Basic Books.

McLuhan, M. (1960, May 18). *Marshall McLuhan: The global village.* Retrieved March 29, 2009, from CBC Digital Archives: http://www.cbc.ca/archives/categories/arts-entertainment/media/marshall-mcluhan-the-man-and-his-message/world-is-a-global-village.html

McLuhan, M. (1962). *The Gutenberg galaxy: The making of typographic man.* Toronto: University of Toronto Press.

Mezirow, J., Taylor, E. W., & Associates (Eds.). (2009). *Transformative learning in practice: Insights from community, workplace, and higher education.* San Francisco: Jossey-Bass.

Miller, P. (1994). Accounting and objectivity: The invention of calculating selves and calculable spaces. In A. Megill (Ed.), *Rethinking objectivity* (pp. 239–264). Durham, NC: Duke University Press.

Miller, P. M. (2007). Examining boundary-spanning leadership in university-school-community partnerships. *Journal of School Public Relations, 28*(2), 189–211.

Miller, P. M., & Hafner, M. M. (2008). Moving toward dialogical collaboration: A critical examination of a university-school-community partnership. *Educational Administration Quarterly, 44*(1), 66–110.

Mitchell, T. D. (2007). Critical service-learning as social justice education: A case study of the Citizen Scholar Program. *Equity & Excellence in Education, 40*(2), 101–112.

Mitra, D. L. (2008). Balancing power in communities of practice: An examination of increasing student voice through school-based youth-adult partnerships. *Journal of Educational Change, 9*(3), 221–242.

Moses, R., Perry, T., Delpit, L., & Cortes, E., Jr. (2008). *Quality education as a constitutional right: Creating a grassroots movement to transform public schools.* Boston: Beacon.

Munin, A., & Speight, S. L. (2010). Factors influencing the ally development of college students. *Equity and Excellence in Education, 43*(2), 249–264.

Musil, C. M. (2009). Educating students for personal and social responsibility: The Civic Learning Spiral. In B. Jacoby and Associates (Eds.), *Civic engagement in higher education: Concepts and practices* (pp. 49–68). San Francisco: Jossey-Bass.

Musil, C. M. (2011). Remapping education for social responsibility: Civic, global, and U.S. diversity. In J. Saltmarsh & M. Hartley (Eds.), *'To serve a larger purpose': Engagement for democracy and the transformation of higher education* (pp. 238–264). Philadelphia: Temple University Press.

National Association of Social Workers. (2008). *Code of ethics of the National Association of Social Workers*. Retrieved April 3, 2012, from National Association of Social Workers: http://www.naswdc.org/pubs/code/code.asp (Original work published 1996).

National Commission on Excellence in Education. (1983, April). *A nation at risk: The imperative for educational reform*. Retrieved February 24, 2005, from http://www2.ed.gov/pubs/NatAtRisk/index.html

National Education Association [NEA]. (n.d.). *Code of ethics*. Retrieved June 4, 2013, from http://www.nea.org/home/30442.htm

National Leadership Council for Liberal Education & America's Promise [NLC-LEAP]. (2007). *College learning for the new global century*. Washington, DC: Association of American Colleges and Universities (AAC&U).

National Task Force on Civic Learning and Democratic Engagement [NTFCLDE]. (2012, January). *A crucible moment: College learning and democracy's future*. Washington, DC: Association of American Colleges and Universities. Retrieved March 3, 2012, from The Civic Learning and Democratic Engagement Project: http://www.civiclearning.org/SupportDocs/Crucible_508F.pdf

Newfield, C. (2003). *Ivy and industry: Business and the making of the American university, 1880–1980*. Durham, NC: Duke University Press.

Newfield, C. (2008). *Unmaking the public university: The forty-year assault on the middle class*. Cambridge, MA: Harvard University Press.

Noel, J. (1999). On the varieties of phronesis. *Educational Philosophy and Theory, 31*(3), 273–289.

Nussbaum, M. C. (2006). Education and democratic citizenship: Capabilities and quality education. *Journal of Human Development and Capabilities, 7*(3), 385–395.

Nussbaum, M. C. (2009, Summer). Education for profit, education for freedom. *Liberal Education*, 6–13.

Nussbaum, M. C., & Sen, A. (Eds.). (1993). *The quality of life*. New York: Oxford University Press.

Nyberg, D. (2008). The morality of everyday activities: Not the right, but the good thing to do. *Journal of Business Ethics, 81*, 587–598.

Ostrander, S. A. (2004). Democracy, civic participation, and the university: A comparative study of civic engagement on five campuses. *Nonprofit and Voluntary Sector Quarterly, 33*(1), 74–93.

Page, S. E. (2007). *The difference: How the power of diversity creates better groups, firms, schools, and societies*. Princeton, NJ: Princeton University Press.

Palmer, P. J. (2007, November–December). A new professional: The aims of education revisited. *Change, 39*(6), 6–12. Retrieved April 7, 2009, from http://www.changemag.org/Archives/BackIssues/November-December2007/full-new-professional.html

Peck, M. S. (1990). *The different drum: Community-making and peace*. London: Arrow.

Peter D. Hart Research Associates. (2006). *How should colleges prepare students to succeed in today's global economy?* Washington, DC: Author.

Peters, M. A. (2011). *Neoliberalism and after? Education, social policy, and the crisis of Western capitalism.* New York: Peter Lang.

Peters, M. A., & Olssen, M. (2011). Neoliberalism, higher education, and knowledge capitalism. In M. A. Peters, *Neoliberalism and after? Education, social policy, and the crisis of western capitalism* (pp. 42–74). New York: Peter Lang.

Peters, S. J. (2004). Educating the civic professional: Reconfigurations and resistances. *Michigan Journal of Community Service-Learning, 11*(1), 47–58.

Pettigrew, T. (2008). Future directions for intergroup contact theory and research. *International Journal of Intercultural Relations, 32*(3), 187–199.

Preskill, S. (2005, Spring). Fundi—The enduring leadership legacy of civil rights activist Ella Baker. *Advancing Women in Leadership Online Journal, 18.*

Pruitt, B., & Thomas, P. (2007). *Democratic dialogue—A handbook for practitioners.* Retrieved October 14, 2009, from http://www.democraticdialoguenetwork.org

Pugin, V. (April 2007). *La politique d'éducation prioritaire: Bilans et perspectives [The politics of priority education: Review and perspectives].* Lyon, France: Millénaire: Le Centre Ressources Prospectives du Grand Lyon.

Putnam, R. (2007). E pluribus unum: Diversity and community in the twenty-first century. The 2006 Johan Skytte Prize Lecture. *Scandinavian Political Studies, 30*(2), 137–174.

Quigley, S. A. (2011). Academic identity: A modern perspective. *Educate~, 11*(1), 20–30.

Randall, G. E. (2000, November). *Understanding professional self-regulation.* Retrieved January 5, 2013, from Ontario Association of Veterinary Technicians: http://www.oavt.org/self_regulation/docs/about_selfreg_randall.pdf

Reason, R. D., Broido, E. M., Davis, T. L., & Evans, N. J. (Eds.). (2005, Summer). *Developing social justice allies: New directions for student services* (vol. 110). San Francisco: Jossey-Bass.

Reay, D. (2004). 'It's all becoming a habitus': Beyond the habitual use of habitus in educational research. *British Journal of Sociology of Education, 25*(4), 431–444.

Rhoads, R. A. (1997). *Community service and higher learning: Explorations of the caring self.* Albany: State University of New York Press.

Rhoads, R. A., & Liu, A. (2008). Globalization, social movements, and the American university: Implications for research and practice. In J. C. Smart (Ed.), *Higher education: Handbook of theory and research* (pp. 273–315). Dordrecht: Springer Science + Business Media.

Ricoeur, P. (2004). *Memory, history, forgetting* (K. Blamey & D. Pellauer, Trans.) Chicago: University of Chicago Press.

Robeyns, I. (2005, March). The capability approach: A theoretical survey. *Journal of Human Development, 6*(1), 93–117.

Rodgers, C. (2002). Defining reflection: Another look at John Dewey and reflective thinking. *Teachers College Record, 102*(4), 842–866.

Rojzman, C. (2008). *Sortir de la violence par le conflit [Overcoming violence through conflict].* Paris: La Découverte.

Rojzman, C. (2009). *Bien vivre avec les autres [Living in harmony with others].* Paris: Larousse.

Rojzman, C., & Pillods, S. (1999). *How to live together.* St. Kilda, AU: Acland.

Rojzman, C., & Rojzman, T. (2006). *C'est pas moi, c'est lui: Ne plus être victime des autres [It's not me, it's him: How to stop being a victim].* Paris: JC Lattes.

Ross, L. M. (2002, August). American higher education and community engagement: A historical perspective. In M. Martinez (Ed.), *Lasting engagement: Building and sustaining a commitment to community outreach, development, and collaboration* Vol. 1 (pp. 1–17). Washington, DC: U.S. Department of Housing and Community Development, Office of University Partnerships.

Salamon, L. M., Sokolowski, S. W., & List, R. (2003). *Global civil society: An overview.* Baltimore, MD: Johns Hopkins Institute for Policy Studies, Center for Civil Society Studies.

Salovey, P., & Mayer, J. D. (1990). Emotional intelligence. *Imagination, Cognition and Personality, 9*(3), 185–211.

Saltmarsh, J., & Hartley, M. (2011). To serve a larger purpose. In J. Saltmarsh & M. Hartley (Eds.), *'To serve a larger purpose': Engagement for democracy and the transformation of higher education* (pp. 1–12). Philadelphia: Temple University Press.

Sandel, M. J. (2012). *What money can't buy: The moral limits of markets*. New York: Farrar, Straus and Giroux.

Sandmann, L. R., Thornton, C. H., & Jaeger, A. J. (Eds.). (2009). *Institutionalizing community engagement in higher education: The first wave of Carnegie classified institutions.* San Francisco: Jossey-Bass.

Sandy, M., & Holland, B. A. (2006). Different worlds and common ground: Community partner perspectives on campus-community partnerships. *Michigan Journal of Community Service Learning, 13*(1), 30–43.

Schön, D. A. (1990). *Educating the reflective practitioner.* San Francisco: Jossey-Bass.

Schraad-Tischler, D. (2011, October 27). *Social justice in the OECD: How do the member states compare? Sustainable governance indicators 2011.* Retrieved November 10, 2011, from SGI: http://www.sgi-network.org/pdf/SGI11_Social_Justice_OECD.pdf

Schram, S. (2012). Phronetic social science: An idea whose time has come. In B. Flyvbjerg, T. Landman, & S. Schram (Eds.), *Real social science: Applied phronesis* (pp. 15–26). New York: Cambridge University Press.

Schwandt, T. A. (2005). Modeling our understanding of the practice fields. *Pedagogy, Culture and Society, 13*(3), 313–332.

Sellman, D. (2012). Reclaiming competence for professional phronesis. In E. A. Kinsella & A. Pitman (Eds.), *Phronesis as professional knowledge: Practical wisdom in the professions* (pp. 115–130). Rotterdam: Sense.

Senge, P. M., Scharmer, O. C., Jaworski, J., & Flowers, B. S. (2004). *Presence: Human purpose and the field of the future.* Cambridge, MA: Society for Organizational Learning.

Sergiovanni, T. J. (2005). Organization, market and community as strategies for change: What works best for deep changes in schools. In A. Hargreaves (Ed.), *Extending educational change* (pp. 296–315). Dordrecht: Springer.

Shirley, D. (1997). *Community organizing for school reform.* Austin: University of Texas Press.

Shotter, J. (2012). Knowledge in transition: The role of prospective, descriptive concepts in a practice-situated, hermeneutical-phronetic social science. *Management Learning, 43*(3), 245–260.

Shulman, L. S. (2004). *The wisdom of practice: Essays on teaching, learning and learning to teach.* San Francisco: Jossey-Bass.

Shulman, L. S. (2007). Response to comments: Practical wisdom in the service of professional practice. *Educational Researcher, 36*(9), 560–563.

Shulman, L. S., Golde, C. M., Bueschel, A. C., & Garabedian, K. J. (2006). Reclaiming education's doctorates: A critique and a proposal. *Educational Researcher, 35(3),* 25–32.

Small Group Skills. (n.d.). HCI consulting. Retrieved November 3, 2009, from http://www.hci.com.au/hcisite2/toolkit/smallgro.htm#Skills for leading and participating

Solbrekke, T. D., & Englund, T. (2011). Bringing professional responsibility back in. *Studies in Higher Education, 36*(7), 847–861.

Solomon, R. C. (1992). Corporate roles, personal virtues: An Aristotelian approach to business ethics. *Business Ethics Quarterly, 2*(3), 317–339.

Solomon, R. C. (2008). Free enterprise, sympathy, and virtue. In P. J. Zak (Ed.), *Moral markets: The critical role of values in the economy* (pp. 16–41). Princeton: Princeton University Press.

Solorzano, D., Ceja, M., & Yosso, T. (2000). Critical race theory, racial microaggressions, and campus racial climate: The experiences of African American college students. *Journal of Negro Education, 69*(1/2), 60–73.

Stanton, T. K. (2008). New times demand new scholarship: Opportunities and challenges for civic engagement at research universities. *Education, Citizenship and Social Justice, 3*(1), 19–42.

Stanton, T. K., Giles, D. E., & Cruz, N. I. (1999). *Service learning: A movement's pioneers reflect on its origins, practice, and future.* San Francisco: Jossey-Bass.

Staub, E. (2003a). Notes on cultures of violence, cultures of caring and peace, and the fulfillment of basic human needs. *Political Psychology, 24*(1), 1–21.

Staub, E. (2003b). *The psychology of good and evil: Why children, adults, and groups help and harm others.* New York: Cambridge University Press.

Steinberg, K. S., Hatcher, J. A., & Bringle, R. G. (2011, Spring). Civic-minded graduate: A north star. *Michigan Journal of Community-Service Learning, 17,* 19–33.

Stiglitz, J. (2003, October 17). *We have to make globalization work for all.* Retrieved January 25, 2005, from YaleGlobal Online: http://yaleglobal.yale.edu/content/we-have-make-globalization-work-all

St. John, G. (Ed.). (2008). *Victor Turner and contemporary cultural performance.* New York: Berghahn.

Stoecker, R., Tryon, E. A., & Hilgendorf, A. (Eds.). (2009). *The unheard voices: Community organizations and service learning.* Philadelphia: Temple University Press.

Stoll, L., Bolam, R., McMahon, A., Wallace, M., & Thomas, S. (2006). Professional learning communities: A review of the literature. *Journal of Educational Change, 7,* 221–258.

Stone, C. N. (2001). Civic capacity and urban education. *Urban Affairs Review, 36*(5), 599–619. Retrieved July 1, 2013, from http://www.gvpt.umd.edu/stone/prolo.html

Stone, C. N. (2005). Civic capacity: What, why, and from whence. In S. Fuhrman & M. Lazerson (Eds.), *The public schools* (pp. 209–243). New York: Oxford University Press.

Sullivan, W. (2005). *Work and integrity: The crisis and promise of professionalism in America* (2nd ed.). San Francisco: Jossey-Bass.

Susskind, L. (1999). *A short guide to consensus building: An alternative to Robert's Rules of Order for groups, organizations and ad hoc assemblies that want to operate by consensus.* (L. Susskind, S. McKearnan, & J. Thomas-Larmer, Eds.). Retrieved April 14, 2012, from MIT-Harvard Public Dispute Program: http://web.mit.edu/publicdisputes/practice/shortguide.pdf

Swadener, B. B., & Lubeck, S. (1995). The social construction of children and families-at-risk: An introduction. In B. B. Swadener & S. Lubeck (Eds.), *Children and families 'at promise': Deconstructing the discourse of risk* (pp. 1–14). Albany: State University of New York Press.

Swim, J. K., Hyer, L. L., Cohen, L. L., Fitzgerald, D. C., & Bylsma, W. H. (2003, February). African American college students' experiences with everyday racism: Characteristics of and responses to these incidents. *Journal of Black Psychology, 29*(1), 38–67.

Tarpinian, A. (2010, January 6). Politique et école. La dimension anthropologique [Politics and schools: Anthropological perspectives]. Retrieved February 1, 2010, from *Psychologie de la Motivation*: http://www.le-cercle-psy.fr/politique-et-ecole-la-dimension-anthropologique_sh_24792

Taylor, C., Appiah, K. A., Habermas, J., Rockefeller, S. C., Walzer, M., & Wolf, S. (1994). Multiculturalism: Examining the politics of recognition. (A. Gutmann, Ed.) Princeton: Princeton University Press.

Taylor, M. M. (2004). Critical challenges of the learning Red Zone: Senior managers in empowering organizational change. *The Innovation Journal: The Public Sector Innovation Journal, 9*(1), 1–17.

The citizen professional idea. (n.d.). Citizen Professional Center, University of Minnesota. Retrieved May 25, 2012, from http://www.cehd.umn.edu/fsos/projects/cpc/idea.asp

The Innovation Center for Community and Youth Development; National 4-H Council; National Network for Youth; Youth Leadership Institute. (2003). *Youth-adult partnerships: A training manual*. Authors. Retrieved May 6, 2005, from http://www.ca4h.org/files/2424.pdf

Thompson, C., Schaefer, E., & Brad, H. (2003). *White men challenging racism: 35 personal stories*. Durham, NC: Duke University Press.

Thompson, S. (2006). *The political theory of recognition: A critical introduction*. Cambridge: Polity.

Thomson, A. M., Perry, J. L., & Miller, T. K. (2009). Conceptualizing and measuring collaboration. *Journal of Public Administration Research and Theory, 19*(1), 23–56.

Tishman, S., & Andrade, A. (1995). Thinking dispositions: A review of current theories, practices, and issues. Unpublished manuscript, Harvard University, Cambridge, MA. Retrieved January 6, 2013, from http://learnweb.harvard.edu/alps/thinking/docs/dispositions.htm

Torre, M. E., Fine, M., Stoudt, B. G., & Fox, M. (2012). Critical participatory action research as public science, pp. 1–31. Retrieved February 14, 2013, from https://archive.org/details/TorreEtAl.2012CriticalPARAsPublicScience

Toulmin, S. (1990). *Cosmopolis: The hidden agenda of modernity*. Chicago: University of Chicago Press.

Toulmin, S. (1996). Concluding methodological reflections: Elitism and democracy among the sciences. In S. Toulmin & B. Gustavsen (Eds.), *Beyond theory: Changing organizations through participation* (pp. 203–225). Amsterdam: John Benjamins.

Toulmin, S. (2003). *Return to reason*. Cambridge, MA: Harvard University Press.

Trevino, J. (2001). *Talcott Parsons today: His theory and legacy in contemporary sociology*. Lanham, MD: Rowman & Littlefield.

Truth and memory. (n.d.). Retrieved January 26, 2012, from International Center for Transitional Justice: http://www.ictj.org/our-work/transitional-justice-issues/truth-and-memory

Tschannen-Moran, M. (2004). *Trust matters: Leadership for successful schools*. San Francisco: Jossey-Bass.

Tyack, D. B. (1974). *The one best system: A history of American urban education*. Cambridge, MA: Harvard University Press.

van Manen, M. (2007). Phenomenology of practice. *Phenomenology & Practice, 1*, 11–30.
von Mises, L. (1947). *Bureaucracy. Introduction*. Retrieved January 9, 2012, from Ludwig von Mises Institute: http://mises.org/etexts/mises/bureaucracy/introduction.asp
Waddock, S. A. (1991). Typology of social partnership organizations. *Administration and Society, 22*(4), 480–515.
Wade, R. (Ed.). (1997). *Community service-learning: A guide to including service in the public school curriculum*. Albany: State University of New York Press.
Washington, P., & Gracie, D. (1994). *Other sheep I have*. Philadelphia: Temple University Press.
Webster-Wright, A. (2009). Reframing professional development through understanding authentic professional learning. *Review of Educational Research, 79*(2), 702–739.
Weick, K. E., Sutcliffe, K. M., & Obstfeld, D. (2005). Organizing and the process of sensemaking. *Organization Science, 16*(4), 409–421.
Wenger, E. (2006, June). *Communities of practice: A brief introduction*. Retrieved December 3, 2012, from http://www.ewenger.com/theory/index.htm
Wheatley, M. J. (2010). *Leadership and the new science; Discovering order in a chaotic world* (3rd ed.). San Francisco: Berrett-Koehler.
White, B. P. (2010). Power, privilege, and the public: The dynamics of community-university collaboration. *New Directions for Higher Education, 2010*(152), 67–74.
Winnicott, D. W. (1987). *Babies and their mothers*. Cambridge, MA: Perseus.
Wood, D. J., & Gray, B. (1991). Toward a comprehensive theory of collaboration. *Journal of Applied Behavioral Science, 27*(2), 139–162.
Workgroup for Community Health and Development, University of Kansas. (2013). *Community-based participatory action research*. Retrieved September 11, 2013, from The Community Tool Box: http://ctb.ku.edu/en/tablecontents/sub_section_main_1349.aspx
Yalom, I. D., & Leszcz, M. (2005). *The theory and practice of group psychotherapy* (5th ed.). New York: Basic Books.
Yalowitz, B. (2005). *Trespassing: Criss-crossing the university-community borderline*. Paper presented at the Annual Conference on Social Theory, Politics, and the Arts. University of Oregon.
Yalowitz, B. (2011). The black bottom: Making community-based performance in West Philadelphia. In B. Adair, B. Filene, & L. Koloski (Eds.), *Letting go? Sharing historical authority in a user-generated world* (pp. 156–173). Philadelphia: Pew Center for Arts and Heritage.
Yankelovich, D. (1999). *The magic of dialogue: Transforming conflict into cooperation*. New York: Simon & Schuster.
Young, I. M. (2000). *Inclusion and democracy*. Oxford: Oxford University Press.
Young, I. M. (2011). The five faces of oppression. In I. M. Young (Ed.), *Justice and the politics of difference* (pp. 39–65). Princeton, NJ: Princeton University Press. (Original work published 1990).

INDEX

AAC&U *see* Association of American Colleges and Universities
accountability: as extension of modern rationality 54–5; as measurement, in education 59, 65–6; in new public management 65; neoliberal logic of 64–5, 120; in partnership relationships 169; as professional self-regulation 76, 98n1; as technology of power 67, 77
action research: in CFW 117, 119, 130n9; in collective intelligence process 206–7; in professional learning communities 93; in reflection/sensemaking cycle 127; for social advocacy work 80; in teacher Allen's classroom research project 102
Addams, Jane 20, 79–80
advantage: emotional 123–4; social 121, 124
agency: as aspect of habitus 112, 120; expressed as violence and rebellion to authority 15, 210; released through community stories 166, 226; as restored hope 226; in TST practice 201–2, 206; from victimhood to responsible 202
ally: defined 173, 183; different aspects of 151; as exchange relation 174; problem with teacher as 204–5; resonance as alternative to 173–4; struggles with being a white ally 178
Anzaldúa, Gloria 73, 74, 86

Argyris, C. 123
Aristotle 104–6; elite views by 130n5; *see also* habitus-field-capital interaction; phronesis
asset-based community development 36, 138, 160n12
Association of American Colleges and Universities 37, 48, 50, 98n4
assumptions 68; awareness of, through reflection 114; deficit-based 86, 146, 155; as obstacles to democratic engagement 69; open-mindedness and 105, 139; paradigmatic, of liberalism and neoliberalism 54, 60, 62, 63–4, 68; paradigmatic, of Modernity 42, 55–7, 68, 76; of practice, as scientific problem solving 58, 101–3, 138–9; questioning, in service-learning 142, 145, 154–5; of situated, phronetic practice 103–4; unexamined, of *normal* professional identity and practice 42, 58, 60, 74, 86–7, 110, 120, 138, 142, 146, 210
authority: embodied in normalized roles 90–1, 93, 146–7, 157; formal 27; legitimized through discourses and technologies of power 40, 57; *see also* habitus-field-capital interaction

Banks, J. 45
Barber, B. R. 84
Barker, D. W. 44–5

binary opposites: 8, 15, 55, 68; vs. complexity 198, 202, 204–5; victim-oppressor 192–3, 201–2
border pedagogy: cultivating identities for 180–1, 183; and de-centering higher education partners 180, 186, 224, 226; defined 175; joint poetry workshop in 181–3; need for occasional insider view in 180–1, 183; and refusing to lead a segregated life 184–5; as space for challenges and affirmations 175; storytelling circle in 175–9; teacher as vulnerable self in 179, 184; *see also* habitus; *third space*
border-crossing 74; barriers to 22–5, 67–8; capacities for 15, 86–91, 190; as disruption of Self-Other relations 121; supports for 125–6; *see also third space*
border-crossing democratic professional: and Civic Learning Spiral 88–90; cultivating the development of 119–22, 125–9, 156–9,185–7, 212–13, 220–1; and spaces for change 91–6; staying in zone of discomfort 74; summary of characteristics of 96–7; three practices for 14–16, 221–8; *see also* border-crossing partnership framework
border-crossing partnership framework 99, 113–16, 221–2
border-crossing practice, in cases: building collective intelligence 119, 150, 206–7; constructing and enacting the (particular) good 117–19, 145, 152–4, 157; creating spaces for transformation 117, 118, 122, 151, 158–9, 187, 200–3, 207–10; cultivating qualities and embodying virtues 117, 119, 120, 137–40, 149, 185–6, 197, 212; disturbing the habitus 117–18, 122–5, 139, 141, 144, 155–6, 187, 204; interrupting oppressive normalcies 140–1, 158, 193–4, 196–7 201–2; making sense of situations 121–1, 145, 146–9, 195, 202, 207, 212; surfacing suppressed narratives 187–8, 204; *see also* circle of friends; developmental leadership; habitus-field-capital interaction
borderland 41; as colonial outpost 42; as space for disrupting oppressive normalcies 74; *see also third space*
borders; defined xii; different from boundaries xii

Bourdieu, P. 91, 111–14
Boyer, E. 46, 47, 50–1, 53, 79,
Boyte H. 11, 13, 48, 88, 94–5, 98n7
Bringle, R. G. 98n3
Brint, S. 75, 77, 92
Brookfield, S. 68
Brown v. Board of Education 163, 176
bureaucracy: different from and being replaced by networks 5–6, 7; as framework for change-oriented action 91; as modern organizational form 58–9; neoliberal thought and 63
business ethics 110–11; *see also* ethics

calculative rationality *see* accountability
Campus Compact 45, 48, 49
capabilities approach 138
capital 113; knowledge as 120; social 34, 86; *see also* habitus-field-capital interaction
Carnegie classification of community engagement 46, 51, 52–3
Cary, Lorene 166, 169–70, 170–1, 172
Castells, M. 5
Center for Democracy and Citizenship 78
CFW *see* Change from Within Programme
Change from Within Programme 116–19, 149, 212
Chevannes, P. 92, 116–17, 119, 133
circle of friends 88, 92, 96, 110, 116, 129, 212; *see also* community of practice
citizen artist 164
civic capacity: through border-crossing collaboration 205; cultivating, in multicultural democracies 193–4; defined 190–1
Civic Engagement VALUE Rubric 50
civic engagement; defined 49–50, 52–3; democratic 45, 91; Hull House enactment of 79; incorporating diversity and global citizenship 88; partnership approach to, in Change from Within Programme 116; and democratic public work xiv, 48, 94
Civic Learning Spiral 84, 88–90, 94, 96
civic-minded professional 83–6; and orientations to citizenship 87
Clayton, P. & Ash, S. 142
CLS *see* Civic Learning Spiral
collaboration; alternative practices for 30–2; barriers to, in Addams-Lincoln case 33–6; and boundary spanning

29–30; cross-border contrasted to boundary spanning 37; defined 28–9; process for 29, 30–4
collaborative dynamics 32–5; in Addams-Lincoln case 35–6; integrating process and outcomes 86
collective intelligence 15–16, 227–8; in Change from Within case 127; in Maville case 206–7, 210–12; missed opportunities for 68, 150, 158; as a new kind of wisdom 220–1; and assumptions of modernity and neoliberalism 68
community: defined 92; crossing borders to build 153–6; as framework to inform change-oriented action 91–2
community needs: constructions of 134, 152, 153–4; identifying through community-based research 154; meeting authentic 50, 134, 152–4
community of practice 92–3, 110; *see also* circle of friends
community partners: assets/capacities of 138–9, 164; and community storytelling 169; critique of Cantril, in Addams-Lincoln case 83; perspective on quality partnerships 36–7; voice of 27–8, 50
community-arts process 164–5, 168–9
community-based research 80; across borders 206–7; in collective intelligence process 202–4, 207–8, 209–10; about partnership dynamics, in Addams-Lincoln case 22–3; in service learning 142, 154; *see also* dialogue
consensus decision making 31–2, 108, 223; compared to Roberts' Rules of Order 27, 31
constructing and enacting the good 109–11, 140, 186, 212, 219; *see also* border-crossing practice
critical friend 139, 159n5
critical incident: defined 133; in service-learning practice 144, 145, 158, 227; and shift in consciousness 153

deliberation; defined 31–2, 110–11; in Addams-Lincoln case 35; in situational ethics 111
democracy, participatory 94, 190
democratic civic professional: associational life of 94–5, 96; border-crossing capacities of 87–8, 90–1;

three constructs for 85–6, 88–90; *see also* border-crossing democratic professional; third space
developmental leadership 80–1; *see also* border-crossing practice
Dewey, J. 49, 78–9, 105
dialogue: and civic engagement outcomes 86, 89; and collective intelligence 209–10; in community arts 165; community engagement as 37; as life-affirming 209; vs. monologue 80; qualities needed for 154, 155; wise practitioner's dispositions for 106
difference 15
discourse 40–1
dispositions: of border-crossing civic professional 106–7; in Civic Learning Spiral 89; defined 101; experiences that affirm 127–8; part of professional identity 76, 84–6, 96; *see also* habitus
disturbing/interrupting oppressive normalcies xiv, 14–15, 41, 218–19, 220, 223–4; in Addams-Lincoln case 35, 41–2; in Advocate case 224; in Maville case 197, 199, 201, 207, 210; in Upland case 138, 140–1, 142, 144, 148–9, 155, 157–8; *see also* assumptions; Self-Other transformation
diversity 8–9; and civic engagement 50, 85, 88; and collective intelligence 16; *see also* difference
double-loop learning 93, 123

Ehrlich, T. 49
embodying the virtues 104–7; in Change from Within case 212; in Maville case 212; *see also* border-crossing practice
emotional advantage 124
emotional intelligence 90–1; leader's capacity for 77, 87, 146; *see also* power
emotions: absent from scientific problem solving 101–2; and being a man 119; control over, by traditional professional 75–6, 138; disturbed, in border-crossing 121–3, 127; intellect versus, in Modernity 55; learning from 74, 90, 96, 127, 133, 142, 229; part of habitus 112, 125; and pathological institutions 73–4, 194; personal, interpersonal, and organizational 96; surfacing repressed 230; *see also* border pedagogy; resonance; Transformational Social Therapy

250 Index

engagement: campus 51–2; democratic 44–5; faculty 50–1, 54; higher education xiii–xiv; outreach and democratic as different forms of xiv; institutionalization of 53–4; and land-grant universities 46, 52, 60; and mission of higher education 50; movement 46–8; multiple forms of xiii–xiv, 51–3, 60; and research 52–4, 79; student 46, 48–50; at University of Chicago and Hull House 80–1
Enlightenment *see* Modernity
ethics: and associations' codes of conduct 83, 91, 110; of engaged professional 86–8; and gap between statements and practice 110; of social trustee professional 76–8; situational vs. universal 110, 121, 140; virtue 104–5; *see also* constructing and enacting the good
evaluation 43n4; as sensemaking 107–8; *see also* action research
everyday racism 42
expert 77, 78–9; challenges to 77; exemplified by Cantril, in Addams-Lincoln case 67, 81–3; negative views of, by community partners 36, 39; *normal* assumptions of 39, 42, 111; outreach as *normal* practice of 44, 53, 59, 83; as an orientation to practice 101

Felman, S. 123
field 112–13; *see also* habitus-field-capital interaction
Flyvbjerg, B. 99, 108, 109, 110, 142
Foucault, M. 40, 42, 59, 66, 220
free market *see* neoliberalism
Freire, P. 37, 49, 80, 209

Gadamer, H.-G. 104, 106
good, the: as collective 'happiness' 105; situation specific 223; *see also* constructing and enacting the good

Habermas, J. 57
habitus: in border pedagogy 179; defined 112; disturbing, in border crossing 121; emotional 138–9, 212; of expert professional 120; influenced by affiliations and authority systems 112, 124–5; interaction with field 195; orientation and dispositions of 101, 125–6; transforming 186–7, 194; *see also* habitus-field-capital interaction; border-crossing practice

habitus-field-capital interaction 111, 114, 220; illustrated in Change from Within case 120–9; and phronesis 113–16, 220
Harkavy, I. 79, 80
Hatcher, J. 48, 49, 86, 98
Honneth, A. 9
Hurtsthouse, R. 105

icebreakers 128
ignorance: and desire to ignore 138, 155; as resistance to learning 123

Kemmis, S. 80, 100
Kettering Foundation 43n4, 45
knowledge for practice 100, 101–3, 218–19; *see also* border-crossing practice
Kretzmann & McKnight 133, 138

Lacan, J. 123
leadership: contradictions in 170; developmental 80–1, 146, 147–8, 225–6; task-oriented 146–7
dignity, lives worthy of: as goal of phronetic practice 99–100, 105, 148; *see also* constructing and enacting the good
Lukes, S. 40

making sense of the situation 107–9; in Change from Within case 120, 121, 122; in Maville case 201, 202, 203, 205–6, 210, 212; students in Jamaica service learning program 108–9; in Upland case 136, 138–9, 145, 148–9, 154–6; *see also* border-crossing practice
market fundamentalism 63; privatization of public services in 63–4; *see also* neoliberalism
mask: and building trust 210; to hide vulnerabilities 123, 138, 193, 196, 201; of in-group unity 204; intellectualizing as 206
McIntosh, P. 155
McLuhan, M. 5, 56
mistrust 124; and unmet human needs 193–4; *see also* Transformational Social Therapy; trust
Modernity 54–6; and binary opposites 55; dominant approach to knowledge in 57–8; Enlightenment influence on 54–6, 57, 62, 101; and higher education 56; and modern *man* 56–7; oppressive normalcies associated with 218–19; Others in 60; Renaissance influence on

Index **251**

54–5; *see also* bureaucracy; technical/instrumental orientation
murals: as activist art in Church of the Advocate 171–2
Musil, C. 37, 50, 88, 98n4

National Task Force on Civil Learning and Democratic Engagement 37, 44, 48
neoliberalism: continuity with Modernity 54–5, 57; and economic *man* 66–7; freedom as market choice 63; impact on higher education of 65–6; origins of 61–2; partnership approaches in 6–7, 64–5; promoting calculative identities 64; two orientations of 62–3; *see also* accountability
network society 5–7
Newfield, C. 64
Noel, J. 104, 108
normalcies: defined 14; of the habitus 114; part of Modernity 224; and public comment sessions 34; in Self-Other relations 122, 225; and service learning course structure 142; supporting enactment of academic identity 53; as technologies of power 14, 41; *see also* disturbing/interrupting oppressive normalcies
normalization process 40; in creation of neoliberal economic man 66–7; examples of 41, 59, 67
Nussbaum, M. 59, 108
Nyberg, D. 110–11

oppression 15; embodied 90; intersecting 225; recognizing existence of 88; transmuted into community art 164; *see also* Self-Other transformation
oral history research 164, 168–9; as democratic civic work 185, 187–8
orientation: defined 101; *see also* habitus
Others 8; constructed as 36; counter discourses of 42, 45, 60, 80; exotic 177; students as 121; violence toward 196; as pervasive injustice 225; *see also* Modernity; Self-Other transformation

Palmer, P. 73–4, 90, 212
participatory democracy *see* democracy, participatory
phronesis 99–100, 104–5; different from technique 104; and power 110, 142; supports for wise practice 122, 125–9; and virtue ethics 105; *see also* border-crossing practice, in cases; constructing and enacting the good; embodying the virtues; habitus-field-capital interaction; making sense of the situation;
planning, practitioner-oriented: as community engagement, in Maville case 210, 227–8; *see* action research
plantation metaphor 42
power: as capacity to act 104, 112, 191; to change oneself, in Upland case 152; and critical emotional intelligence 90; disguised as rationality/efficiency 42, 78, 83, 220; as lens in Addams-Lincoln case 39–42; multiple faces of 34–40; of the normal 40–1; sharing, by changing unequal relations 170–3, 186; powerlessness, and civic professional's task 222, 227
practice turn 100, 103
practice: defined 100–1; *normalized*, in teacher Allen's research 102–3; as scientific problem solving, critique of 101–2, 110; *see also* border-crossing practice; practitioner knowledge; learning for ch 5
practitioner/participant-situation interaction 156, 158, 220
professional: defined 75–6; as social trustee 77; three aspects of being a 75–7; as wise practitioner 106; *see also* democratic civic professional; expert professional
professional learning community 95; *see also* community of practice

qualities: of reflective practitioner 105–6; *see also* virtues

reciprocity 174
reflection: qualities/virtues that foster 105, 125, 137; in service-learning 49, 133, 142–4, 155–6; as support for wise practice in Change from Within case 126–7
reflective practitioner 103
relationships, healing [ch 8]: and race and class divides 170–1
Renaissance *see* Modernity
repressed knowledge 124
request for proposals; as technology of power 41; in Addams-Lincoln case; in ch6;

resonance 173–4, 177; and Self-Other transformation 224; *see also* ally
responsibility: as embodied virtue 105; in sensemaking 109; *see also* civic responsibility; professional responsibility; responsabilization (in TST case 201, 205, 209); and responsible agent 105
RFP *see* request for proposals
Rodgers, C. 105–6
Rojzman, C. 190, 191, 195, 196–8, 213n2

Saltmarsh & Hartley 52
Schön, D. 103, 109
Schwandt, T. 101–3
Self-Other binary 8–9, 15
Self-Other transformation: and Civic Learning Spiral 88; and collective intelligence 206; in cross-border collaboration 37; through de-centering, in Advocate case 226; defined 9, 15; and developmental leadership 225–6; through habitus-field-capital interaction 129; in Hull House 79–80; as task of democratic civic professional 224–7
Self-Other: binary, illustrated by Cantril and Harris (Addams-Lincoln case); and invisibility of capacities 225; and Other's loss of hope 225; and social injustice
Sergiovanni, T. 91–2, 93, 96
service-learning 48–9; as counternormative pedagogy 142–4; course structure for wise practice 142; *see also* disturbing/interrupting normalcies
Shotter, J. 107, 109, 148
Shulman. L. 103, 108
situation: defined 107; distinguished from context 107
situational ethics *see* ethics
social justice; defined 9–10; importance of recognitive, for community partners 36, 219; Otherness as denial of 220, 225; self-determination and recognitive aspects of, in Addams-Lincoln case 38–9, 60, 83
social partnerships xiii; across social divides xiv; engaging in xii; as networked organizational arrangements xiii, xiv; *see also* border crossing
social trustee professional 78–9

Solomon, R. 105, 106, 110, 120
Sullivan, W. 77, 85

teaching *see* border pedagogy; service learning, counternormative pedagogy
technical/instrumental orientation: different from community-oriented practices 95; to knowledge 57–8; in positivism 58; and *normal* construction of the professional 77, 218; in Schwandt's model 1 101–2; in scientific management 79; value efficiency and expert control 58–9
thinking tools: defined 17–18; how to use 38
third space 74, 90, 93–6, 129, 158, 220
Toulmin, S. 55–6, 104, 110
Transformational Social Therapy: building trust through expression of emotions 207, 210; changing relations to authority 194, 196, 201, 211; creating a 'group' 196–7; facilitator as wise practitioner 197–9; fostering autonomy and self-determination 194, 198; motivation to participate 199, 210; and expression of negative emotions 194, 203; as phronetic practice 197–8; and repairing relationships 198, 205, 207–8, 210; theory of action 193–4; *see also* violence
trust: as aspect of social capital 34; barriers to 167–8; building 167–8, 209, 210; defined 124; dimensions of 33–4; in Change from Within case 124–5; through power sharing 168; as principal element in shared motivation 33–4; through TST process 208
TST *see* Transformational Social Therapy

violence: defined, in TST 194, 196; differentiated from conflict 196; and pathological organizations and settings195, 196, 210, 211–12; and Self-Other divides 8, 36; symbolic 124; of structured social inequality 111–12; transforming into conflict, in TST 196; and unmet human needs 193–4; *see also* everyday racism; Transformational Social Therapy, theory of action
virtues: defined 104–5; cultivated not learned 106; developmental nature of 106–7; *see also* embodying the virtues
vulnerability 206, 209

Waddock, S. xiii
Washington, Father Paul 162, 171
Wenger, E. 92
What Works Clearinghouse 102, 130
white privilege 155–6

youth engagement: as a value 145; and adult leaders' habitus 145–6, 149–50; service learning for 150–3
youth-adult partnership and normal adult behaviors 203, 208